Bill Frindall was born in Epsom, Surrey, on the first day of the timeless Test in Durban. Educated at Reigate Grammar School, he then spent six and a half cricket seasons at the RAF before becoming a full-time cricket statistician in 1966 when he joined the *Test Match Special* team. About to start his 42nd season in its Golden Jubilee year, he is the programme's longest-serving member and has now scored more than 350 Test matches.

He has been the editor of *Playfair Cricket Annual* since 1986 and is the author of many other major publications, including *The Wisden Book of Test Cricket*, as well as being the cricket statistician for *The Times*. He publishes and retails his own linear scoring book. A professional speaker, he specialises in anecdotes from the TMS box. He is Patron of the German Cricket Board and of their Umpires and Scorers Association, President of the BBC Cricket Club, former President of British Blind Sport (1984–2004), and was awarded an Honorary Doctorate of Technology by Staffordshire University. Created MBE in 2004, he lives in Wiltshire with his wife Debbie, daughter Alice and five cats.

BEARDERS

MY LIFE IN CRICKET

BILL FRINDALL

An Orion paperback

First published in Great Britain in 2006
by Orion
This paperback edition published in 2007
by Orion Books Ltd,
Orion House, 5 Upper St Martin's Lane,
London WC2H 9EA

1 3 5 7 9 10 8 6 4 2

A CIP catalogue record for this book is available
from the British Library.

ISBN 978-0-7528-8137-9

Printed and bound in Great Britain by
Mackays of Chatham plc, Chatham, Kent

The Orion Publishing Group's policy is to use papers that
are natural, renewable and recyclable products and
made from wood grown in sustainable forests. The logging
and manufacturing processes are expected to conform to
the environmental regulations of the country of origin.

www.orionbooks.co.uk

CONTENTS

To ALICE KATHARINE

A late joy
and
a constant source of delight

ACKNOWLEDGEMENTS

So many people, most completely unwittingly, have helped me pursue this extraordinary cricketing journey and deserve considerable thanks. My late parents, whose ghastly shopping expeditions motivated me to escape to cricket grounds. Jack Glenister, who, terrified by the prospect of controlling two classes on a rained-off sports afternoon, taught me how to score. The local scorer who failed to turn up and allowed me to usurp his role. My aunt Jean who taught me to read and catch a ball. Reigate Grammar School, Banstead Cricket Club and the Royal Air Force who coached me and gave me abundant opportunities to play cricket. The BBC who risked employing me and have put up with me for 40 summers. The many commentators whom I have corrected and interrupted – sorry Blowers! My nearest and dearest, and constant friends, who have accepted that cricket always comes first. The cavalcade of international cricketing talent whose exploits have given me such pleasure to chronicle. The Maltamaniacs for allowing me to lead them astray on four continents. My wife, Debbie, for much sound advice and encouragement. And particularly Ian Marshall, editor supreme, with whom I have worked on sundry volumes spanning two decades, for bravely commissioning this book.

FIRST STEPS

J OHN ARLOTT, one of radio's most celebrated broadcasters, arrived a few minutes before play started, wearing a camouflage MASH jacket and carrying an enormous briefcase, which I assumed contained his library for that match. It didn't. It contained his lunch – two bottles of claret, a large wine glass, a vine-root corkscrew, cheese, biscuits, a plate, cutlery and, underneath them all, cricket's pocket bible, *Playfair*.

We were introduced and John immediately tried to put me at ease. His first words to me were, 'Hello. Welcome. What do you give to the woman who has everything?'

The scene was a cramped, ramshackle eyrie, set on stilts overlooking a rain-swept cricket ground at Worcester. Even months of meticulous research and a dawn arrival for my first cricket broadcast had not prepared me for such a question.

'Encouragement?' I ventured, helplessly.

'No,' he growled triumphantly. 'Penicillin.'

My dismay at failing to answer such an obvious riddle was swiftly removed by the great man's next remarks.

'I hear you like driving. Well, I like drinking. We're going to get on well.'

And we did, for fifteen wonderful summers, until John hung up his microphone and moved his library and cellar to the Channel Islands.

One of the thirstiest souls ever to have been let loose on this planet, the Sage of Alresford took me under his wing like a surrogate son and immediately filled me with confidence and Chardonnay.

With a scorecard and stopwatch as his only props, he proceeded to give a three-minute match preview for the BBC World Service. Finishing precisely within his allotted time, he opened his case to reveal the famous lunch. It rained for most of the three days and my baptism was painless. John's kindness towards and interest in novice writers and broadcasters was unlimited. He was to have a tremendous influence on my life. No one helped me more with wise advice and encouragement during that first season. After the first session of my debut at Worcester, he inspired much-needed confidence by saying, 'You'll do. You've got a scorer's mind. You can focus on the play and obliterate everything happening in this box.' Perhaps my two years in a NATO war room had provided the perfect training.

Few people are destined to spend their working lives indulging in their favourite hobby. To earn a living doing something you would gladly do for free is everyone's dream. Hooked on cricket since the age of eight when a great uncle took me to watch a club match, I often dreamed of playing for England, but never did I expect to be granted forty summers and several winters watching international cricket from the best seat in the house.

Every life has its key moments. Some may emerge through hindsight, while others are glaringly apparent as soon as they happen. My decision to apply for the position of *Test Match Special*'s scorer/statistician when Arthur Wrigley suddenly passed away became a key moment only when I was eventually offered the job. Even that inspired piece of obituary watching would not have occurred had I not been taught to score by a desperate master on a rainy day at primary school. A few days later I was taken to a match where they needed a scorer and a remarkable career was born. Timing is everything, though, and had I not just ended a seven-year stint in the RAF shortly before my predecessor's demise, I would have been unable to apply for his job – but I'm jumping the gun. Most attempts at autobiography seem to start at birth, so I had better stick to the rules of this game.

My innings began on Friday, 3 March 1939, exactly six months before Neville Chamberlain called 'Play' in the Hitler war. More appropriately, my arrival coincided with the start of the famous timeless Test between South Africa and England at Durban. The longest cricket match ever, that epic contest between South Africa and England began when I was three and a half hours old and ended in an improbable draw some eleven days later. After 43 hours and 16 minutes of actual playing time, England, with five wickets in hand, were just 42 tantalising runs short of victory when rain deprived them of the final session possible before they had to catch a train to Cape Town and board their ship for home.

Sadly, I cannot claim to have been aware of these fascinating facts until many moons later. I had emerged into Epsom District Hospital after a protracted and painful run-up involving an instrument with a long handle. After the ordeal, my mother, 4´ 10˝ short, and I were both given brandy. Apparently, I enjoyed it much more than she did. Fathers were not encouraged to witness births in those days, so Dad was spared the drama. At home and without a phone, he had been told not to worry unless a policeman called. He had a fearful shock when one did and told him that both mother and infant were on the danger list.

When Mother and I had recovered, my parents addressed the task of naming me. They had complicated this chore by anticipating a daughter. In the absence of any scientific means of establishing the gender of their embryo Frindall, they had resorted to the old detection ploy featuring a wedding ring dangled over the bump. Even though Dad was a research chemist and Mother had been a staff nurse, they got it completely wrong. To appease their mothers, they had eventually agreed on Susan Florence Elizabeth. Totally unprepared for a male, they resorted to naming me after their dog, Bill, adding my father's family middle name of Howard. It was not a good omen for the hound, a snappy multibreed, as he was immediately given his marching orders in case he bit me. As my running costs mounted, my parents had to choose between keeping their car or me. The vote probably went to a recount.

I slept through most of World War Two, spending much of it in an improvised shelter in the cupboard under the stairs, but without the magic assistance available to Harry Potter when he was imprisoned in similar accommodation. Apparently, I even slept when a bomb dropped smack in the middle of our garden shed and buried itself somewhere in the earth beneath, having failed to explode. We were evacuated immediately to my grandparents' house a few miles away in Kingswood, opposite the ground where I was to score my first cricket match. Troops searching, unsuccessfully, for the bomb reduced the garden to a chalky rubble. All they found were its fins. From those they deduced that it was a thousand-pounder made in Germany. Wartime regulations prevented our returning until the bomb had been found and defused but by now it had worked its way through the chalk into an underground stream where, presumably, it still rests. Eventually, Herbert Morrison, Home Secretary and Minister of Home Security in Churchill's War Cabinet, was persuaded to sign a letter certifying that our beloved bomb had never existed. We returned to a white garden and a complete absence of kitchen equipment.

My wartime memories extend little further than those two events. My father, Arthur Howard Frindall, was then a research technician specialising in yeast fermentation at the Great Burgh department of the Distillers Company. His work became more diverse once the war began. He never divulged his secret duties but they were sufficiently important to prevent him from being recruited by the fighting forces. The closest he got to armed conflict was fire-watching duty on the roof of Great Burgh, once the home of Jeremiah Colman, the mustard magnate. My father was a quiet chap whose main interests were reading, crossword puzzles, gardening, carpentry and cricket. He was born in Merton, then part of Surrey, in December 1909, the last of five offspring of a solicitor's senior clerk. Although I have never found time to research its origins, my surname is believed to have evolved from Friendall (Friend of All) with origins in the West Country. I spotted one in a playbill for an eighteenth-century restoration comedy.

My mother, Evelyn Violet, was born in Paddington five days after Dad, curiously the first of five children whereas he had been the last. Her father, then chief buyer at a departmental store in Clapham, was a McNeill of Barra, descendant of a particularly vicious little Scottish pirate. Unfortunately for my father, Evelyn Violet had inherited many of her forebear's characteristics. Dad hated rows and would either retire to his shed or engage in a prolonged sulk. His death certificate may well have been the first to list 'Nagging' as the cause.

My early years were spent in a surreal wartime world of gas masks, blackouts, air-raid sirens, rationing coupons, wrecked buildings and the curious wired, synthetic glass that replaced hundreds of fractured shop windows. Before we reached VE Day and the street party, I was sent to a nearby private school. Few children can have had a more bizarre start to their formal education. The academy in question was sited in a semi-detached house run by a couple called Smith. Mrs Smith taught the infants in the living room. I was expelled before I qualified for promotion to Mr Smith's emporium, which was housed enticingly in an upstairs bedroom. His class of juniors included several much older girls whom I later thought I recognised among the cast of St Trinians.

Mrs Smith and I did not gel. She soon discovered that not only had I inherited a musical bypass, but also that I was quite unable to dance or skip. Luckily, Auntie Jean McNeill, my mother's younger sister, was also a teacher. It was she who taught me to read and, far more importantly, to catch a ball. She also taught me how to tell the time. One hot summer afternoon Mrs Smith had moved her class into the garden and asked if any child could tell the time. I eagerly accepted the challenge and was sent back into the house to inspect the large electric clock on the mantelpiece. To my horror, it had a third hand. I had been taught two-handed clocks. In desperation, I unplugged the monster and hauled it outside to show an appalled Mrs Smith.

Although that reckless act did not result in my expulsion, fate did not delay the inevitable for long. My burgeoning artistic talents made up for some of my many shortcomings and rare happy moments involved drawing pictures in a sand tray. I had just completed a masterpiece dominated by a house and flowers when a wretched girl deliberately jogged the tray. My lovely picture vanished, a red mist appeared, I up-ended the tray of sand over the girl's head and was quickly despatched into the state education system at Banstead County Primary School.

I was eight when great uncle Jack Trevillian took me to Beckenham to watch my first senior cricket match. A Cornishman who had married a maternal aunt, he was devoted to cricket. His only son, Tony, had been on the verge of the Kent team when the war began. An RAF navigator, he was shot down and killed in the Battle of Britain. Preceding John Arlott by two decades, Uncle Jack adopted me as his surrogate son. On that sunny spring day the Foxgrove Road ground looked an absolute picture. I have a vivid memory of being sat between my great uncle and Dad in the stand at the Pavilion End. Ringed by blossoming horse-chestnut trees, we looked down the pitch towards a backcloth dominated by two Victorian tennis pavilions. For many years the ground staged the Beckenham tennis championships and the outfield doubled as the main courts. I was hooked on cricket from that day, the first and most influential key moment of my life. Not until 2002 did I visit that ground again. Then it was to play under the captaincy of Derek Underwood for the Primary Club against the hosts. Four young players, determined to overcome the disappointments of their frequent first-ball dismissals, started the Primary Club at Beckenham in 1955 and it has grown into a worldwide charity, responsible for vast contributions to sport for the blind and partially sighted.

Opening the batting for Beckenham on that fateful spring day in 1947 were E.W. 'Jim' Swanton and A.W.H. Mallett, a remarkable duo to find in a club twenty years before league cricket arrived in the south of England. Jim Swanton stayed locally with an aunt when he played for the club. Not long released from the Japanese POW camp that built the

Burma Railway as a routine exercise, he was to become the doyen of cricket writers and reach the impressive age of 93. An outstanding summariser of a day's play, he was a long-established member of the *Test Match Special* team when I joined it nineteen years later. Tony Mallett, tall, craggy and pipe smoking, was a contemporary and friend of Trevor Bailey at Dulwich College. They also shared wartime service in the Royal Marines. Mallett played for Oxford University and Kent, became an outstanding schoolmaster and emigrated to Cape Town. There we met in 1980 when my charity touring team, the Maltamaniacs, played the Western Province Club on the Test ground at Newlands. He also sired Nick Mallett, later to become South Africa's rugby coach. According to Mallett *fils*, the act of conception occurred above the music room at Haileybury.

The following year, soon after my ninth birthday, we emigrated to Canada. Like so many parents with young families in those dark, ration-riddled years immediately after the war, mine were enticed by a higher quality of life in the Commonwealth countries. My father's closest colleague in the research department had been offered a job in Jamaica and a second post was available there for Dad. Meanwhile, nearly all of Mother's family, including three sets of aunts and uncles with their children plus Grandad, were heading out to Vancouver. As Mother inevitably got her own way, we went to Vancouver. That decision was another key moment. Had we moved to Jamaica where Dad was guaranteed work, I would probably have completed my education there. In spite of my addiction to cricket, it is unlikely that there would have been sufficient broadcasting opportunities for me to develop the career I now have.

Dad ventured to British Columbia on the strength of an interview but failed to get the job. We stayed for a year during which he had several temporary posts. Then fate intervened and he received an unexpected letter from his old employers, offering him control of a new department back at Great Burgh. Gratefully, we beat a hasty retreat home and, within two years, all of the family had returned to England. Canada was also recovering from the war and, not surprisingly, the best posts were going to Canadians. Astonishingly, my 66-year-old Grandad refused a job because it had no prospects.

Although the Canadian Experience proved to be a traumatic and costly mission for my parents, it provided a highly memorable series of adventures for me. On the outward journey, our aircraft developed engine trouble in mid-Atlantic and we made a dramatic emergency landing in the Azores at 3 a.m. local time. After crossing the tarmac between an alarming avenue of Portuguese soldiers armed with rifles, we were welcomed with a lavish three-course meal and I enjoyed my first glass of white wine – another key moment. We spent three days on Santa Maria, the lack of telephone communication compelling a twice-daily journey between the airport and our hotel some five miles distant. On one occasion, we reboarded the stricken aircraft and began to taxi to the main runway, but after a very loud explosion and a Goon Show sound effect of metal hitting tarmac, we juddered to a halt. With great relief, we all returned to the hotel. There, each night, an American pilot consumed much falling-over water and selected the small glass panels behind the bar as a target for his empty glasses. Within an hour of one of these escapades, his plane was cleared for take-off and a somewhat reluctant herd of passengers followed in his unsteady wake.

A replacement aircraft eventually arrived for us and we began a second attempt to reach Canada. When the intercom announced next morning that we should prepare for our landing in Sydney, I asked Dad if we were on the right plane. In April 1948, Sydney airport in Nova Scotia consisted simply of a large grassy field and an impressive log cabin. Inside it, I was introduced to white bread, real eggs, bananas, waffles with maple syrup and Coca-Cola. Wartime bread had been available in a muddy brown colour, while eggs had come in powdered form in waxy cartons. We proceeded to Vancouver on a series of exciting domestic flights. The final leg of the fourteen-day marathon was made on the maiden flight of Trans Canada Airline's newest aircraft and I was treated to a lengthy visit to the flight deck as we crossed the Rockies and approached Vancouver Airport at sunset. By dusk, yellow lights on a black backcloth provided a spectacular map of the city, with the main road to the east glowing in a dazzling straight line.

My introduction to Vancouver at ground level was memorable for its awfulness. Our hotel was situated in a squalid downtown area. Its entrance hall was lined with battered upright chairs and beside each one was set a brass spittoon. Mother had not enjoyed the journey and, presented with this setting late at night, she was not at her best. Her mood darkened when we were shown to rooms bearing dramatic scars of recent battles. A wardrobe door had been separated from its hinges and the shredded curtains were heavily bloodstained. When she scalded her hand on water from the cold tap, we forfeited the advance payment of a week's booking and joined the filthy rich at the five-star Hotel Sylvia in English Bay.

Within a week we had decamped to a motel beside the major highway I had seen from the air. The other half of our semi-detached cabin was occupied by a large number of Chinamen. All was quiet during the day but after dusk a steady flow of vans arrived and a constant babble of voices and running water emanated from next door. Eventually, Mother could stand the racket no longer and sent for the motel's owner, Mrs Law. When that robust Irish lady discovered that her Oriental guests were using the bathroom to wash hundreds of cabbages for market, the scrubbers were swiftly despatched.

Soon after our arrival I developed measles. It lingered for a month, unimpeded by visits from a doctor who sat on my bed inhaling heavily from a cigarette as he examined me. My chances of recovery had virtually been written off when Mrs Law brought me a jug of steaming hot toddy. I have a vivid memory of this vast Irish galleon moving under full sail across the yard, jug held high, apron ties flying, declaring, 'This will either kill or cure him. If it's the first, we'll bury him on the lot.' With that choice ringing in my ears, I drank most of the brew. Two days later I woke up miraculously cured.

While Dad made daily pilgrimages to job interviews in the city, I wandered down the road watching a road gang digging a deep ditch alongside the pavement (sidewalk in Canadian terms). They soon employed me as their drinks waiter, sending me to buy bottles of pop and rewarding me with nickels and dimes. It was the first money I had ever earned. Luckily, there was no jealousy as Dad soon acquired a job in a cod liver oil factory. That career lasted exactly one day. Mother wouldn't allow him inside the front door when he returned wearing overalls reeking of fish. His next employment was at a jam factory. He assured me that the fact that we were never short of fruit was not in any way linked to the company going bankrupt five months later. By this time we had bought a house in one of the eastern suburbs. Dad had been out of work for three months before he was reprieved by the Distillers' offer and we returned home.

Canada provided some important firsts in my education. It introduced me to two enormous, multisectioned broadsheet newspapers and a vast public library. I also made my first appearance on radio. The *Daily Province* arrived on our porch neatly rolled and thrown on the pedal by a cycling newsboy. Its pages included a generous section for children, which even ran its own club. As a prize for winning one of its painting competitions, I was invited on stage at one of its monthly radio shows, and so Vancouver's Radio CKWX Playhouse became the venue for my broadcasting debut. For answering a question about pirates I won a dartboard. Vancouver's public library housed a substantial section for children and motivated my appetite for reading. However, any thoughts that I might have harboured about progressing well during my year at Richard McBride's School were severely dashed when, forty-four years later, I showed my report to the current headmaster. 'We don't want you back,' was his only comment.

Although cricket has never been a major sport in Canada, the earliest references to it being played in that country go back to 1785 – three years before Australia's first white settlement was built at Botany Bay. The first two countries to play international cricket were not England and Australia but Canada and America in 1844, thirty-three years before the first official Test match, and an English team toured the United States two years before one journeyed to Australia.

When Sir Donald Bradman visited Vancouver in 1932, on an

Australian tour that doubled as his honeymoon, he described the Brockton Point ground as the world's most beautifully situated cricket venue. The setting, beside a busy harbour, dominated by a backcloth of mountains, with the Lions Gate Suspension Bridge and Stanley National Park's giant trees and colourful gardens close by, is absolutely breathtaking. In 1994 I had the honour of opening the bowling there for the MCC.

We began our journey home in March 1949 by traversing America on a succession of fairly primitive Greyhound buses. The expedition took three weeks, with alternate nights spent on the bus. The highlight was the Columbia River Highway, with its massive waterfalls and sheer drop to a meandering river far below. At Salt Lake City we visited the Mormon Temple and Mother tried to explain what Mormons did. When she mentioned they had more than one wife, Dad muttered, 'How ghastly!' A disappointing lack of gangsters spoilt Chicago for me.

Eventually, we reached Halifax, Nova Scotia, where it rained non-stop for three days before we boarded RMS *Aquitania* for Southampton. The last of the four-funnel Cunard liners, it had dark panelling and was ornately furnished, and its decks housed a cinema, library, shops, hairdressers, a games room where I learned to play table tennis, and a lounge with a resident band. The voyage was a little rough early on and my parents remained in their cabin for the first two days. Seasickness depends on your ears, apparently, and even on the roughest water I don't suffer from it. When she had recovered sufficiently, Mother attended the ship's church service, claiming that it was her first visit for nineteen years. Fortunately, the *Aquitania* survived her rare commune with the Almighty, although it was soon running on just two engines and a year later it was despatched to the breakers' yard. My 'Abstract of the Ship's Log' shows that we covered 2782 nautical miles in six days and 42 minutes.

FIRST NOTCHES

BACK IN SURREY, we lived as paying guests at Cestria, my grandparents' house in Kingswood, where we had been evacuated during the unexploded bomb episode. It became our home for a year while a plot of land was found and a bungalow built at Epsom Downs. Cestria, a gloomy 1920s house with stuccoed interior walls and a décor relying heavily on dark brown, had been inherited by Dad's widowed sister-in-law, Pauline, usually known as Paul. Its saving grace was an acre of tree-surrounded garden with a lawn just large enough for cricket. I was distraught when Paul banned my Test matches with Dad after I straight drove a rubber ball through the roof of the conservatory and then beheaded several of her beloved gladioli with my trademark cow shot. Fortunately for my burgeoning cricket skills, Paul travelled daily to a solicitor's office in London and visited her brother on Sunday afternoons. My teacher once asked me about my aunt's work. 'She solicits,' I answered innocently. Thankfully, Paul's time-keeping was punctilious and Dad and I could play cricket every evening until her train was due, using her ten-minute walk from the station to hide the gear and repair any damage. Dad would resurrect any felled gladioli using matchsticks, a method guaranteed to keep the stem intact until the bloom appeared to have perished through natural causes. Sunday afternoons allowed several hours of cricket and we were careful to move the pitch to avoid excessive wear on the lawn.

Stump holes were filled in, straight drives banned and mows into the gladdies penalised.

All went well until Sid, Paul's gardener, made an unexpected Sabbath visit. I never saw Sid without his flat cap and a scowl. Nature had not been kind to him as he had copped a cleft palate and a hairlip. He hated cricket, especially when it threatened 'his' garden. That day he stayed until Paul returned and then his extraordinary high-pitched nasal tones rang out – 'That bloody Bill has been playing sodding cricket again and flattened my effing gladioli.'

Few schools can have had a more wonderful setting than Tadworth County Primary. Perched atop a terraced garden, the Victorian stone building was surrounded by untamed heath. An area the size of a small cricket ground had been cleared and there we played during all our breaks. The Canada hiatus had caused me to miss virtually a year's education and handicapped my sitting the eleven plus exam to secure a grammar school place. I was promised a new bike if I passed and eternal damnation if I failed. Fortunately, Beryl Agate, my form teacher, was exceptionally skilful and encouraging, with a well-developed sense of humour. When she showed us how to do cartwheels, she won every boy's admiration as they introduced us to the delights of her French knickers.

Tadworth employed five members of staff and one of them, Jack Glenister, was to provide the key moment that was to shape the rest of my life by teaching me how to score a cricket match.

It all happened by accident. Games afternoon was the highlight of our school week, especially in the summer. So when it rained heavily throughout the morning, we could only stare grimly out of the windows, knowing that we would be confined to the classroom. A drastic post-war shortage of male teachers had led to a scheme whereby demobbed servicemen were fast-tracked into teaching by a condensed training course. Mr Glenister had recently completed this two-year deal after leaving the RAF and it was he who was given the short straw of taking the top two classes that rain-swept afternoon. His brief was to teach us anything he fancied about sport. Fortunately for me, he was an enthusiastic cricketer who opened the batting for Epsom. He had spotted a small, unused scorebook in the stationery cupboard. Removing its staples, he separated the tiny pages and gave one set to each of us. He had forfeited his lunch break to chalk up the entire lay-out of a scorebook page on the blackboard. We then played an imaginary innings. Every run had to be recorded in three places – alongside the batsman's name, in the bowler's little overs square and then crossed off the side's tally block. I was absolutely enthralled and the two hours sped past. Probably an eight-year-old Stewart Storey was the only other member of that young audience who will have any recall of that wonderful afternoon. An outstanding schoolboy games player, Storey was to play fifteen seasons for Surrey and, but for the untimely arrival of Basil D'Oliveira, would almost certainly have represented England.

Jack Glenister flourished well into his eighties and confessed to boasting frequently that he was the man who taught Bill Frindall how to score. In his final years I enjoyed several lunches with him. After a few drinks he would proudly reveal many well-kept secrets about his years at Tadworth, including his colourful adventures with a young music mistress.

Behind the houses opposite Cestria spread the Kingswood offices of the Legal & General Assurance Society and its Temple Bar Sports Club. To escape my parents' dreaded shopping expeditions, I had taken to watching their cricket team. Auntie Paul had accidentally initiated this when she took me to meet the head gardener. A genial man, he suggested that I should go up past the swimming pool and watch the cricket. He then led my aunt towards his greenhouses. At the age of ten one doesn't question such actions.

The teams were practising on the outfield. I watched for a while, hoping to have the chance of a bowl. One of the players came over to me and told me that their scorer hadn't turned up.

'Sonny, do you know how to score?'

'Yes,' I replied eagerly, 'I was taught at school on Tuesday.'

He looked at me so incredulously that I was convinced he thought I was lying. No one is ever formally taught how to score. Most newcomers to the role sit next to an experienced scorer and learn on the hoof. I couldn't believe my good fortune when, having introduced himself as Nick Nicolson, captain of Temple Bar 2nd XI, he handed me the score-book and led me to the scorers' table. Jack Glenister must have taught me well because at the end of the match everything balanced. Besides being given a free tea, I was rewarded with a glass of ginger beer. Happily, Nick seemed impressed by my efforts and, to my immense delight, I was invited to escape shopping the following Saturday.

I scored for the 2nd XI for the remainder of the season and, on one memorable occasion when they were a player short, was roped in to play. I didn't bat or bowl and had to score when we batted. Nevertheless, I count it as my debut in senior cricket and, having appeared in more matches than I should have done in this twenty-first century, I can claim to have extended my playing career over seven decades.

Now completely hooked on the game, I persuaded Dad to embark on a massive cricket project with dice. We played the entire county championship in its standard two-innings format and with all seven-teen counties meeting their sixteen opponents on a home and away basis. He procured reams of foolscap squared paper and we played most evenings and during rainy weekends. We both wanted to be Surrey and neither of us wanted to be Yorkshire. After five winters, half the original players had retired and one had died. We called a halt with the task still unfinished.

To my immense relief I duly passed the eleven plus and gained a place at Reigate Grammar School. Spared eternal damnation, I received the promised bicycle. The final term at Tadworth passed swiftly. I can recall only the art class when I drew a picture of Kingswood Church. It instilled a love of sketching that has remained with me ever since.

In April 1950, I received a letter from Nick inviting me to become Temple Bar 2nd XI's official scorer. I was probably more thrilled by that invitation than by the prospect of going to Reigate. Bronzed and athletic, Nick was inevitably accompanied by attractive girls. That season he missed several matches through back strain. For the first time I was taken by car to their away games. My chauffeur was Jimmy Clark, the vice-captain. A jovial little chap with curly fair hair, glasses and a wide smile, he batted and kept wicket in spite of his hands being crippled by Dupuytren's contractures, a condition with which I was to become all too familiar. He eventually took over the captaincy and many years later I used to meet him in the pavilion at The Oval, where he would watch every Test match from the upper deck. In 1993, when he was 85, he visited the *TMS* box and, to Jonathan Agnew's immense amusement, presented me with a photograph of a Temple Bar team taken in 1954. It includes a shy, skinny, 15-year-old beardless wonder, sporting a school blazer with a pen-filled breast pocket.

When Temple Bar were without a fixture, I would be dragged off to Croydon by my parents. One Saturday we visited a large department store, where the television section's screens were showing cricket. I watched them while my parents continued their meanderings. Probably thinking that a young spectator would encourage trade, an assistant brought me a chair and I managed to spend the entire afternoon watching England play West Indies at Trent Bridge. Two very young spin bowlers, Sonny Ramadhin and Alf Valentine, were weaving their spells against Reg Simpson and Cyril Washbrook. Ram and Val, who had been selected for the tour of England after just two first-class matches apiece, had shared 18 wickets and bowled West Indies to their first-ever Test victory in England at Lord's. Egbert Moore, aka 'Lord Beginner', had celebrated this historic event with the game's most famous calypso. It starts 'Cricket, lovely cricket!' At Trent Bridge, 'those two little pals of mine, Ramadhin and Valentine' had shared just four wickets as England were dismissed for 223. West Indies had replied with 558 (Frank Worrell 261, Everton Weekes 120) and England's openers were in the process of sharing a record series opening stand of 212 while I watched. Ramadhin bowled with his cap on and sleeves buttoned at the wrists. His fast arm action and variety of spin and flight were fascinating to watch, even in black and white and with cameras at just one end of the ground. The left-handed Valentine was taller and gangling, with a higher, bouncing trajectory. When he arrived in England, his batting and fielding were so poor that he was sent to an optician. His first glasses (thick-lensed) improved things a little.

Not only was this my first sight of professional cricket but it was the first time I had seen any sport on television. It was an historic debut for that medium, too, as this was the inaugural cricket transmission from Nottingham. Prior to the opening of the Sutton Coldfield transmitter, television coverage of Test cricket had been restricted to London. It was also my introduction to Brian Johnston. Some of the houses in the adjacent Fox Road had balconies allowing a free view of the play. He asked the producer to get a camera to focus on the people who were watching from there. A television must have been on in one of the rooms behind because they soon started waving. Suddenly, it began to rain and the players trotted off the field – all except the tall Jamaican fast bowler Hines Johnson, who remained near the pitch, obviously enjoying the refreshing shower. When the rain became heavy, he calmly slipped under the covers, emerging from his shelter to great applause when the sun returned. From that day, I read every article on cricket that I could find and fought with Dad over the county scores at breakfast.

In September 1950 I started at Reigate Grammar School and we moved to our new bungalow. My bedroom was swiftly transformed into my first cricket office. My favourite subjects were the ones I was to take at A Level – English, History and Art. A congenitally inaccurate ear made languages a trial and music a nightmare. The first hint of my musical bypass came when I was eight and my class was issued with recorders. I was the first child not to be given one, on the grounds that it would be a total waste of the instrument's valuable time. That condition was confirmed by two events in my first year at Reigate. Looking reasonably angelic, I was selected for the front row of the junior choir but ordered to mime and not utter a sound. Then, at Christmas, came an unfortunate general knowledge quiz and the question that was to haunt the rest of my life at that establishment because I was the only boy who got it wrong. 'Who composed Handel's "Largo"?' I guessed that it was a piece of music and, after agonising between the two composers I had heard of, did a mental toss-up and chose Mozart. It was a close thing because I almost put Beethoven.

Dad's carpentry skills sadly missed a generation and I was too ashamed to take home a lidded box I had spent two terms making. The dovetail joints were OK but I could not plane straight. My bizarre effort, with its lid perched on sides that arched upwards in the middle, was placed on the woodwork master's desk as a warning. An elderly science assistant, Mr Woodhead, spotted it and asked if he could have it for his chemistry lab. Of all the boxes made by that class, mine was the only one to be put to any use.

A large rabbit I lovingly crafted needed two people to remove it from the pottery kiln. Saddest was my attempt at puppetry. My task was to make an ugly sister for a production of *Cinderella* and I certainly succeeded. Overestimating the measures, I had poor Mother boiling up endless saucepans of newspapers to manufacture a vast quantity of papier mâché. When my sorry effort lurched on stage and sat on a small bench, it catapulted its sister into the wings. When it stood up, its head and neck disappeared above the proscenium arch. I was taken ill with flu after the first night and Mr Sweatman, the art master, had to undertake major surgery and a complete restringing before the next performance. It was the only puppet he omitted to keep in his collection and the last I attempted to make.

My first sight of live professional cricket came in 1951 when Dad took me to Kennington Oval to watch the second day of Surrey's championship match against Middlesex. Rain had reduced Saturday's play in this local derby to ninety minutes. These were the days of uncovered pitches and moisture was still in the surface when the for-midable Alec Bedser began bowling to Bill Edrich and Jack Robertson. Perched on hired cushions on stark bench seating, we watched from midwicket in the Harleyford Road terrace, facing the gas holders and with the pavilion on our right. The small cream radio and TV com-mentary boxes were balanced on the flat roof on our side of the pavilion. Recall of Surrey's chocolate-coloured caps, with the sun highlighting the players' pale cream shirts and trousers against the green outfield, remains vivid. Bedser soon had Edrich caught in the gully by the burly, dignified Jim Laker, and loud, prolonged applause heralded the arrival of Denis Compton. He had a distinctive walk – possibly because of his knee injuries from playing soccer for Arsenal – and a stage presence that only the truly great sportsmen possess. Very much a personal hero, he exuded fun and pleasure when he was batting and I had longed to see him play that famous sweep. With both protagonists close to the peaks of their careers, their battle provided outstanding entertainment.

Play took place from 11.30 a.m. to 1.30 p.m. before a forty-minute interval. I had already finished my favourite cheese and beetroot sandwiches, housed in one of those famous red Oxo tins, and emptied my bottle of Tizer. During the interval we walked round the back of the pavilion and, for one shilling, I bought a copy of Jack Parker's benefit booklet. It remains a prized possession. At just three and a half inches high and nearly ten inches wide, it has a unique format and includes thirty-five pages of cricket strip cartoons featuring coaching tips from most of the top English players of the day. Surprisingly, no other beneficiary has thought of producing something similar.

After lunch, the pitch eased and Compton looked in total command. Although economical, Laker and Tony Lock found little turn and it was again Big Alec who made the breakthrough. First he had Dewes caught by Arthur McIntyre, the sprightly wicket-keeper who nearly always stood up to Bedser. It was a very long walk down the pavilion steps at The Oval, through the white picket gate held open by the senior steward, and across the vast playing area to the far Vauxhall End. Harry Sharp took guard, lost his middle stump to Bedser's next ball, and retraced his journey, a trudge completed in absolute silence until a few people clapped sympathetically as he neared the gate. Three decades later, when he was the Middlesex scorer, I unwisely asked if he remembered that innings. 'Burned on my heart,' he growled, 'but Alec was a bowler you could be proud to get out to.'

At tea, Compton was in the nineties and I was looking forward to the Brylcreem Boy's century. Such dreams were cruelly dashed when Dad insisted that we must leave at once as he had promised Mother we would be back home for tea by 6 p.m. A very disappointed beardless wonder accompanied his father in sulky silence, burying himself in the Parker coaching strips. I probably blamed Dad for not doing a McIntyre and standing up to Mother. Next morning he grabbed the paper before I could see it, turned to the cricket scores and tried not to show his relief when he read 'D.C.S. Compton c Surridge b Lock 97'.

Over the next few seasons I spent many happy hours with Dad at The Oval. Most of our visits coincided with Surrey's halcyon days when, under the captaincy of Stuart Surridge, they won five consecutive championships. Dad's visits were legitimate as he could rearrange his research shifts. Mine were not. His neat writing and Mother's copious knowledge of illnesses combined to produce notes of fictitious maladies that would have done credit to an ace forger. Not until I reached my final year at Reigate did any member of staff twig that I was only ill when Surrey were playing at home.

Apart from an occasional emergency call-up for Temple Bar and some form games at school, my playing career remained largely dormant until 1953 when I was picked for the school junior eleven. I played every lunchtime on the tarmac playground with a tennis ball. The wicket was chalked on a pillar of an air-raid shelter and whoever caught or bowled the batsman took over the bat. Once, in racing to hold a catch in the deep, I collided with another lad and fractured my left collarbone. The only benefit of being sufficiently injured to be taken to hospital while at Reigate was the mode of transport. Tony Emery, a tall, studious history master with a handlebar moustache and three and a half vintage Bentleys (he shared the fourth), would cart the victim to neighbouring Redhill in one of his incredibly noisy open chariots. Emery introduced voluntary calligraphy classes and taught me the style of writing that I have used continuously since the start of my RAF career.

The arrival of Lindsay Hassett's Australians dominated the start of the 1953 summer, before the Queen's coronation took centre stage on 2 June. School closed and we were all expected to watch the service and procession on television. Most families without a set bought or rented one for this event. My parents were totally addicted to their wireless, so I listened to the service for a while before playing cricket with a lad who lived close by. His father, Gerry Bush, was an outstanding opening batsman at Banstead. Seeing me bat and bowl prompted him to suggest that, if I were interested, he would recommend me to the manager of the Banstead Colts. His kindness led to me eventually being invited to captain that team and to enjoying more than a decade in the senior sides.

Two other key moments occurred during that coronation summer. The first happened on the opening morning of the Ashes series and involved the school caretaker. The splendidly named Sergeant Major Cuss was also mainstay of the school's Combined Cadet Force, of which august body I was later to become an occasional member. His house, surrounded by a waist-high picket fence, was sited on the deep-cover boundary of the playground. By standing on tiptoe against the wooden railings, it was just possible to see his television. On Test match days, Mr Cuss would eat his lunch while sitting in front of the screen. Fed up with the young Frindall peering through his window, towards the end of the previous year he had actually invited the little pest to join him. Much jealousy ensued. Rather than invite the entire school into his front room he had evolved a cunning plan. Finding an abandoned blackboard, he sited it beside his front door. In return for the bonus of a ringside seat, I had to chalk up the latest team and individual scores at the end of each over or when a wicket fell. A loud cheer rang around the playground when they read 'Australia 2 for 1, Hole b Bedser 0'. Basic training for my broadcasting career?

The next defining moment also involved televised cricket, which I managed to watch at a neighbour's house. When I heard the radio commentary competing from the kitchen through a serving hatch, I muted the TV's sound in favour of John Arlott's familiar burr to see what the effect was. My host was entranced and whenever both broadcasts were available – neither then covered the entire day's play – she would back up the silent picture with the radio commentary. This eventually became a popular combination throughout the country and, after he had been sacked by TV and joined *Test Match Special*, Brian Johnston used to rejoice in goading Jim Laker, then a TV commentator, with this information. 'They're ignorant,' was always Jim's growled response.

Although many famous people from all walks of life have appeared on *TMS* and I have appeared alongside a variety of others for Lord's Taverners cricket teams, Seretse Khama was the first truly great man I met. I had read about Ruth Williams, a Croydon typist who had met and married this African chief while he was studying Law at Oxford. Because he had wed outside his tribe he was banned from his chieftainship and exiled from Bechuanaland. I discovered that the Khamas lived just eight miles away so I cycled to their house, autograph book in pocket. Mrs Khama warmly welcomed my intrusion but her infant son took one look at me and was sick. Seretse, the first black person I had met, greeted me warmly and they both wrote kind messages in my book. I had no idea that I was briefly in the company of one of the most compassionate and important leaders of the twentieth century. Allowed to return home as a private citizen three years later, his chieftainship was eventually restored and he became the first prime minister of Bechuanaland and subsequently Botswana's first president.

Coronation year brought a memorable hat-trick of long-awaited achievements by British sportsmen and teams. Stanley Matthews at last won a Cup final medal when Blackpool beat Bolton Wanderers 4–3 at Wembley. Gordon Richards, champion jockey for twenty-six years, finally rode a Derby winner, Pinza, at his twenty-eighth attempt. His knighthood had been announced shortly before the race and there can have been few more popular victories at Epsom. Then, after four tense drawn Tests, England beat Australia on a sundrenched afternoon at The Oval to regain the Ashes after nineteen years, their longest period without them. Denis Compton swept the winning runs and inspired Brian Johnston's excited double proclamation, 'It's the Ashes! It's the Ashes!' as the crowd swarmed on to the outfield.

Playing cricket had begun to attract me more than scoring, although I continued to keep the book for Temple Bar until I got into the school 2nd XI in 1955. My reward of ginger beer was converted first into shandy and eventually into bitter. One of their players, Jack Hill, a fine batsman-keeper, became scorer for Surrey and was the first to use at county level the scorebook that I designed and published. As early as 1950, Jack had predicted that I would score for England one day. He was almost right.

Jack is the only batsman whose departure I have noted on a scoresheet as 'Retired Bored'. Having savaged 70 in an hour off a wilting Old Whitgiftian attack, he stood waiting for the next over to begin. The skipper had bowled the previous one and was trying desperately to persuade someone else to have a go. When this standoff continued, Jack took off his gloves, shoved his bat under his arm and strode back to the pavilion.

'How were you out?' I asked.

'Bored,' he replied with a grin.

I was selected for the school 2nd XI as an opening batsman and occasional off-spinner. They already had four opening bowlers. My proudest schoolboy feat was to carry my bat for an unbeaten 35 out of 57 in 95 minutes. I spent the following two seasons in the 1st XI achieving little of note with the bat, but catching everything within reach at forward short-leg. To my immense disappointment, I was not given a bowl until my very last match. Then, at Guildford Royal Grammar, an establishment soon to educate Bob Willis, when our five major bowlers had failed to break a partnership of 50, I was at last given my chance. My second ball swung away, clipped the edge and was held by Tony Johnson, later to gain a doctorate, lecture in history at Cardiff University and become my oldest friend. I then bowled a left-hander with a shooter and left Reigate with 1st XI career figures of 3-0-7-2. The award of my cap was promulgated posthumously, as far as my schooldays were concerned, by an announcement in the school journal the following Christmas.

Our kindly umpire, Mr Woodhead, saviour of my curved carpentry, encouragingly remarked that, had I been given regular bowling opportunities, I would have made a successful new-ball bowler. In two house matches immediately before the Guildford finale I had returned a combined analysis of 13.3-4-24-11. One team was dismissed for 11 in 7.1 overs, the lowest total of any match I have ever played in. There were seven ducks and the highest scorer was extras.

While captaining Banstead Colts, I scored a then career-best 42 against Sutton and played my first games for their third and fourth senior elevens. Banstead's ground was owned by a Church Trust and they were not allowed to play Sunday matches, so I joined a local Sunday club. Their skipper, Reg Cassidy, an extrovert and supremely enthusiastic wicket-keeper-batsman from Liverpool, gave me my earliest opportunities with the new ball at adult level. Throughout July and August I played whenever invitations came my way and appeared in 44 matches that season.

In my final year at Reigate, I was able to study in the prefects' room and listen to Test match commentaries. The 1957 season was the first in which BBC Radio broadcast Test cricket ball-by-ball throughout the day, and the programme's current name, *Test Match Special*, was introduced. The opening match of the West Indies series reintroduced Test cricket to Birmingham after a hiatus of 28 years. It was a memorable match. After Ramadhin (7 for 49) had skittled out England for 186, the tourists had amassed 474. England drooped to 113 for 3 before Peter May (285 not out) and Colin Cowdrey (154) added a monumental 411 together. The commentary provided compulsive listening, especially when England declared at 583 for 4 and reduced West Indies to 72 for 7 before time ran out.

In the sixth form I became fascinated by the history of architecture and won the sixth-form art prize by sketching and reviewing half a dozen old buildings in Epsom, mostly pubs. Mr Sweatman, the ugly sister episode long forgotten, improved my sketching and lettering skills so that I sailed through the A level art exam. Despite my cricket activities, I managed to pass all three A levels and the general paper. It probably helped that for an entire week prior to the exams I decanted from school and, accompanied only by a crate of brown ale, revised assiduously in the garden. Having chosen to study architecture, I was awarded a Surrey Exhibition and a place at the Kingston School of Art.

My career in architecture lasted precisely one term. Two major factors conspired to end it. The first was cricket. I had not realised the amount of studying that would be involved, although I was well aware that the course would take six years. I was far too hooked on cricket to give it second best. The second was Dad's deteriorating health. The Canada Experience had taken its toll, exacerbating a congenital heart problem and causing high blood pressure. Nowadays beta-blockers and even surgery would probably have restored him to reasonable health but neither was available in the 1950s. With heavy mortgage outgoings he could not afford to restore the full cost of my studies. Although I loved making measured drawing and drafting plans, I probably only wanted to design cathedrals. I was slightly put off the first day when our structural engineering lecturer informed us that we had made a ghastly mistake. 'You should have become doctors,' he advised his startled audience. 'They can bury their mistakes. You'll have to keep walking past yours.'

The decision made, I felt incredible relief. The downside was the fact that, having terminated my full-time education, I was now liable for two years of National Service. The final phase of my training for *Test Match Special* was about to begin.

THREE

ROYAL AIR FORCE SERVICE

ALTHOUGH ESCAPING from architecture and full-time educa-tion had made me liable for National Service, it was unlikely that I would be called up before the autumn. Needing to find some employ-ment that would allow me to play cricket, I began full-time work in the production department of a London book publisher for a weekly – or weakly – wage of £6. Unwittingly, I was to learn much about pub-lishing that would stand me in good stead when I began compiling and writing books.

Lutterworth's proprietors were the United Society for Christian Literature. Facing their entrance somewhat inappropriately were the offices of two of Britain's raunchier publications, *Blighty* and *News of the World*. Just around the corner in Fleet Street was Jack Hobbs's Sports Shop. Although now retired, Sir John Berry Hobbs, 'The Master', occasionally visited it from his home in Hove and I once caught a glimpse of him inside the shop. How I envied those who had watched him scoring some of those first-class aggregates of 61,237 runs and 197 hundreds, world-record tallies that will never be equalled. John Arlott became his close friend and began organising lunches in London for the great man's birthdays on 16 December. The guest list was confined mainly to Surrey cricketers and leading cricket writers. These celebrations have continued uninterrupted since Sir Jack's death in 1963, but with a place still laid for him. The Master's Club itself has even survived the passing of its president, John Arlott, in 1991. It meets bi-annually at The Oval, once in mid-season on the first morning of a county championship match and, secondly, for the birthday lunch. Membership, by invitation, is limited to 81 – the number of years of Sir Jack's life – and it was a huge honour when John asked me if I would like to join that élite group.

After a few weeks' experience of the drudgery of office life at the Lutterworth Press, I knew I would not be returning to publishing. The production department was not large. I was one of four assistants squeezed into a room the size of the *Test Match Special* commentary box in the Media Centre 'spaceship' at Lord's. The manager had a similarly sized room to himself on the other side of a thin partition. A kind man and a good explainer, he had the added quality of an interest in cricket. This was very handy when Banstead selected me for a midweek 1st XI match and I had to request a day off. As the cricket season gathered momentum and my new-ball bowling became more effective, such requests mounted. His solution was to set me various projects and leave me to adjust my working hours accordingly. Between us we invented flexitime.

I had registered for National Service in January but was not called for my medical for four months. At Tavistock House I coughed and was counted. As I had a brace of everything I should have, I was despatched to the Medical Board Centre in Croydon that afternoon. There, a tuning fork confirmed partial deafness from measles and formally ended my non-existent hopes of becoming a pilot. Colour blindness tests involving a book of charts, featuring tiny coloured circles, and an Indian doctor ended in pure farce. Unwittingly, I created some bizarre record by identifying large numerals among these tiny circles of varied colours that could be seen only by those suffering from rare extremes of colour interpretation disorders. To see one was unusual. To identify six was unheard of. He switched the pages and even hid the book, suddenly producing it again when he thought my attention was elsewhere. His eyes gleamed wildly. It was all to no avail. I could still see just the numbers I had originally identified.

'Oh, my God,' he screamed, like a demented Peter Sellers. 'What are we to do? Please say you can see a 49 on this page and I will pass you. Please!' I refused. I could see a 13 and that was all. I was sent outside. Other medics were called. They peered round the door at me, probably expecting to see an alien. I gave them my best impression of Alec Guinness smiling. Eventually, I suspect by a narrow vote, I was passed fit to serve Her Majesty. I had already been guaranteed selection for the RAF because of my Combined Cadet Corps (CCC) service at Reigate, and I was told to expect to be in a blue uniform by August.

The following week, the assistant production manager failed to appear and was never seen again. With scant ceremony and no pay increase, I was elevated to his post. This grand new title and promotion from ledgers to cards controlling paper and binding did not postpone my decision to leave the Lutterworth Press – and publishing – in late July. I had decided to devote my energies entirely to playing cricket until I was called up. September arrived but my official brown envelope had not. I cycled into Epsom and searched for a temporary job. Woolworth's immediately signed me on to unpack their delivery trucks and rack their goods for £8 a week. I worked with two other lads and it was great fun. The top floor of the shop was virtually a vast barren attic and we would play cricket up there in our breaks. One of my rare offside strokes, middled just behind square, plucked out a secret panel leading to a hidden area under the eaves. It housed a mattress and occasionally a mistress, as it turned out to be a nesting area for a young member of the management team and an attractive blonde sales assistant. 'Woolies' had obviously added a casting couch to its array of plastic flowers.

During 1958 I managed to escape on to the cricket field 44 times, all for various Banstead teams and clubs. By now, I was batting in the lower order, if at all, and averaged a princely 4.83. My bowling figures, 94 wickets at 10.93, 40 of the dismissals being bowled, revealed how my game was developing. I had four five-wicket analyses, including one of 6 for 15 after an all-night party. Surprisingly, I managed to hold 17 catches, the most I was ever to latch on to in a season, a stat that will amaze many who saw my embarrassing efforts in later years when I became handicapped – literally – by Dupuytren's contractures partially contracting my hands.

Eventually, the brown envelope arrived with my travel orders and a rail warrant to Bedford. My service career began at RAF Cardington on Monday, 8 December. Formerly the base of the RAF Balloons Unit, the station's vast airship hangars that had housed R-100 and its mates still survived, giant fortresses with red warning lights on their summits. RAF No. 2 Reception Unit was my home for a week. Because of my CCC experience, I was made senior man of the sixteen inmates of Hut 428 and given the responsibility of ensuring that the stove was clean, its coke polished and everything within the hut kept to surgical cleanliness. We were given our service numbers, issued with identity cards (Form 1250) and presented with enough kit to last us for two years. As we were found items to fit us, a process that took four days, we had to replace that article of our civilian attire. Apart from the airfolk stationed at Cardington, everyone wandered around the camp in a delightfully bohemian mixture of uniform and civvies. The effect of this conglomerate disarray was similar to that shown in the castle courtyard of the old black and white film, *The Colditz Story*.

One of our 104 weeks of service had passed before about sixty conscripts, including myself, were cleared to travel by special train to the Recruit Training Centre at RAF Bridgnorth in Shropshire. All went serenely until, after a five-hour journey, we disembarked. As if released from hell, a swarm of corporal drill instructors (DIs) descended on us, shouting and screaming as though we had just tried to escape from a POW camp. We were herded into trucks and transported like cattle to the training centre. It was the start of eight weeks of shouting, marching and bull that constituted our basic training. In such situations, everyone mucks in together and those with a sense of humour fare best. It is essential to be positive. I determined that I was going to enjoy my two years and make the RAF pay a heavy price for that slice of my life.

A sound piece of advice in the services is do not volunteer for anything. The classic scenario is, 'Any musicians here? Good, move that piano!' I forgot this edict at Bridgnorth when a corporal taking us on fatigues asked if any of us were good at painting. 'Watercolours or oils, corporal?' I asked innocently, having yet to dabble in oils. 'I mean ordinary effing painting, son. You'll do.' Given a vast drum of grey paint and a small brush, I was taken to the cookhouse, where several hundred new coat hooks had been mounted on unpainted wood. Four hours later, my work completed, I was revisited by the corporal. 'Very good, son. Very impressive. Right. I'm going off on a thirty-six now. Have your lunch and then report to one of the other corporals.' He was referring to a 36-hour pass to escape the camp but I thought he meant he was going on a bus. It mattered not. I guessed that he had not warned any of the other corporals to expect a visit from 'Painter Will' and so I vanished for the rest of the weekend.

Reigate Grammar School had introduced hockey during my final year. As few boys had played it before, they recruited the cricket 1st XI. Our first game was played away against the local County Grammar School for Girls. We decided to nudge and push delicately past their defenders and not go for any savage blows. After they had laid out our goalkeeper in the second minute, we moved swiftly on to Plan B. There were many injured shins (female), much bad language (female) and a 6–1 victory (male). I am assured that the fixture was never repeated before that girls' academy closed. My second volunteering risk, for a station hockey trial, bore better fruit than the first and I was selected for the RAF Bridgnorth hockey XI. After a reasonable debut, I was picked for a match at RAF Stafford. This was wonderful news as my flight (the RAF thought it was a bird and divided its employees into flights and wings) was due to spend two nights on a Resource and Initiative Camp in tents on the snowy mountains of north Wales. Just as they were leaving, I was summoned to the station CO's office and told that the hockey match had been cancelled because of the icy weather. I gambled and did not pass this message on to my squadron commander. Off went fifty-seven recruits, while three of us kept a low profile in our hut, emerging only to thieve coke for our stove or feed in the mess. My two comrades in escape had exploited their minor childhood maladies to gain medical exemption. On the third day the others returned, a sad, bedraggled, unshaven, cold, saturated and dispirited shambles. The snow on the mountainside had thawed the previous night causing torrents of freezing water to swamp their tents.

The most significant event of the Bridgnorth episode was our trade testing. I returned top marks in academic subjects and virtually none in those concerned with engineering or anything even slightly technical. The officer who interviewed me with these contrasting results before him greeted me with a wan smile. 'We must protect our aircraft from you, Frindall,' he said. He offered me a commission as a dental officer if I cared to sign on for an extra year. I had experienced enough agony in dental surgeries on two continents for me not to want to work in one. This left two alternatives – clerk accounts or clerk progress. Clerk progress, a junior version of clerk statistics, was rated the top clerical trade and there was keen competition to be selected for its training course. Asked if my choice would affect my chances of playing cricket, he assured me that if I was good enough, I would have every opportunity to play any sport regardless of what trade I was in. That being the case, I opted for clerk progress. Whenever I posed myself a question about my working future, the answer always involved cricket in some capacity.

After the confinements, bull and frozen wastes of Bridgnorth, the Trade Training camp at RAF Hereford was a veritable paradise. The atmosphere was relaxed, the training staff pleasant, the work interesting and the city of Hereford itself such a delight, with its ancient buildings and views along the Wye valley, that I determined one day to live there. The RAF camp at Creden Hill, a short bus ride out of the city, is now the headquarters of the Strategic Air Service. There I began my six-week clerk progress course and I was immediately selected for their hockey team. By now, I realised that anyone even moderately handy at a sport would have every opportunity and encouragement to engage in it in the services. As soon as it was known that I was keen to play hockey and cricket, I was almost given a separate contract. Officers responsible for supervising my official duties had to bow to the demands of team selectors and were very happy to do so. Luckily, I was not engaged on operational or shift work and the trade of clerk progress was to prove ideal.

At the end of the course we took the final exams and eventually learned that all but two of our class of twenty-two had passed. Somehow I finished with top marks and was automatically promoted from AC2 to the dizzy heights of AC1. The decision that was to determine where we spent the final twenty months of our conscription was indeed a key moment and we awaited our postings from Records Office with some trepidation. Our fates were announced in alphabetical order by Flying Officer Chang. 'Airclaftsman Flindall,' the Burmese officer intoned. He paused and then to a chorus of indrawn breaths and merriment he proclaimed, 'Belsen.' My heart stopped. Never mind the terrible location – think of two cricket seasons in Germany! Chang looked disconcerted and then summoned me to his desk. He handed me the posting notice. It read 'RAF BENSON'. Situated halfway between Oxford and Reading, it was just sixty miles from home.

One member of our course came from a wealthy Hereford family and his parents threw the final party. We all availed ourselves of the copious amounts of booze on offer and I tried whisky for the first time. Obviously, I tried far too hard. I have a surreal recollection of sitting in the back of a car and having the arm attached to my hand clasping my Form 1250 held out of the window as we passed the guardroom. I was put to bed and awoke early next morning with a monumental headache. For some reason I had torn my two bedsheets into thin bandage-like strips. All our bedding had to be returned before we left camp that morning. Carefully, I assembled the strips and arranged them between the folded blankets in the standard bed pack. To the casual observer, just the edge of the sheets showed. Undo the pack and it would be a different tale. We lined up. In trepidation I carefully handed the bedding store clerk my pack. Those behind me held their breath. The clerk ticked my name, casually lifted my pack and threw it over his shoulder on to the pile behind him. It disintegrated in midair, the sheet strips flying like bunting. Miraculously, the clerk did not look round but just continued with the next pack and somehow I got away with it. Like Brian Johnston, who revealed that he had first got drunk in almost identical circumstances, I have never touched whisky again.

RAF Benson was by far the best organised and most scenically attractive station I served on during my seven cricket seasons in the Royal Britannic Airworks. Set in the Chilterns and close to the Thames, it was one of the few camps to be methodically designed so that its operational and domestic compartments were totally separate. The station's ambience hardly mattered, such was my relief that it was within easy reach of home and cricket at Banstead.

After an eight-hour journey, I arrived at Benson just in time for tea. Having collected my food and found a space at a long table, I was asked to pass the ketchup. A danger bell rang in the back of my brain as I recognised the voice. Looking up, I saw the grinning face of my *bête noire* from Reigate. Because our names were next to each other in the register, I spent several years sitting alongside him. A large bullish lad, he would tear pages out of my exercise books, spray ink at me and generally be rather fun company. Having once taken him on physically, I decided that when my injuries eventually healed it might be wiser to turn the other cheek next time. He was frightened of only one man, our form master, Mr Bowles. A fit and exceedingly strong rugby forward, Mr Bowles had an exceptionally powerful follow through when aiming a gym shoe at a backside in need of punishment. As Mr Bowles was chalking on the board ten feet in front of our twin desk, he aimed a water pistol at the nape of a lad sat immediately in front of him. To gain maximum effect he turned round and winked at the back of the class as he fired his weapon. He thus missed seeing his victim drop a pencil and bend down to retrieve it. The jet of water sailed harmlessly above a prone blazer, passed over Mr Bowles's right shoulder and neatly obliterated the word he was chalking. That famous follow through was soon exacting splendid revenge. Thoughts that his cheating and cribbing had passed unnoticed were dispelled by a brilliantly terse comment on his end-of-term report – 'He is forging his way steadily ahead.'

It was inevitable that his final day at Reigate would be dramatic. Having uncoupled a goods train in a siding at Redhill, he spotted the railway police arriving at the school entrance and barricaded himself inside a second-floor classroom. Finding a crate of empty milk bottles, he opened the window and began hurling them at a female teacher as she crossed the playground to her chemistry lab. He was expelled, presumably dealt with by the authorities and encouraged to join the RAF as a boy cadet. Benson was his first posting, but as he had nudged a local girl into a delicate condition, he was being posted to Kenya the following day. To quote Neddy Seagoon, 'I never saw him again.'

Before I could attempt to wreck Benson's Motor Transport (MT) Section with my embryo Kardex expertise, I was detached on a special mission by one of that office's senior NCOs. Sgt Les Smith had played wartime cricket alongside Jim Laker for RAF Egypt and was a fine all-rounder. His major ambition since arriving at Benson had been to construct a decent practice pitch but he required a fellow enthusiast to provide his work force. Les had even prepared detailed plans of the dimensions and strata of varied rock, stones and shale that were to form the base below the jute matting. For my first fortnight, instead of starting office work at 8 a.m., I had a leisurely breakfast before reporting to Sgt Smith's married quarters for mid-morning coffee. We would then stroll over to the cricket ground and work on the magic pitch. We dug out a vast trench, supervised the various fillings, rolled the shale level and carefully laid the mat. We erected the netting and then, of course, we had to practise on it daily to test for any inconsistencies of bounce. Besides elementary statistics and office management, the RAF taught me the art of skiving or work evasion. Les Smith was a skiver supreme and passed on many tips. An invaluable one was that if you were on an unauthorised or even nefarious errand, if you walked purposefully and carried a sheet of paper, no one would ever question your mission. Unfortunately, training in advanced shirking has proved of absolutely no use in my self-employed role of the past forty years.

My training file must have contained a note of warning about my ability to wreck parades because I was never asked to attend a formal one at Benson. The station housed the Queen's Flight and some of the world's leaders were flown there *en route* to Chequers. I did manage to stand in a security guard for Dwight D. Eisenhower, 34th President of the United States, without mishap or mayhem. As he passed my position, he raised both arms as though signalling a six and gave a broad smile. Prime Minister Harold Macmillan beside him was in more serious mood.

Cricket soon occupied most of my summer days, with weekend matches for various Banstead teams and midweek ones for RAF Benson and the squadron team. Those middle months of 1959 were among the happiest of my life. Once you had escaped from the bull and bawling of the training camps, life in the RAF was a delightfully cushy number indeed. Members of the station cricket teams could even have their boots and pads whitened by delivering them to the sports section. Weeks of net practice had improved my batting and a drop to number eight gave me licence to slog if we batted first and were planning to declare.

A successful spell of swing bowling in the trial match, when my six wickets included a hat-trick, ensured selection for the first match at RAF White Waltham. That station, close to Maidenhead, had been the scene of my only school CCC camp, my maiden experience of gliding, and my first attempt to fry mushrooms plucked off the airfield in butter nicked from the cookhouse. Now it provided a happy debut with a handy undefeated pre-declaration slog preceding figures of 5 for 22 from 12 overs to earn a 73 run win. Other five-wicket hauls earned me selection for Transport Command, while, at Banstead, a return of 6 for 24 for the 2nd XI earned me a Saturday debut in the top side. I had never felt fitter in my life and was bowling with good pace and rhythm. Then I began to notice a nagging ache in my lower back and slight numbness in the left leg. Little niggles in the undercarriage are part and parcel of a bowler's burden and I have always tried to ignore them. This time it wasn't such a good idea and my back virtually seized up overnight. A visit to the Medical Officer resulted in a slipped disc being diagnosed and my spending the next fortnight on a bed of boards in hospital at RAF Halton, near Aylesbury. They wanted to keep me longer but I dressed and climbed the hill that had overlooked my bed for all those bleak hours to prove that I should leave. A chiropractor's manipulations helped with the back's resurrection. Alarmingly, he advised that my lying on boards had merely weakened the supporting muscles. Many years later, X-rays revealed that I had actually fractured two discs. The only good news to reach me during my incarceration concerned my promotion to LAC (Leading Aircraftman) and a substantial weekly pay-rise of about £1.

Told not to bowl fast again for six months, I spent the rest of the season reverting to occasional off-spin and opening the batting, mainly for the exotically named village clubs of Berrick Salome and Warborough and Shillingford. So capricious were their pitches that any batsman reaching double figures was revered as a latent Len Hutton. Compelled to graft by my dodgy back, I bored my way to 13, 16 not out, 0 and 10.

The director of Benson's Stage Club, Juliana Goss, persuaded me to audition for their next production, the comedy *Sailor Beware*. A splendid galleon of a lady, she had worked with Tony Hancock in his early days as a comedian and remembered him as being very thin, extremely nervous and so lacking in confidence that, after each performance, he would ask everyone if he had been OK. She played the role of Emma Hornett, which Peggy Mount had made famous, and chose me for the part of her downtrodden husband, Henry. To be asked to play the male lead on the back of a stage career spread over ten years and consisting of just two roles, and those a fir tree in Hiawatha and first commoner in *Julius Caesar*, was asking a lot. I relished the chance, though, and photographs of me as a 60-year-old drunken ferret keeper do look embarrassingly recent. My attempts to cope with a false moustache were discarded early in rehearsals and I decided to grow one. To do this I had to make a formal application to my CO that may even have had to be registered at the Air Ministry. The moustache remained with me for the remainder of my RAF career, gradually being extended into modest handlebar proportions after I was commissioned.

My 'Henry' was well received. A scout from the British Forces Network came to the show and I was chosen to appear in a half-hour play to be recorded at their Millbank studio. My stage experiences have proved invaluable training for public speaking. They gave me confidence to brave an audience and also taught me to project my voice. Thankfully, I was to discover that it is much easier to make an after-dinner speech using your own material than it is to remember lines of a script.

Like most RAF stations, Benson had its own broadcasting system. Most of the time it would transmit BBC programmes but in the evenings and at weekends, volunteers from the station's staff and their families would present material of their own. As Julie Goss was heavily involved with Radio Benson, I was invited to help out as an announcer. In no time I had been ambushed into the role of film critic, which at least earned me a permanent free seat in the station cinema. When she scripted a weekly skit on RAF life entitled 'Airmen at Large', she cast me in the lead. This again was invaluable training for *Test Match Special* because it gave me confidence to speak on air and to edit my comments to fit in with gaps in play and commentary. Without that experience, I probably would never have been allowed the luxury of my own BBC microphone. She also involved me in the station's panto as one of the custard-pie throwing broker's men. That same week I was asked to do a stint as a waiter in the officers' mess. I had nightmares about confusing the two roles.

Another interest that compensated for my back problems was Maureen Doris Wesson. Some mischievously suggested that she might have caused them. Joining the Banstead Wayfarers in 1957 had proved to be another key moment, not because I was immediately appointed their fixture secretary, but because I met my future wife. Maureen was their scorer and her brothers, Bevan and Clive, both played for the team on Sundays. As far as Maureen and I were concerned, it was a case of mutual dislike at first sight. It didn't help when I discovered that she hated being called 'Little Mo'. All the Wessons were midgets. The boys were just over five feet tall and Maureen was barely the same height as my mother. This was a tremendous disadvantage for her because I had received prolonged advanced training in dealing with the disruptive capabilities of tiny women. I got on very well with Bev, a stylish batsman who had represented Surrey Schools, and also with Clive, whose lack of inches allowed him to flight the slowest of off-breaks and lure many batsmen to their doom.

I had played several matches for the Wayfarers before an accident tempted Maureen to befriend me. It happened while I was fielding for Banstead at backward short-leg to the bowling of Charlie Millsom. A unique character and the subject of a complete chapter in Ronald Mason's *Sing All a Green Willow*, Charlie bowled one long-hop a season. Recognising the annual event later than the batsman, who clobbered it straight at my left temple, I managed to get part of my left hand to the missile and deflected some of the force. They ran a single as I went down and that annoyed me. I refused to go off as I was bowling at the other end and had taken a couple of wickets. After a long break I began the next over, hit the offender on the pads and the umpire's finger went up, possibly in sympathy but I think it was fairly plumb. I finished with 4 for 35 and a spectacular, multicoloured bruise. Next day I felt fine but the white of my eye was blood red and I had a massive shiner. Such was my enthusiasm and madness that I insisted on playing for the Wayfarers and it was then that Maureen succumbed to her maternal interests and showed genuine concern for my welfare. For me, this was unknown territory and I was smitten.

We started going out and the relationship blossomed throughout my first year in the RAF. By the end of 1959, we had decided to risk becoming a divorce statistic and I had to give serious thought to my future career. I was gaining valuable experience by frequently being left in charge of the Tech Manning office. In fact, I was rather enjoying life in the RAF, especially the statistical work, while the opportunities for playing cricket appeared endless. There was also a chance that my excursions into acting and broadcasting might bear fruit. Even my draftsmanship skills, a by-product of my term at the Kingston School of Art, were proving useful and I was able to inflate my RAF pittance with the proceeds of some varied art commissions. On the strength of my three A levels, I gained a certificate of eligibility from London University to read for a degree in economics. Eventually, I horrified my National Service colleagues by taking a serious look at my career prospects in the RAF if I signed on for another three years. Then came a note from Records Office announcing that I had been posted a dozen miles north-west to RAF Abingdon.

My move to Abingdon heralded the start of a year of major decisions. These inevitably produced key moments, two of which were exceedingly traumatic. In fact, I took two plunges within a month. First, I ended my National Service stint by signing on in the RAF for an additional three-year term. Three weeks later, I married Maureen in the village church a few hundred yards from Banstead cricket ground and we set up house in Long Wittenham, a sleepy Thames-side hamlet.

I soon reduced my working week to three days by playing cricket on Wednesdays and studying economics at Oxford Polytechnic (now Oxford Brookes University) on Fridays. Then, just as this very pleasant schedule was running smoothly, I was despatched to Lincolnshire for a six-week statistics course. No sooner had I successfully passed this and taken advantage of the instructor's slow dictation of notes to hone my permanently adopted italic script, than I contracted glandular fever. Bizarrely, I was twice promoted during my sick leave, reaching the lofty rank of corporal after the briefest of time as a senior aircraftman (SAC). Until all signs of my virus had vanished, the RAF could not permit my return to duty. Happily, minor traces remained for several months although, curiously, after a few weeks, I was fit enough to play cricket.

Like Gilbert's Wandering Minstrel, my 1960 season was a thing of shreds and patches. With breaks for the Lincolnshire course and illness,

I managed to play in sixteen matches, involving seven different teams spread over five counties. Those involving Abingdon Town gave most pleasure. Their players were mostly doctors of science working at nearby Harwell and Culham, while their ground, in a delightful setting close to the Thames, faced the stately spire of St Helen's Church and a Benedictine Abbey.

Maureen was admitted to Epsom District Hospital, where I had started my own innings twenty-one years earlier, while I was playing my last match of the season at Felbridge in Sussex. This was long before the days of mobile phones and I was blissfully unaware of this dramatic news, as were her two siblings who were with me. It was not until I returned to my in-laws late that night after enthusiastically celebrating a return of 5 for 37 that I discovered that I had become a father. Next morning came the emotional thunderbolt. Raymond Ernest Howard had arrived by Caesarean section without his left thumb and radius (the shorter, thicker forearm bone). Only parents who have had to face the birth of a first child who is afflicted to any degree will know the reaction that hit Maureen and me that Monday morning. The nursing staff could not have been more sympathetic and comforting but forty-five years have done little to soften that gut-wrenching shock. At that stage, we feared that he might have other abnormalities, but mercifully there were no major ones. Soon Raymond was beginning a long series of visits to London's major children's hospital in Great Ormond Street for tests and periodic surgery. A friendly, cheerful lad, he overcame the problems of a shortened left arm and became very keen on cricket. In retrospect, we should have named him Leonard after the great Hutton, whose left arm had been noticeably reduced by a compound fracture sustained during a wartime accident in an Army gymnasium.

The RAF could not have been more considerate. They awarded me compassionate leave and posted me to RAF Northolt in Middlesex so that we could be nearer Great Ormond Street Hospital for Raymond's treatment. Eventually, we found a flat in Sutton in Surrey and I bought a Lambretta scooter to commute to Northolt.

In the summer of 1961, Richie Benaud's Australians retained the Ashes when they won the fourth Test at Old Trafford to take a 2–1 lead in the five-match rubber. It was Benaud himself who scuppered England's charge to victory by pitching his leg-breaks into the rough from around the wicket to take 5 for 12 in 25 balls. The series was full of incident and I managed to hear much of it on *Test Match Special*. The RAF allowed me a 50-match season that was spread over nine counties and my back withstood its greatest workload to date – 498.5 overs. In the 490th of those, fairly close to Christmas, I took my hundredth wicket of the season, the first time I had achieved such a feat. The RAF Northolt team was the best organised of any I was to find in the service. We won eight and lost just three of our 15 matches and my 32 wickets at 11.25, together with 117 runs at 16.71, earned me a 1st XI cap.

More crucially, that performance considerably affected the remainder of my RAF career as it gained me a significant visit to Command Headquarters. I was interviewed by a senior officer who had been appointed CO of a Joint Services Trials Unit at RAAF Edinburgh near Adelaide. I suspect that he might have rehearsed his sales pitch: 'My establishment of personnel numbers eleven men, Frindall, and, as a cricketer, it has given me an idea. I need a corporal clerk statistics, but more importantly I need an opening bowler who can bat at number eight. You, Frindall, are he. I might add that, handy cricketer though you are, this will almost certainly be the only time you are selected for a tour of Australia. What is more, you will be there for four years and, as a statistician, I'm sure you will have calculated that, with English seasons at each end, you will have six summers in those four years.'

The only drawback was that I would have to increase, yet again, the length of my service to accommodate this tour of duty, but the opportunity was far too tempting to refuse. I signed on for an extra two years and applied for the posting. After six weeks the Air Ministry delivered its blunt message: 'Application refused. Subject to Cosmic Top Secret clearance, you will be attached to NATO at HQ Allied Air Forces Central Europe, Fontainebleau.' Even though this was considered to be an exceptionally plum posting, to me it was shattering news. This edict condemned me to a two-and-a-half-year tour of duty in France and I feared there would be no cricket, except the wicketless sort where you used the bat to defend your legs. Later, I discovered that I had indeed been selected for the Adelaide mission but was diverted to Fontainebleau when another corporal clerk stats was found to be providing unauthorised favours for a senior officer's wife. Sadly, she was sent home, too. I was to wait another fourteen years before visiting Australia.

With Raymond still undergoing treatment in London, it was decided that he would be based with my in-laws if Maureen joined me in France. Overseas living-out allowances were generous but the cost of rented accommodation in Fontainebleau was very high and there was a waiting period of eighteen months for NATO flats. The Commander in Chief of HQ AAFCE was Air Chief Marshal the Earl of Bandon. A colourful and thirsty character, the 'Abandoned Earl' featured in scores of memorable anecdotes. He had opened a swimming pool in Singapore by diving into it clad in his pyjamas. At the coronation, he was controlling the RAF's fly past from the roof of Buckingham Palace when one of his subordinates, desperate for a pee, relieved himself behind a chimney. The Earl formally charged him with 'pissing on the Queen's roof'. As the Earl was very fond of lamb, meat that was then unobtainable in France, he authorised his aircraft to fly his ADC to Northolt, where a staff car was regularly provided to collect supplies from a local butcher. Such imports were forbidden, but the Earl was able to smuggle in his tasty contraband via his own airstrip at Melun.

I managed to sneak a lift with the Earl's emergency rations to search out alternative accommodation in Fontainebleau. Apart from the Canada migration, I had not previously ventured outside England. I discovered that my choice lay between renting a houseboat on the Seine and importing a large caravan. An enterprising Frenchman had recently bought a field in a village ten miles south of Fontainebleau. I was taken to meet him and discovered that he had installed 240 volt power and mains drainage. His site boasted just four mobile homes but there was space for at least twenty more. He offered me commission of a month's free rent for every caravan I introduced to his field. When I left eighteen months later, I had boosted the tally to twenty-four. The real bonus was that I was able to sell my caravan and recoup all my outgoings when I left. That Melun visit also unveiled the extraordinary news that cricket was played at Fontainebleau, Versailles and in Paris.

My trusty Lambretta gained me another major prize in the form of a full NATO driving licence. One of my first tasks was to go into the historic town of Fontainebleau and register for NATO petrol coupons. As NATO licences for two-wheeled vehicles did not exist, I was issued with a four-wheel one which entitled me to drive pretty well anything. I bought a second-hand Ford Anglia and an RAF driver bravely took me on what he termed 'driving destruction' on evening runs that must have terrified the villagers close to our caravan site. I had never previously sat behind a steering wheel of anything apart from a wooden car Dad built me when I was four. Gradually I got the hang of it and I comfortably survived my first solo trip, a highly ambitious expedition to Paris to collect the newly arrived Maureen.

Soon I was driving around Europe. A chance meeting with Colonel P.C. Williams led to a major expansion of cricket at Fontainebleau. Discovering my enthusiasm for the game, Pat Williams contacted me and said that if I could find the fixtures he could obtain NATO funds to enable us to tour outside France. The RAF, Army and a Combined Services team already had a number of regular fixtures on a matting pitch laid on bitumen-covered concrete at the Camp Guynemer sports stadium. This schedule was swiftly expanded to encompass trips to Geneva, Germany and The Hague. Pat Williams was near retirement. Asked what he intended to do, he would reply, 'Beachcomb around the Med.' Two years later he was installed as Secretary of Sussex County Cricket Club.

Geneva Cricket Club played on a matting pitch laid on grass within the running circuit of an athletics ground. Single-brick walls marked the inner and outer extremities of the running track. Hits that stopped at the inner wall counted two and those that crossed the lanes to the far wall were boundaries. In the first game, batting at five, I was run out for 1. I can recall it vividly. The mat had shrunk and the edges were stretched to make it reach the 22 yards with the result that the crease appeared as a curve. My bat had passed the nearer part of the arc but not its wider extremities. Aircent (Allied Air Forces Central Europe) won two low-scoring matches and the scorecard shows me catching their top scorer in the second match, an all-rounder called Buzo who would have given John Arlott great delight.

In Germany, we completed a double victory against the BAOR (British Army of the Rhine) Cup winners and, having motored 300 miles to The Hague, we rather stupidly bowled out the Commonwealth Cricket Club before lunch and were heading home by teatime. Their main all-rounder was a Lancastrian who had furnished his flat with a dozen bar stools nicked from local pubs. Our hosts were greatly amused to discover that one of our players was named Dicky Dykes. Dinner in an Indonesian restaurant instilled my love of spicy dishes.

The first known reference to cricket occurs on 10 March 1300 in the Wardrobe Account of King Edward I with a note of 'creag' being played at Newenden in Kent. The game was almost certainly being played in France by that time, too. By 1478 'criquet' was being referred to in Flanders. Horace Walpole, fourth Earl of Orford, recorded cricket being played in Paris in 1766 and there is reference to a match at St Omer *circa* 1777. A different sort of contest at Waterloo probably put the French off cricket and the next reference to a match of any significance came eighty-eight years later. The most significant date in the history of French cricket is 1890 when a group of British businessmen founded the Standard Athletic Club at Meudon. Their members were swollen by engineers imported to construct the Eiffel Tower.

Cricketwise, France's main claim to fame is that it staged the only game of Olympic cricket. The two-day match was played at the Velodrome de Vincennes, a cycling stadium, as part of the Great Exposition in 1900, and was retrospectively awarded Olympic status in 1912. England (117 and 145 for 5 declared) beat France (78 and 26) by 158 runs. England were represented by the Devon County Wanderers, a combination of the old boys of Blundell's School in Tiverton and Castle Cary CC in Somerset, while the home side was composed mainly of English members of the Standard Athletic and Albion Clubs living in Paris. England received silver medals (and models of the eleven-year-old Eiffel Tower) and France were awarded bronze ones.

As well as playing for the Aircent, Afcent (Allied Forces Central Europe) and RAF teams in Fontainebleau, I frequently drove to Paris to play for Standard Athletic. Situated in woodland, it was primarily a tennis and football club. I don't recall any Frenchmen playing cricket in the two seasons I was there. The pitch was jute matting on rolled shale and it was a batting paradise. I used to open the bowling with a delightful Nigerian teacher who rejoiced in the splendid name of Rex Akpofure. He lived up to it by bowling fast and clogging the ball into the tennis courts and adjacent swimming pool. Our wicket-keeper and opening batsman was a dexterous Indian called Badrinath. I have no idea what his first name was. Everyone called him Badri. He was one of the best keepers I've seen outside the first-class game and his batting was as wristy and elegant as that of Azharuddin. Our captain, Sindbad 'Mike' Vail, was an American who, like Sir Paul Getty several decades later, fell in love with the game while in England.

A major player in the Standard Athletic team of the early sixties was a James Robertson Justice lookalike called Commander (Engineer) Jack Hodges. During après cricket drinks at his sumptuous apartment, I asked him what had been his proudest feat on the cricket field. He extracted a leather-bound *Wisden* from his shelves and turned to the score of a two-day match at Lord's between the Royal Navy and the RAF in July 1949. He had joined the number four batsman, a young national serviceman, with the score 91 for 7. They were still together at the declaration some 192 runs later, Jack's share being 58. His partner, who scored 162, was one writer Peter Barker Howard May, the future Surrey and England captain, who had made his first-class debut for the Combined Services against Hampshire at Aldershot the previous season.

After a few months working on servicing schedules in the RAF Motor Pool, I was moved to the international building where my main task was to spend two days a month in a war room in the bowels of Fontainebleau Forest. There we rehearsed World War Three. It proved to be excellent practice for my six- and seven-hour stints on *Test Match Special*. I quickly learnt to concentrate for long periods as I recorded hits and misses of launched missiles. Now that more than four decades separate me from the secret action, I can reveal that we lost 15 wars to 2 during my stint there.

My RAF CO, Squadron Leader Greenaway, recommended me for a commission and, after interviews in Germany, gruelling manoeuvres at RAF Biggin Hill, prolonged square-bashing at RAF Thetford in wintry Norfolk, I began the final stage of my service career as a Pilot Officer. I was almost instantly promoted to Flying Officer, because of my previous service, and could add the evocative abbreviation of 'Fg Off' after my name.

My posting to RAF Leeming, a Flying Training station just south of Catterick and close to the A1, was as station accountant officer. After I had done the job for several weeks, I was sent to Lincolnshire to learn how to do it properly. The first thing I did was to find out who was secretary of Grantham Cricket Club and offer my services as a player. In the second of my two appearances for them, against the Leicestershire village of Buckminster, I took 6 for 30 in 16 overs as we dismissed them for 65. Four of my victims were bowled, the first of them taking my wickets tally for the season to 100.

Returning to Yorkshire, I played regularly for Northallerton in the North Yorkshire and South Durham League. This was my first taste of league cricket and I relished the competitive edge that it added to the matches. Most of the pitches helped seam bowlers and I took 27 wickets at 16.00 in my 10 matches. It helped that my opening partner was a 17-year-old left-arm quick bowler, Arthur ('Rocker') Robinson, who was destined to play 84 first-class matches for Yorkshire. I averaged only 9 with the bat but twice top-scored, first with 27 out of 49 all out in a nine-wicket defeat at Barnard Castle, and second with 38 out of 116 to tie at Stokesley. Batting second, we were 43 for 6 when I went in. Here's the local press report: 'But W. Frindall (38) hit out with gusto and with the luck going Northallerton's way and the tailenders scrambling precious runs, the tie was reached. Frindall, going for the winning run, hit out only to be caught on the far boundary.' I had just put one on to the pavilion roof and, with the field brought in, found the lone missionary at long-on. I still swear he was in the next field!

Albert Gaskell umpired many of our Sunday 'friendly' matches. An excellent umpire who was on the minor counties list, he was an extremely large and thirsty unit. Unless you ran in from a wide angle, you had to treat him as a roundabout and both 'Rocker' and I developed odd kinks in the final parts of our approaches to the wicket. Albert spent two seasons on the first-class list but both were heavily rain-affected. He grew larger and redder as the sales of Tadcaster ale climbed and he was forced to retire. His wife, a lovely neat little lady, often watched cricket on television. A reporter once asked her if she looked for Albert when she tuned in to a game.

'Don't have to look for him,' she replied. 'If it's large and white and moves, it's Albert. If it doesn't, it's sightscreen.'

We weren't on the phone in our rented accommodation. One morning as I was preparing to make my debut for the Adastrians at Ampleforth College, a colleague from Leeming knocked on the door. He had to impart the news that my father had died the previous night. I had visited Dad in Epsom Hospital a few days earlier, where he seemed to be recovering well from a heart attack, but on the eve of going home he had had another massive coronary. He was 54. Modern drugs and surgery would probably have prolonged his life by twenty years.

Dad had been advised not to play cricket after we returned from Vancouver so I never saw him play in a match. He bowled and batted against me hundreds of times in back gardens, on untamed fields and even, naughtily, on a remote putting green on Epsom Downs. He bowled quickish off-breaks and batted down the order. His highest score was 49 and his best bowling 9 for 45. I determined to better both

of them and eventually I succeeded but I probably played several hundred more games than he did. Bob Honess is the only cricketer who
played alongside both of us. A laboratory technician at Great Burgh
before joining the RAF, he played for the Distillers with Dad. Having
joined Legal & General, he played countless years for Temple Bar,
including the match where I made my scoring debut in 1949. We were
to play alongside each other many times after I left the RAF, and in
1980 he toured South Africa with my Maltamaniacs.

Dad's death left Mother alone in Epsom and I decided not to prolong my career in the RAF. I had no real idea what I wanted to do apart
from being involved with cricket. On my final day I shaved off my
apology for a handlebar moustache, put it into an envelope and handed it in to stores with the rest of my service kit. It was a symbolic ges-
ture to mark the end of a service career that had provided me with a
university of life, an academy of cricket and, unwittingly, a thorough
training for the unexpected dream career ahead.

FOUR

GOING FREELANCE

M Y SOLE AIM when I left the RAF in 1965 was to find work in cricket, preferably involving administration or reporting. I never even considered scoring. Apart from standing in, as players have to when their team doesn't have a scorer, I had not acted as an official scorer at club level since 1955 when I began playing regularly. Until the right opportunity presented itself, I was prepared to take any work to support my young family, a second son, Stuart William, having been born in Yorkshire at RAF Catterick hospital in March. Meanwhile, I continued playing cricket for Banstead and, occasionally, as a guest for the Legal & General Assurance Society's team, Temple Bar. While I was waiting to bat for them, I was headhunted. They just happened to be looking for a trainee insurance inspector in their City office. Although the work sounded fairly unexciting, it had the great advantage of being flexible. Inspectors could check on their agents during the morning and play cricket in the afternoon. This had enormous appeal. After the briefest interview with a former captain from my scoring days at Kingswood, I began work in Fenchurch Street and five days later took 8 for 29 for Banstead 1st XI.

Then, on 30 October, Arthur Wrigley, BBC Radio's scorer since 1934, died of cancer in a Stockport hospital, following emergency surgery. His premature demise proved to be the key moment of them all and my life changed. Arthur was only 53 and had pioneered a role born out of Hedley Verity's phenomenal bowling performance against Australia at Lord's in 1934. In those early days of cricket broadcasting, Test matches were covered by a lone reporter accompanied by an engineer with all his gear housed in a haversack. Initially, the MCC would not permit live broadcasting from within the Lord's ground and Howard Marshall, their cricket reporter, had to broadcast from a room rented in a house nearby. On one occasion he had to halt a piano lesson in the room above. At the 1934 Test, Marshall was broadcasting his reports from a tiny balcony above the home dressing room. Australia had easily won the opening Test at Trent Bridge. This second Test began on a Friday. England won the toss, batted and scored 440, with Maurice Leyland and Les Ames scoring hundreds. No other England keeper scored a century against Australia until Alan Knott did so in 1974–75. At stumps on Saturday, Australia were 192 for 2, with Bill Brown 103 not out and, crucially, Bradman out for 36. With the pitch uncovered, heavy rain on the rest day produced a 'sticky dog' and Verity's left-arm spin was virtually unplayable. He took 14 wickets for 80 runs on that third day as Australia were dismissed for 284 and 118. His match analysis of 15 for 104 has been surpassed for England in Ashes Tests only by Jim Laker's 19 for 90. During the final hour, when Verity took the last six wickets, Marshall's reports were in constant demand. He was compelled to provide virtually ball-by-ball commentary without a scorer and with only a primitive scoreboard visible. He had no idea what Verity's figures were. It was to be England's only Ashes victory at Lord's in the twentieth century.

When Marshall returned to Broadcasting House he asked for a scorer for the third Test at Old Trafford. He was flatly refused and advised to bribe a groundstaff boy with a two-guinea match fee. Marshall went to the office of the Lancashire Secretary, Captain Howard. He was in luck. Lancashire had just signed a young leg-spinner on to their groundstaff and he also happened to be training as an accountant. His name was Arthur Wrigley and he became the first BBC scorer and statistician. His 31-year reign was broken only by wartime service in the RAF and occasional appearances by Roy Webber or Jack Price.

I heard the news of his death on a radio bulletin. Having been a devoted listener to radio commentaries since 1950, I had heard his name mentioned many times. Very occasionally, he was allowed to say something. I wondered who would score for *TMS* the following summer. Then came the vision. I could do it. I had collected a reasonable number of cricket books and knew a fair amount of cricket history. The RAF had trained me in statistics and accountancy. I had served in a NATO war room and had learnt to concentrate for long periods. So I looked up the BBC's phone number and asked the operator who was in charge of cricket. After much research she told me it was Mr Charles Max-Muller and he was Head of Outside Broadcasts (Sound). She told me not to omit the hyphen or the brackets and on no account to put 'Radio' instead of 'Sound'. I got out my Basildon Bond pad and used my neatest calligraphy. Not having a photocopier – they probably didn't exist then – I cannot reveal what I wrote. Certainly not anything along the lines of 'Dear Sir, I hear you are going to be one short in the scoring department next season.'

To my amazement, I received a reply a few days later inviting me to visit Mr Max-Muller for an interview on 5 November. It was the first time I had seen Broadcasting House, let alone entered that historic Art Deco sanctuary. A secretary met me in the foyer and guided me along a maze of corridors to the Head of Outside Broadcasts office. Inside were Charles Max-Muller seated behind a formidably exalted desk, cricket producer Michael Hastings and the jovial cricket correspondent Brian Johnston. I had met Johnners when he played in a memorial match for one of the Ashtead players a few weeks earlier. I meekly accepted the offer of a cup of tea. It was swiftly delivered with BBC emblazoned on the cup, spoon and sugar cube wrapper. The corporation had obviously had a petty pilfering problem. The rattle of the cup on the saucer revealed the state of my nerves.

Max-Muller broke the ice by asking what had made me think I could do Wrigley's job. I told them about my scoring history and RAF training. Then I handed round the three loose-leaf scrapbooks I had kept containing scores, reports, cuttings and photos of my playing career. Luckily, Brian turned to a purple passage where I had taken 20 wickets in three innings on dodgy pitches in Lincolnshire. 'I don't know about scoring for us, he'd better ruddy well play,' exclaimed Johnners.

After the briefest discussion, Mr Max-Muller offered me regular Saturday scoring work at eight guineas a day. They felt duty bound to offer the Test matches to two others, Michael Fordham and Arnold Whipp, who had regularly scored for them at county matches. I accepted the Saturday work provisionally because I was reluctant to end my Saturday playing career. League cricket was about to be introduced to the south, thanks almost entirely to the efforts of former Surrey, Northamptonshire and England batsman, Raman Subba Row. Banstead were to play in the new Surrey Championship and I had established myself as an opening bowler in the 1st XI, captained by Derek Pratt (Surrey and Bedfordshire) and including his brother, Ron (Surrey), and former England keeper Roy Swetman – nor would Saturday work rescue me from insurance inspecting.

I returned to my Fenchurch Street training and kept quiet about the BBC offer. Mike Smith's MCC team was touring Australia and I rose early to practise my scoring from the radio commentaries on the final hour's play. In 1953 I had been given a copy of the third edition of *The MCC Book for the Young Cricketer*. Illustrating an article on statistics and TV scoring by Roy Webber was a linear sheet recording India's 58 all out at Old Trafford the previous season. I had drawn up similar sheets on squared paper and recorded the occasional session of play over the intervening years. Now I seriously reviewed them in case I did score county games the following summer and I made some substantial revisions, as you will see if you compare pages 54 and 55 with my example in the chapter on my scoring system.

I also worked out the touring team's batting and bowling averages. When I compared them with those published in the national press, I found a considerable number of discrepancies. Their figures were obtained from the Press Association and so I visited their offices in Fleet Street and asked if I could see the person who compiled them. A dishy girl clerk came to the counter clutching a school exercise book. She showed me some of the pages and it wasn't hard to spot that she had made some entries against the wrong players.

I seized my chance and contacted the sports editors of five national newspapers, pointing out that their MCC averages were up the creek and telling them why. They each asked me to visit them. When I started work at Fenchurch Street I was told that 'lunch must be taken between twelve and three'. The five newspaper offices were all to the west of mine. *The Times* was in Printing House Square near Blackfriars Bridge, the *Daily Telegraph* and *Express* were near neighbours in Fleet Street, the *Sun* was at Covent Garden in Endell Street and the *Guardian* was on the way back, near High Holborn. By leaving on the stroke of noon, I managed to complete the entire circuit by foot, stopping only for a liquid lunch, and arrive back just in time for tea and biscuits at 3 o'clock. All five editors invited me to supply the averages henceforth. Each wanted two copies and typed. Each paid a different fee per set. *The Times* paid least (£2), then came the *Telegraph* (£3), *Guardian* (3 guineas) and *Express* (£5). Frank Nicklin, benevolent son of Derbyshire and sports editor of the *Sun*, knowing who paid most, asked me how much the *Express* had offered. '£5,' I told him. 'I'll pay you five guineas but I want them here first,' countered Frank.

Although I had gained the commissions, a few hurdles still had to be overcome. There was no internet to pick up the scores, no computer to calculate the averages quickly, and no time to type them out. Somehow I coped. During a Test match I could pick up most of the stats from the radio commentary. Any missing details I obtained from an acquaintance on the sports desk of the *Evening News*. I compiled the averages during the train journey from Cheam to London Bridge. My first stop at Fenchurch Street was at the typing pool where I had befriended a cricket fan. At noon I would collect ten copies of the averages from her and set out on my three-hour trek.

During the cricket season, Arthur Wrigley had written a Monday column for the *Express*. John Morgan, their sports editor, told me that if I got the Test match job, he would like me to take this over. Knowing

Third Test at Manchester 1952 — INDIA 1st Innings

BOWLER	BATSMEN		BOWLER	SCORE AT END OF OVER / TIME	BATSMEN		COMMENTS
				12·25	Roy	Mankad	
Bedser	······	40000X	:	4	0	0 *Adhikari*	Cover drive (1st)
	000X1 ·	·····0	Trueman	5	1 *Hazare*	0	
Bedser	000000	······		5 · 12·40	1	0	
	······	00000X	Trueman	5	1	0 *Umrigar*	
Bedser	000004	······		9 · 12·49	5 (1)	0	Square cut slash (6th)
	······	400000	Trueman	13	5	4 (1)	Edged through gullies (1st)
Bedser	000000	······		13 · 12·55	5	4	
	······	000000	Trueman	13	5	4	
Bedser	000004	······		17 · 1· 2	9 (2)	4	Mid wicket (6th)
	······	00X0X4	Trueman	21 · 1·10	9	4 *Phadkar / Manjrekar*	Turn to leg (6th)
Bedser	00003 ·	·····0		24	12	4 (1)	
	01····	··0200	Trueman	27 · 1·17	13	6	Trueman off—holding side
Bedser	0000† ·	·····1		29	13	7	1 Leg-Bye
	··0001	41····	Laker	35 · 1·24	14	12 (2)	Late cut (1st)
Bedser	000000	······		35	14	12	
	··0000	01····	Laker	36	14	13	
Bedser ·	······	000001		37 · 1·30	14	14	
LUNCH				37-5	14†	14†	
				2·13			
	······	20024X	Trueman	45	14	0 *Divetia*	Bumper hooked (5th)
Bedser	020000	······		47	16	0	
	······	04X020	Trueman	53 · 2.19	16	2 *Ramchand*	50 in 76 mins.
Bedser	X00000	······		53	0 *Sen*	2	
	··4X	XI··	Trueman	58 · 2·33	4	1† *Ahmed*	Turn to leg (3rd)

58 all out in 85 minutes — Follow-on 289 behind.

SUMMARY	FALL OF WKT.	TIME IN	OUT	MINS. BAT.	RUNS ADDED	
V. Mankad c Lock b Bedser (square short-leg)	4	1/4	12.25	12.30	5	4	1 four
P. Roy c Hutton b Trueman (1st slip)	0	2/4	12.25	12.35	10	4	
H. R. Adhikari c Graveney b Trueman (silly mid-off)	0	3/5	12.30	12.45	15	1	
V. S. Hazare b Bedser	16	8/53	12.35	2.25	70	49	2 fours
P. R. Umrigar b Trueman	4	4/17	12.45	1.5	20	12	1 four
D. G. Phadkar c Sheppard b Trueman (gully—fine hard catch)	0	5/17	1.5	1.8	3	0	
V. L. Manjrekar c Ikin b Trueman (point—skier off impossible ball)	22	6/45	1.8	2.13	25	28	3 fours
R. V. Divecha b Trueman	4	7/51	2.13	2.20	7	6	1 four
G. S. Ramchard c Graveney b Trueman (cover)	2	9/53	2.20	2.28	8	2	
P. Sen c Lock b Trueman (off leg glance)	4	10/58	2.25	2.30	5	5	1 four
Ghulam Ahmed not out	1	-	2.28	—	2	5	
Extras (LB)	1						
	58						

COMMENTS ON PLAY	BOWLING ANALYSIS

	Bedser	Trueman	Laker
Whole field close to bat—if through it is four.	1-0-4-1	1-0-1-1	1-0-6-0
	2-1-4-1	2-1-1-2	2-0-7-0
Good low catch by Lock to dismiss Mankad off turn to leg.	3-1-8-1	3-1-5-2	Lunch
	4-2-8-1	4-2-5-2	
Batsmen on the retreat.	5-2-12-1	5-2-9-4	
	6-2-15-1	6-2-12-4	
Trueman off with side strain—? stitch.	7-2-16-1	7-2-20-5	
	8-3-16-1	8-2-26-6	
Manjrekar received impossible ball, it came straight up at him and he skied it.	9-3-17-1	8.4-2-31-8	
	Lunch		
Fielding brilliant.	10-3-19-1		
	11-4-19-2		

The B.B.C's. T.V. Scoring Chart

Here are the entries made by Roy Webber during the third Test v. India, at Manchester, in 1952. As explained in his article, it gives the complete record of every ball bowled, and other information not included in the normal scorebook ruling. Fall of wickets is indicated by ' x ' and extras by ' † ' (details in ' comments ').

that two others would have to refuse a dream job, my chances of accepting his offer were extremely slim. Meanwhile, the five sports desks started asking me for other stats and to solve various queries. My section of the Fenchurch Street office soon became known as the cricket reporting agency and my superiors were not amused.

Arthur Wrigley had set the questions for a BBC Radio panel game called *Sporting Chance* and I was invited to take over this work. Unfortunately, I also had to supply the answers. All sports were involved except horse racing which, for some unfathomable reason, was considered unsuitable. The thirty-minute programmes involved a panel of three sports commentators competing against a panel of four schoolboys. The four schools scoring the most points in the preliminary programmes went through to the semi-finals, the winners of that round competing in a grand final. For my first winter, I just set the questions, but after my first season with *TMS*, I also took part in the recording sessions, sitting next to the question master, usually Alun Williams but occasionally Brian Johnston, keeping score and acting as adjudicator. Geoff Dobson, the producer, was a delightful man who quickly put me at ease and inspired confidence. The panel of Maurice Edelston, Liam Nolan and Norman Cuddeford were all great fun, their combined knowledge covering most sports. I made my debut for *Sporting Chance* in the main hall of Haberdashers' Aske's School at Elstree in February 1967.

I was spared researching questions on boxing. The programme had attracted the attention of one Arthur McArten, an authority on the sport, who provided stats for a number of publications and regularly sent Geoff batches of questions, which he passed to me. When his questions were used in the programmes he was usually credited as 'Arthur McArten of the Isle of Wight'. I soon exhausted the first supply of questions and asked Geoff for some more. They arrived in an envelope bearing a royal crest. Thinking that perhaps Mr McArten was an alias for one of the royal family, I tore open the envelope and discovered that he was in fact a guest of Her Majesty in Parkhurst Prison. I wrote back thanking him for his questions and got an immediate reply. He thanked me for thanking him and enclosed a pass with an invitation to drop in and see him the next time I was passing. I had never visited the Isle of Wight, but decided to do so the next season when I was scoring a match in Portsmouth. My widowed mother sometimes accompanied me to county matches and she asked if she could come. McArten duly sent another pass.

Our taxi dropped us outside a vast wall with an enormous gate. I rang the ancient bell pull and a small grill opened at face height. A cap peak appeared, two beady eyes peered through at me and a gruff voice asked me to hold up our passes. The door opened with heavy squeaking sounds and we were ushered across a yard to a large wooden hut. Inside were a dozen lantern-jawed ladies bearing cakes. I had visions of the hardware hidden under the icing. I expected to go into a dark room and be separated from the prisoner by wire mesh as in the films. Instead, we were taken to a modern NAAFI-like canteen with a large, light room furnished with sets of tables and chairs. Arthur was barely five feet tall, bald and with a broad Glaswegian accent. On the table in front of him was an enormous bouquet of flowers and what looked like a framed picture wrapped in brown paper and string. With great courtesy he presented my mother with the flowers. Overwhelmed, she thanked him and asked if he had bought them from the prison florist.

'No,' Arthur replied. 'My mate's a trusty. He looks after the prison gardens.' Arthur handed me the wrapped picture but asked me not to open it until I had left the prison. It turned out to be an oil painting of me, taken from a photograph but clad in a blue and white striped prison shirt. Its frame was an old prison notice board.

Mother asked him what he was in for. When he told her 'petty larceny' and admitted that he had spent most of his last thirty years in jail, she rebuked him with, 'You can't be much good at it. What went wrong last time?' Arthur described a scam worthy of an Ealing comedy script. He had rented a haberdasher's shop with a flat above it, close to Euston Station, and had acquired a British Railways uniform, pass and bicycle. He would leave his shop after midnight and tour a few of the neighbouring railway stations, passing himself off as a relief porter. The staff at every mainline terminus knew him as 'Mac' and would welcome him into their rest rooms with a mug of tea. Mac would offer to check on security. The real porters would eagerly hand him the keys, grateful that they didn't have to leave the comfort of their warm room in the middle of the night. Mac would head for the parcels room and check for promising loot. When he found one he fancied, he would take from his pocket a gummed label addressed to his shop and stick it over the address on the parcel. Returning the keys and assuring his mates that all was well, Mac would cycle home to bed and await the delivery of his swag the next morning. It took the quick-thinking railway police two years to outwit him by adding an extra label to parcels. They caught him when he inadvertently stuck his own label over part of theirs.

I was involved with *Sporting Chance* until it ended in 1968. With regular journeys to Belfast and Glasgow, I did more flying with the Beeb than I had done in my entire RAF career. Jonathan Lord was one of the schoolboy panel when we visited Dollar Academy in Clackmannanshire. A cricket nut and fervent Hampshire supporter, he has kept in touch ever since with a letter and card every Christmas. His bumper bundles of sweets have become a feature of Lord's Test matches.

In 1967 we recorded a special Christmas edition in the Winter Gardens at Harrogate, with the BBC panel pitted against Yorkshire County Cricket Club in the shape of Fred Trueman, Phil Sharpe and Tony 'Nick' Nicholson. Nick had taken 9 for 62 against Sussex at Eastbourne the previous season and I was asked to set a question featuring this career-best performance. Nick had been unable to answer any other question, so when Alun asked, 'Who were the two bowlers who took nine wickets in an innings for their counties last season?' Nick pressed his buzzer with great enthusiasm. Thinking he was still in the dressing room, he answered, 'Well, I was one fucker and John Cotton were t'other.' Fred's response was unprintable and the hall erupted into gales of laughter. Everyone hushed when our ashen-faced producer emerged from his desk behind the stage curtain and we had to record the question again. He still had to edit out more laughter when Nick's second attempt had an unfortunate pause – 'Well, I was one … of them and John Cotton were t'other.'

Early in 1966, I received a phone call from Michael Tuke-Hastings's secretary at the BBC, who asked if I could consult my diary as her boss wanted to take me to lunch. I borrowed a diary and we agreed a date, 26 January, and a venue, Verey's restaurant in Regent Street, a short walk from Broadcasting House. It was another defining moment. Neither Fordham (teacher's pay in Maidstone) nor Whipp (bus timetables in Manchester) was prepared to abandon a safe, pensionable job. Within a few years both had departed this world. Michael Fordham married Roy Webber's widow and had a heart attack lifting her luggage out of a taxi in Miami. Arnold Whipp was washed off a rock while birdwatching in the Dee Estuary. I promise that I was not responsible for a reprise of *Kind Hearts and Coronets*, where a distant heir to a title murders the dozen relatives separating him from it. Nevertheless, the BBC did lose five scorers in as many years. Michael Tuke-Hastings (the Tuke was a recent addition, his mother's maiden name being added to ward off paternity petitions and other unsavoury post addressed to another Michael Hastings) offered me the *TMS* job on a three-match trial basis. Years later I asked Johnners if anyone else had applied.

'Well, yes, Bearders,' he said, 'but we weren't going to tell you. There was just one. A New Zealander with poor handwriting living in Auckland – but it was a very close thing.'

The offer, together with a long list of West Indies tour matches and county championship bookings, was confirmed a fortnight later. I contacted the *Express* and was duly commissioned to write a weekly column throughout the season. Then I spent the rest of the winter compiling records and building up my cricket library. To show how prices have changed, I was able to purchase twenty-four editions of *Wisden*, including the valuable 1939–45 wartime ones, for £11.

On 18 February 1966 I finished work at Legal & General and officially began my career as a freelance cricket statistician. On reflection, it was a brave step to take with just the BBC's guarantee of £1000 for the summer as confirmed income. For many years I expected to wake up and find that it had ended, or been a dream, and I would have to find a proper job. The short time I spent at Fenchurch Street had convinced me that if I ever did have to find another job, it would not involve trainloads of misery or a crowded office. Hard work, kind clients and many slices of good fortune have kept me going beyond official retirement age. Three epigrams have guided me: 'If a job's worth doing, it's worth doing well', 'The Lord helps those who help themselves' and 'Smile and the world smiles with you.'

Anyone joining the ranks of the self-employed needs a knowledgeable and honest accountant. There are many pitfalls and also a useful number of legal loopholes in the system. One of my greatest strokes of luck was to have Reginald Edward 'Bill' Warne as my first accountant. We met when I joined Banstead Cricket Club in 1957 during my final year at school. Then 45, he was still an elegant, aggressive and entertaining opening batsman. He was also a sprightly wicket-keeper and he needed to be against my bowling. Being left-handed proved a considerable advantage, too. Banstead was one of the first clubs to start a colts' section and to welcome youngsters to the ranks of its four senior elevens, but to a teenager, the transition from schools to adult cricket could be a daunting one. I shall always be grateful to Bill for many things, but especially for the way he welcomed me into the Banstead dressing room and showed me the ropes. Like John Arlott a few years later, he treated me like a surrogate son and gave me confidence. My respect for him made me determined to direct my thunderbolts on an off-stump line. Bill was blessed with a wonderfully dry sense of humour and a splendidly sharp wit. Once, when my radar strayed dramatically and I did him for three sets of legside boundary byes in one over, he suggested that I purchased a set of blinkers before the next match. Bill Warne may well have been responsible for the first instance of a wicket-keeper sledging his own bowler. He continued playing until he was 47. The end of his career was dramatic. It occurred at Cheam in 1959 when his back suddenly locked. Unable to move a muscle, his final exit from the field of play involved being carried to the pavilion frozen in his wicket-keeping crouch – a cross between Quasimodo and a sedan chair.

Like his father before him, Bill had spent all his working life with Sharpe, Pritchard & Co, renowned solicitors situated in Kingsway, much of it as their chief accountant. We frequently met for a glass or three when I was in London. When he learnt that I was about to become a self-employed freelance cricket statistician, he bravely offered his services as my accountant. His wise counsel and encouragement during those early years proved absolutely invaluable. When he went into semi-retirement in 1973, he handed my accounts over to his elder son, Chris, a senior partner in a firm of accountants in Brighton and a close friend ever since we played some of our early cricket together at Banstead. Bill lived until he was 93, long enough to celebrate England's regaining of the Ashes in his final summer. I was honoured to be invited to give the eulogy at his funeral. It was the easiest of tasks. He was a true gentleman, unfailingly friendly, polite, cheerful, generous and much loved.

Before I scored at my first live outside broadcast, Michael Tuke-Hastings arranged for me to spend a non-broadcasting day in the commentary box at Lord's with Eric York. An occasional scorer for the BBC, Eric was a tremendous help in teaching me how a cricket broadcast worked and what my job would actually entail. Having never seen one, it provided my introduction to commentary boxes, but the one in use at Lord's in 1966 was unlike any others on the circuit. For a start, it was much larger and the desk area far superior to those at the other Test grounds. Sited at the top of the Warner Stand, it did not look down the pitch but over a wide mid-off to a right-handed batsman. When I asked Eric why he didn't want to score the Test matches, he replied, 'Because they're very hard work. You have to concentrate throughout six hours of play and often do two or three jobs at once. Arthur Wrigley and Roy Webber were usually exhausted at the end of a day's play.' I wondered if I had made the right choice.

The following day I drove to a hotel in Worcester, my Hillman Imp

laden with cartons of *Wisden*s and files. The next morning I arrived at
New Road at the same time as the groundstaff. A ground dominated
by a cathedral is a most appropriate place to stage a broadcasting baptism and Worcester has a very special niche in my affections. I still have
very clear recall of that first day – 4 May 1966. ~~Wisden confirms it as the~~
start of the West Indies first-class programme. I shall always remember
it as the day I met John Arlott. Our box then was close to the score box
at the Diglis End. A bedraggled garden shed on stilts, it had been
acquired from Silverstone and was ideal for combating the Severn's
annual floods. I had to borrow a key from the groundsman. When I
managed to force open the door, I unleashed the previous season's
insects, some of them still living. For the next hour I did a poor impression of Mrs Mopp. I had just installed most of my library when our
Midlands producer, Dick Maddock, arrived and his first words were,
'Sorry, Bill, there's no room for all those books. We've got to fit three
commentators in here.'

Dick was a lovely man and an excellent producer who ran Test
match broadcasts from Edgbaston and Trent Bridge. It was he who
introduced me to John Arlott. I remember being highly nervous at the
prospect of meeting the owner of a voice that had already given so
much pleasure for two decades. After the memorable exchange I have
already chronicled, I admitted to being very much in his awe.

'Don't know why,' he growled once. 'My sons aren't.'

For the record, the reigning county champions won the toss and,
surprisingly, batted in poor light with rain threatening. Wes Hall
bowled the first over of my professional scoring career, a maiden to
Don Kenyon from the Diglis End, and the tourists' captain, Gary
Sobers, took the first wicket (D. Kenyon c Hendriks b Sobers 4 – flash-
ing – good catch – low). I had a very easy baptism as rain ended proceedings after 34 minutes, allowed 209 minutes on the second day and
completely washed out the third.

John had taken a dislike to driving after twice nodding off on the
way home from broadcasts and he became my regular passenger on
journeys to Test matches. No one could wish for a more entertaining

companion on a long drive. His fund of anecdotes involving old players and fellow broadcasters was inexhaustible and those journeys provided a unique tutorial in cricket and social history. The one drawback
to his presence in the passenger seat was that he was a desperately poor
navigator. 'Turn left back there,' became his catchphrase.

On the eve of my debut for *Test Match Special*, I collected John from
Waterloo and we drove to Manchester. He fell asleep and woke just as
we reached the city's outskirts. Recognising where he was, he sank
back into his seat with a heavy sigh, and said, 'Hell's teeth! Manchester!
It's the only city in the world where they teach lifeboat drill on the
buses!'

Next morning we breakfasted together before visiting Gibbs's
Bookshop nearby. There he dramatically extended my meagre library
by arranging for me to purchase, at a generous discount, a complete
set of *Scores and Biographies*. Making me a present of two other vital volumes, he even asked how I wanted to be introduced on the air.

I can recall vividly the first ball that I scored for *TMS* and I have a
recording of John Arlott's commentary to confirm what happened to
it – 'Jones, fast left-arm, over the wicket to bowl the first match [ball!]
of the first Test of this series to Hunte. He moves in, bowls to him.
Short. Hunte gets over it and cracks it square away for four wide of
cover's left hand, just fine of square. Four runs off the first ball!'

Thus was my *TMS* career launched at 11.30 on a sunny morning at
Old Trafford on Thursday, 2 June 1966. I remember thinking as I
entered that boundary on my ball-by-ball sheet that this should not
happen in a Test match. I can scarcely remember it happening in any
club match I had either scored or played in. Somehow, that brutal
square-cut of Conrad Hunte's, which echoed around the ground like a
pistol shot and knocked back a paling of the fence, unfettered with
adverts in those days, relaxed my nervous tension. Years later I
recounted that ball to Jeff Jones (who didn't laugh) and Simon Jones,
his son (who did).

The cramped eyrie where we worked was half the size of the box at
Lord's. Access was via a spiral staircase and you had to duck under a

metal pole halfway up. West Indies made 484, Hunte scoring 135 and
Gary Sobers 161. Off-spinners Fred Titmus (5 for 83) and David Allen
(2 for 104 in his final Test) confirmed that the pitch was turning.
England were 163 for 8 at the end of the second day. Poor Colin
Milburn, also making his debut, was run out for a duck when Eric
Russell sent him back. On Saturday they added just four more runs,
spinners Lance Gibbs and David Holford sharing eight wickets.
England followed on and were dismissed for 277 at 5.45 p.m. Milburn
scored 94 off 136 balls before being castled by Gibbs trying to complete
his hundred with a six. I had not proved a good mascot for my country. It was England's first three-day defeat since 1938. It also marked the
end of Mike Smith's 25-match captaincy. First Colin Cowdrey and
then Brian Close would lead the side in the remaining four Tests. Had
they managed to take the match into the fourth day, England would
have scraped a draw. Manchester's normal wet weather returned on
Monday and no cricket would have been possible on the fifth day
either. My baptism was eased by Sobers, using his orthodox and
unorthodox left-arm spin, and Gibbs bowling 24 overs an hour, the
latter taking 10 for 106 in the match. There was no time for the commentators to ask me statistical questions.

I was still in my three-match trial period and I arrived at Lord's for
the second Test not knowing how my Old Trafford efforts had being
rated. At lunch on the first day, Michael Tuke-Hastings spoke to me
over my headphones and said that the job was mine if I wanted it. So,
after just ten sessions, I was confirmed as BBC Radio's scorer and statistician. Nearly forty years have passed and, as no one has telephoned
to say the job is no longer mine, I just keep turning up.

In those early days I didn't have a microphone and had to write any
notes on cards. This took time and often any snippet had become irrelevant by the time I had completed the note. Michael seldom attended
a Test match, preferring to listen to us from a studio in Broadcasting
House. I would have a special feed from him, which the others couldn't
hear. This was just as well because he often yelled obscenities about
their commentary. 'Tell the stupid sod to give the score,' was a cue for

me to flash my prepared card saying 'PLEASE GIVE THE SCORE'.

Eventually, they realised that I could give information briefly and time it not to interfere with play. I was given a lip microphone and a device with two lights. When I pressed a button on it, a red light would go on. The engineers were supposed to notice this and turn my mike on. When they did this, my red light would be replaced by the green one. The first – and only – time I used it was when Alan Gibson took over the commentary and said, 'Good morning, Bill.' I pressed my button, the red light came on and I waited for it to change. Another ball was bowled, runs were scored and still no green light. Alan looked irritated and repeated his greeting somewhat louder in case I had gone deaf. Still no green light. I leant across to his microphone, bolted into the desk in front of him and said, 'Sorry, Alan. I was waiting for a green light. Good morning.' There was much hilarity at the back of the box and the contraption was removed, never to reappear. Since then I have been given a microphone that I am trusted to operate myself.

I could have done with one when I was scoring for Brian at the Essex v. West Indies match at Southend. We were crammed into a tiny hut on the roof of a BBC Outside Broadcasts van. I had the scoresheets and stopwatches balanced on a tiny ledge, my pens squashed into my top pocket and a small bag containing files on players, *Wisden* and *Playfair* on the floor between my feet. Suddenly my head was jerked sharply downwards and towards Brian. He had trodden on the flex linking my headphones to a socket at ground level. To make matters worse, Keith Fletcher was on the brink of his hundred and Brian would want details of his minutes, balls and boundaries. There was no point in saying anything because he had his headphones on and wouldn't have heard me; nor could I dig him in the ribs because he would have yelled or said something that should not have been broadcast. Quickly I wrote a note on a card and handed it to him. At that precise moment Fletcher struck a six over backward square-leg to bring up his hundred.

'And that's his hundred,' announced Johnners. 'It's the first century against Gary Sobers's 1966 West Indians and Bill Frindall's handed me a card to tell me … to lift up my left foot! Oh, my Crippen! I must be treading on his right foot. No, I'm not. I'm treading on his head-phones.'

A few days later our producer received a letter from an overseas lis-tener applying for my job 'in view of the fact that the present incum-bent was inebriated and had fallen under the table at 3.28 p.m. on the first day of the match.'

Gradually, my freelance clientele and outlets grew. Kaye and Ward commissioned me to produce my first book, an update of Roy Webber's *Book of Cricket Records*. Speaking engagements and other statis-tical commissions soon followed. *TMS* was an incredibly effective shop window. Once my name had been mentioned a few times, listeners seemed to remember it, even if they couldn't spell it. One evening, after a day's Test cricket at Lord's, I received a phone call from some-one I had never heard of, thanking me for getting him and his pals into the ground.

'I didn't know I had,' I replied, puzzled.

'Oh yes. We just said we were friends of Bill Frindall's and they let us in without tickets.'

Our flat in Cheam occupied two floors above The Potteries, a china and glassware shop run by a semi-retired couple. When they were short-handed I was called upon to look after the shop. I also rebuilt their storage shed and became a general handyman in their house nearby. My knowledge of china and glass swiftly grew and to the own-ers' amazement as well as my own, I never broke a single item.

Opposite was the sports and gardening tools shop owned and run by Eddie Watts who played 240 matches for Surrey between 1933 and 1949. He had converted his office at the rear of the shop into a den where he kept wine, beer and his cricket mementoes. His former team-mate, Laurie Fishlock, would drop by occasionally and I would get a call from Eddie to join them. A fast-medium right-handed bowler, Eddie took all ten wickets for 67 against Warwickshire at Edgbaston in late August 1939. Warwickshire had followed on, 216 behind and lost three wickets, all to Watts, before stumps on the second day. That evening, umpire Joe Hardstaff senior had enjoyed a few beers with the players. Well into the session, he had told Eddie that he would get all ten tomorrow. Next morning Eddie swung the ball late in a heavy atmosphere and, once he had broken a fourth-wicket stand of 85 between Bob Wyatt and Tom Dollery, he took 6 for 4. Warwickshire were 190 for 9 when Charlie Grove joined the wicket-keeper, John Buckingham. They added 30 and Eddie, after 24 overs, was nearly on his knees. Surrey's skipper, 'Monty' Garland-Wells, had put Stan Squires on at the other end with instructions to bowl his medium-pace wide of the off stump. The first ball of Eddie's 25th over swung in and struck Buckingham's front pad. Eddie made a half-hearted appeal. Hardstaff shot his finger up, yelling, 'That's out and, Eddie, you've got all ten.' Eddie admitted that it probably wouldn't have hit another set. Buckingham remained in his crease staring at his stumps until most of the players had left the ground for World War Two.

Wally Hammond was Eddie's bunny. The wall of his den was covered in pictures of a jubilant Watts facing a distraught Hammond surveying shattered stumps. There must have been a dozen of them. Pride of place went to a Tom Webster cartoon featuring poor Wally being castled about six times and Eddie gloating over the flying stumps. He ran a side called the Surrey Cavaliers, who played in the Old Whitgiftians cricket week. I was lucky enough to be invited to play in several of these games along with many former Surrey stars. Once he brought me on to bowl against Raman Subba Row. I managed to bowl him with an in-ducker (to the left-hander). He had scored 99 but he was incredibly unfazed about it and congratulated me on the ball. A few years later I opened the MCC bowling at Framlingham College and bowled his son with a similar delivery first ball. He was less unfazed. Raman congratulated me on being the only bowler to dismiss them both. Nice to have one obscure record to myself!

I was clean-shaven throughout my first season on the circuit, but by tea each day a dark stubble had appeared. Having had a moustache for six years of my RAF service, I decided to throw away the razor as soon as my broadcasting commitments ended with the Gillette Cup final and grow a full set of whiskers. My first professional bearded appearance was at a film studio where I was helping John Arlott script his commentary for a Rothmans film of the 1966 England v. West Indies series. I arrived before John. When he entered the room, he gulped in amazement and said, 'Hell's teeth, Frindalius. I haven't seen anyone like you since the Reformation!'

Although things were progressing well on the career front, my domestic life was struggling. Maureen gave birth to a daughter, Vanessa Jane, in December 1966 but two years later our marriage had already broken down when I exacerbated the situation by meeting a curvaceous cricket enthusiast from Warwickshire, Jaqueline Seager. We eventually set up home in north London and were married after my divorce came through in 1970. That top (fifth) floor flat in Fortis Green, between East Finchley and Muswell Hill, was to be my home and office for twenty years. Jacky and I were blissfully happy until I began spending my winters working overseas. Her own career in computing developed and I returned from one trip to find that she was working in Luxembourg. At least there wasn't a note saying 'dinner in the cat'. She remarried twenty-five years ago, lives near St Ives, runs a major computer network and we have remained good friends.

If I were ever asked what was my most embarrassing career moment, it would have to be the one that occurred in Derby when Brian Johnston and I were invited to lunch with the Derbyshire committee. About a dozen of us sat on either side of a long table. Johnners asked me to pass him a two-litre bottle of white wine, standing a few feet to my right. It had just come out of some cold water and the label was loose. Not seeing the danger, I lifted the bottle and was just passing it to him when it escaped, leaving me holding a soggy label. It landed with its neck facing down the table and released a tidal surge of wine that rushed along, washing food from plates and soaking laps. Dr Barnes Wallis couldn't have achieved a more traumatic effect with his bouncing bomb.

Some sort of timetable is essential if you are self-employed. Unless you are disciplined about your working hours, you will fail to meet deadlines and lose clients. That is totally unprofessional and the self-employed must always give the impression of being utterly professional. I have already emphasised the importance of a reliable and efficient accountant. Reg Hayter, who ran his own highly successful sports reporting agency, gave me another invaluable piece of advice – never turn down work. If you cannot find time to do it yourself, sub-contract it to someone who can. If you refuse a job, it will go to someone else and you may never be asked again by that client.

I have never regretted my decision to go freelance. It has been hard work at times and I am lucky that the RAF conditioned me into being an early riser. I have been able to set my own agendas and have spent most of the last forty years doing exactly what I wanted to do. Christmas always seems dull by comparison.

FIVE

MY SCORING SYSTEM

M Y SCORING method is based on the linear system, which, until recently, was thought to have originated in Australia and been employed internationally by W.H. ('Bill') Ferguson on the first of his 41 international tours, when he came to England with the 1905 Australians. I found some of Ferguson's linear scoring in an exercise book among a mass of old papers when I visited the offices of the New South Wales Cricket Association in 1976. Doubt concerning this theory was raised early in 2005 by John Kobylecky, who has spent the last decade constructing linear scoresheets of many early Test matches using the original 'box' system scorebooks in conjunction with press reports that covered the matches in almost ball-by-ball detail. He discovered that for the 1899 Ashes series, one Australian newspaper included 'balls faced' in its detailed scorecard, along with 'minutes batted' and 'boundaries hit', for every batsman. Similar details were available for the 1902 series. Then, in the final pages of *My Spin on Cricket*, published to mark the end of his broadcasting career in British television in September 2005, Richie Benaud revealed that in 1994 he had received a letter from the grandson of the man who had invented linear scoring, enclosing an obituary note about the man who was the true source of Bill Ferguson's system, which I had adapted.

The scoring method should be known as the Pendlington system after John Atkinson Pendlington (1861–1914). A great cricket enthusiast, he was born in South Shields, played for Benwell in the Northumberland League and founded the Tyneside Supply Company (which became the British Electrical and Manufacturing Company of Newcastle and London). After reading match reports in *Lillywhite* and *Wisden* one winter, Pendlington thought that it should be possible to devise a scoring method that would record the result of every ball bowled in a match. Richie Benaud wrote:

> He soon had it worked out and took the score at Scarborough in Lord Londesbrough's match against the Australians in 1893 (Mr C.I. Thornton's XI). This record showed, for all time, the number of balls each batsman received from each bowler, and what runs he made from them. It caused much amusement and pleasure to Dr W.G. Grace who was at Scarborough and was presented with the authentic document.

This revelation begs two questions. Why wasn't it employed by official scorers for all major matches henceforth, instead of just by compilers of scorecards for Aussie papers? What happened to that original scoresheet presented to WG?

Bill Ferguson was a remarkable character who began his working life as a filing clerk for a Sydney directory. As a respite from the tedium of filing cards with names of householders and streets all day, he used to spend his lunch hour on the waterfront, gazing longingly at ships bound for exotic destinations.

At the age of 24 Fergie determined to escape from the bondage of his filing chores by travelling abroad. He discovered that the Australian cricket team was about to sail for England and needed a baggage master and scorer. Fearing that a written application to the tour manager would have been lost among a mountain of pre-tour correspondence, and, more to the point, realising that he had no qualifications for the job, Fergie decided upon a more painful approach. Monty Noble, considered by many to have been Australia's greatest all-rounder, had a dental practice in Sydney. During several visits for gold fillings, Bill Ferguson persuaded his dentist to recommend him for the tour. Noble did so but the team set sail for England via New Zealand and Canada without him.

Then, just as his hopes had vanished, a letter arrived from Frank Laver, the tour manager, from the SS *Manuka* 'at sea near Auckland'. ~~Dated 3 February 1905 and carefully preserved until his death~~, it offered Fergie the position of scorer and baggage master for a salary of £2 a week plus train fares.

He made his scoring debut at London's Crystal Palace. The opposition was a Gentlemen of England team led by W.G. Grace and including Pelham Warner, Charles Fry, Archie MacLaren and Gilbert Jessop. In near-freezing conditions he opened the brand new tour scoring book for the first time. Astonishingly, he had managed to camouflage the fact that he had never scored a cricket match in his life. Using a pencil and cribbing from his English colleague, he carefully recorded the first of 1207 tour matches. Back in his hotel room each night, he would ink in the details using one of his Street Directory mapping pens. It must have given him special pleasure to record Monty Noble's innings of 60 and 162 in that match.

Not many matches had passed when Fergie realised that the traditional method of scoring a cricket match was extremely cumbersome and actually recorded very few of the more intricate details of an innings. He must have been aware of the Pendlington method and, using a school exercise book, he recorded the remaining matches in both that and the traditional scorebook. That exercise book, which I discovered thirty years ago in the Sydney offices of the New South Wales Cricket Association, close to where Bill Ferguson filed his directory cards, also contains his first radial scoring charts of individual innings, showing the area of the field into which each scoring stroke was played. The original 1905 tour scorebook was bought from Victor Trumper's estate by a private collector and is now in the Cricket Museum at the MCG. Like many others preserved in the MCC Library at Lord's and at Board offices around the world, it contains Fergie's sketches of pavilions and scenery surrounding each ground. These were carefully drawn in the margins of the scoring section and made his books unique.

By an odd coincidence, I have the same initials as William Henry Ferguson. We met just once. Towards the end of their 1953 tour, the Australians played the Combined Services during the Kingston Festival at Hawkers Sports Ground and, during a tea interval, a certain truant schoolboy had the temerity to visit the scorers' box and ask to see Fergie's famous book. A small, frail old man wearing a brown trilby, he was very kind and patiently showed me the latest sample of his handiwork. His meticulous contributions to the Directory had given him a perfect training for scoring and it was very evident that he took great delight in his work.

After scoring 204 Tests out of the 299 played during his working span of 49 years, he died at Bath in 1957 at the age of 77. In the course of guiding cricketers' luggage on world tours totalling an estimated 614,000 miles, he never lost a bag. Australia's longest-serving Prime Minister, Sir Robert Menzies, paid him the ultimate tribute when he wrote in the foreword to Fergie's autobiography, *Mr Cricket* (Nicholas Kaye 1957): 'There is no better-loved man in the entire cricket world'. Sir Robert, who visited our box at Lord's in 1975, also presented Fergie with the British Empire Medal. As far as I have been able to discover, we are the only two scorers who have been fortunate enough to receive national honours.

When continuous ball-by-ball radio commentaries were introduced, my BBC predecessors soon discovered that the orthodox system of scoring a cricket match did not provide sufficient information for the commentators. Additional sheets had to be kept to record the number of balls faced by each batsman but, short of using a different colour for each bowler, it was impossible to analyse an innings in any detail. Arthur Wrigley (1912–65) and Roy Webber (1914–62) were the pioneer scorers for radio and television respectively. Each adapted the Ferguson method in designing their own sheets.

Before making my debut with *Test Match Special* in 1966, I experimented by scoring some of the 1965–66 Ashes series in Australia from radio commentaries. By the last Test I had redesigned all three sheets and made various alterations to the system itself. With a few minor adjustments, mainly to ward off bizarre questions from Brian Johnston, my original designs have remained unchanged and have been used by many media scorers. In 1972 I designed linear sheets for club and county scorers, or for those who just like scoring for fun. They combine the ball-by-ball and cumulative bowling sheets. Marketed in loose-leaf packs of 100 sheets with sets of interscrew binders, these are now used worldwide and by several first-class teams. When he heard that Ireland was the first international team to use my sheets, John Arlott mischievously quipped, 'Ah, Frindalius, but they've got four scorers.'

The method follows the basic conventions of the standard scoring system described in *Cricket Umpiring and Scoring*, a textbook for umpires and scorers compiled by R.S. Rait Kerr, who was secretary of the MCC from 1936 until 1952. For radio commentaries, the system involves three types of scoresheet – a ball-by-ball record of play (*Sheet 1*), an innings scorecard (*Sheet 2*) and a cumulative record of bowling analyses and extras (*Sheet 3*).

From a brief study of the three sheets you will see that the method is easy to follow. It accommodates more facts during play than the conventional 'box' system, involves less recording during each over, enables the run of play with its timings to be fully reconstructed and yet is still simple to follow. This is especially handy for producers hunting for recordings of specific action from a day's play.

Sheet 1, the ball-by-ball record of play, forms the basis of the scoring method but, unlike the other two sheets, it is not used by commentators. It contains three sections – one for the bowlers, one for the batsmen, and one for recording the totals at the end of each over, or at the fall of a wicket, interval or unscheduled stoppage of play. Each line across these columns records one over, the time when the bowler commences the over being entered in the first column.

The sample *Sheet 1* shows the start of the second Test between England and Australia at Edgbaston in August 2005. You will see that there are two bowling columns (one for each end of the ground), and two batting columns, which list the batsmen in the positions (left or

1ST	BOWLERS				BATSMEN					ENGLAND 1ST INNINGS					
DAY	(RE KOERTZEN) PAVILION END		(BF BOWDEN) CITY END		SCOREBOARD LEFT			SCOREBOARD RIGHT		NOTES	END-OF-OVER TOTALS				
TIME	BOWLER	O.	BOWLER	O.	SCORING	BALLS	6s/4s	SCORING	BALLS	6s/4s		O.	RUNS	W.	'L' BAT	'R' BAT	EXTRAS
					TRESCOTHICK		4B	STRAUSS		4B	Pale cloud · cool						
9·30	LEE	1			4·····4	6					W1 W1	1	1				1
34			GILLESPIE	1				···4·×	6	1		2	5			4	
39	"	2			4··4/3 3/4 44	12	3					3	17		12		
43			"	2				··E1·4/5	12		· De Warne LH·RHp (line to left) M1	4					
47	"	3			1·⊙··4·	19	4				NB1 NB1	5	22		16		2
52½			"	3	··:·:	22		3/2 4·4/5 4·1	15	2	4 Tr (maryan C'nat)	6	27			9	
57	"	4						·······	21		M2	7					
·02			"	4	3/4 4/5 4·1	24	5	3·:·4·	25	3		8	36		21	13	
06	"	5			4··4/2 4·1	28	6	3··::	28		NB2 NB2	9	42		26		3
11			"	5	2····	34						10	44		28		
15	KASPROWICZ	1						·⊙·3·⊙4··	36	4	NB NB NB4 /50 p'ship 48/48 b	11	50			17	5
20			"	6	·4/5·:4·::	40	7					12	54		32		
23½	"	2			4/2 1 ⊙····:	46		9 1	37		4 2/5 Harden NB NB3 1HR	13	56			18	6
29			WARNE	1				P··:4··:	43	5	+ ball deviating/changed -DENNESS (3:31-:34)	14	60			22	
38	"	3			3···4·	52					Clark thickening M3	15					
42			"	2				3··3 7 7/8 ··44·	49	7		16	68			30	
45	"	4			·:···:4/5 4	58					M4	17					
49			"	3	·:9··5·6	61	7/1	1···:1	52			18	77		39	32	
53	"	5			·· 2 3/4 44	66	9/1		53			19	86		47	33	
56			"	4				·:P·PP:	59		M5	20					
59	"	6			··×1·4/2·	72					+ Appeal ctwk M6 sway	21					
2·03			"	5	·1·2	74		6 6 4/2 4/6 4 ·4·1··4	63	8	+ Around to Strauss TRESco/BROCK So: 97'	22	95		50	39	
08	"	7						3/6 3/8 ··44·:	69	10	+Mound 4 over 100 p'ship·100'/141b	23	103			47	
12			"	6	4/2 7·1·6	78	1/10	·6·6	71			24	110		56	48	
16	LEE	6			3/4 4/5 2 ·1·1	81		····3 1/2	74		Around	25	111		57		
20			"	7	4/5 1	82		P 4/2 W	76	10		25³	112	1	58	48	6
23								VAUGHAN								0	
25			"	7	6/7 1	83		·:7·1	2			26	114		59	1	
27	"	7			3/8 1/9 3b 4/3 4 6·4·4·4	89	2/13		2	-	2HR	27	132	1	77	1	6
2·30	LUNCH										M6 NB5 W1	L U N C H				

ENGLAND FIRST INNINGS v AUSTRALIA (SECOND TEST) AT EDGBASTON, BIRMINGHAM ON 4,5,6,7,& AUGUST 2005   TOSS: AUSTRALIA.

IN	OUT	MINS	No.	BATSMAN	HOW OUT	BOWLER	RUNS	WKT	TOTAL	6s	4s	BALLS	NOTES ON DISMISSAL	OVER OUT
10.30	1.33	143	1	ME TRESCOTHICK	c° GILCHRIST	KASPROWICZ	90	2	164	2	15	102	HS v AUS Followed ball ang	33
10.30	12.23	113	2	AJ STRAUSS	BOWLED	WARNE	48	1	112	·	10	76	Played back - bowled through gate by quicker ball.	26
12.24	1.58	54	3	*MP VAUGHAN	c° LEE	GILLESPIE	24	4	187	·	3	41	Hooked bouncer to long-leg - top edge wast stair	37
1.34	1.36	2	4	IR BELL	c° GILCHRIST	KASPROWICZ	6	3	170	·	1	3	Edged ball leaving him.	33
1.57	4.29	152	5	KP PIETERSEN	c° KATICH	LEE	71	8	348	1	10	76	HS Skied ball - deep mid-wicket ran in and dived	67
1.59	3.33	74	6	A FLINTOFF	c° GILCHRIST	GILLESPIE	68	6	290	5	6	62	EMG'A firm-footed square drive. Gillespie's 250th wkt	55
3.34	3.48	14	7	†GO JONES	c° GILCHRIST	KASPROWICZ	1	6	293	·	·	15	Edged lifting ball.	58
3.49	4.23	34	8	AF GILES	LBW	WARNE	23	7	342	·	4	30	Missed sweep at dipping full length ball.	66
4.24	5.26	62	9	MJ HOGGARD	LBW	WARNE	16	10	407	·	2	49	Missed sweep.	80
4.30	4.46	16	10	SJ HARMISON	BOWLED	WARNE	17	9	375	1	2	11	off stump - missed stay.	70
4.47	(5.26)	39	11	SP JONES	NOT OUT		19				1	24		
				EXTRAS	b -	lb 9	w 1	nb 14		24				

TOTAL   (79.1 OVERS; 356 MINUTES)   **407.** ALL OUT at 5.26 pm. (1st day) STUMPS

$\overset{6}{10}$ $\overset{54^2}{54}$ 489 balls (inc. 14 nb + one 5 ball over)

* CAPTAIN   † WICKET-KEEPER.

13 OVERS 2 BALLS / HOUR
5.13 RUNS / OVER
83 RUNS / 100 BALLS

UMPIRES : BF BOWDEN (28) and RE KOERTZEN (64).   REFEREE: R.S. MADUGALLE (76)

BOWLER	O	M	R	W	nb	w	HRS	OVERS	RUNS
LEE	17	1	111	1	9		1	13	56
GILLESPIE	22	3	91	2	3	1	2	14	76
KASPROWICZ	15	3	80	3	3		3	13	65
WARNE	25.1	4	116	4	·		4	14	92
							5	12.1	59
	79.1	11	407	10	14	1			

	RUNS	MINS	OVERS	LAST 50
	50	48	10.4	68
	100	100	22.4	73
	150	130	29.1	40
	200	186	40.4	74
	250	215	49.3	47
	300	266	59.5	68
	350	304	66.5	43
	400	353	78.4	72

LUNCH: 132 - 1.

TEA: 289-4. AUS 157 in 3½ hrs

LUNCH: 132-1. [27 OVERS] TRESCOTHICK 77 [120 MIN] VAUGHAN 1 (6*)

TEA: 289-4. [54 OVERS] PIETERSEN 40 (64) [34.1 MIN] FLINTOFF 68 (72)

AUSTRALIA LAST CONCEDED 400
IN A DAY AT LORD'S IN 1938 (409-5).
(493 TESTS · AUSTRALIA · AGO)

WKT	PARTNERSHIP		RUNS	MINS	BALLS
1st	Trescothick	Strauss	112‡	113	158
2nd	Trescothick	Vaughan	52	29	44
3rd	Vaughan	Bell	6	2	3
4th	Vaughan	Pietersen	17	21	28
5th	Pietersen	Flintoff	103#	74	105
6th	Pietersen	G. Jones	3	14	19
7th	Pietersen	Giles	49	34	45
8th	Pietersen	Hoggard	6	5	8
9th	Hoggard	Harmison	27	16	20
10th	Hoggard	S. Jones	32	39	59
			407		489

‡ E·V·A· # = 100 PARTNERSHIP
$ = 100 runs added at two Edgbaston.

AUSTRALIA BOWLING — FIRST INNINGS

LEE

NB	O	M	R	W	WIDES
	1	0	1	0	3
	2	0	13	0	
	3	0	18	0	4
	4	1	18	0	
	5	1	24	0	5
	6	1	25	0	
	7	1	43	0	8
LUNCH					
	8	1	45	0	
	9	1	56	0	2
	10	1	58	0	
	11	1	72	0	3
TEA					
	12	1	84	0	3
	13	1	90	0	
	14	1	98	1	5
	15	1	108	1	5
	16	1	110	1	
	17		111	1	14.5

GILLESPIE

NB	O	M	R	W	WIDES
	1	0	4	0	
	2	1	4	0	
	3	1	9	0	2
	4	1	18	0	4
	5	1	20	0	
	6	1	24	0	5
LUNCH					
	7	1	27	0	
	8	1	36	0	7
	9	2	36	0	
	10	2	37	0	7
	11	2	39	1	
	12	2	41	1	
	13	2	45	1	8
	14	2	55	1	10
	15	2	64	1	12
TEA					
	16	2	65	2	
	17	3	65	2	
	18	3	67	2	
	19	3	74	2	13
	20	3	76	2	
	21	3	78	2	
	22	3	91	2	14

KASPROWICZ

NB	O	M	R	W	WIDES
	1	0	6	0	
	2	0	8	0	
	3	1	8	0	
	4	2	8	0	
	5	2	17	0	3
	6	3	17	0	
	7	3	25	0	5
LUNCH					
	8	3	36	0	6
	9	3	43	0	7
	10	3	51	2	8
	11	3	63	2	10
TEA					
	12	3	65	2	
	13	3	70	3	11
	14	3	74	3	12
	15	3	80	3	13

WARNE

NB	O	M	R	W	WIDES
	1	0	4	0	
	2	0	12	0	3
	3	0	21	0	3
	4	1	21	0	
	5	1	30	0	4
	6	1	37	0	5
	7	1	40	1	5
LUNCH					
	8	1	42	1	
	9	1	46	1	6
	10	1	50	1	
	11	1	60	1	2
	12	1	66	1	3
	13	1	69	1	
	14	1	71	1	
	15	1	79	1	4
	16	1	88	1	3
	17	1	89	1	3
TEA					
	18	1	94	1	4
	19	2	94	2	
	20	2	100	2	
	21	2	105	3	4
	22	2	111	3	4
	23	2	111	3	
	24	4	111	3	4
	25	4	115	3	4
	25.4	4	116	3	

EXTRAS

B	LB	W	NB	TOTAL
	1		1	1
	1			2
				3
	3			3
	4			4
	8			5
	9			6
				7
				8
				9
				10
				11
				12
				13
				14
				16
				17
				18
				22
				23
				24

CRICKET SCORING SHEET No. 5

Designed and drawn by BILL FRINDALL

right) in which their scores are shown on the scoreboard. Although most grounds now have computerised scoreboards, which give the complete batting order, my sheets were designed for use in England when most boards identified the players by their number on the score-card only. The left/right separation identifies the batsmen in the End-of-Over Totals.

My sheet shows that umpire Rudi Koertzen is standing at the Pavilion (Commentary Box) End, while 'Billy' Bowden is at the City End. Australia won the toss and, to everyone's astonishment, elected to bowl. Ricky Ponting's decision allegedly gave Shane Warne apoplexy, particularly as they had lost the services of Glenn McGrath after he had wrecked his ankle treading on a ball.

The surnames of Marcus Trescothick and Andrew Strauss are entered in the batting columns, with 'LHB' noted alongside to record that they are both left-handed batsmen.

Brett Lee is about to bowl the first ball of the match from our end and I enter his name on the next line of the 'Pavilion End' column. I put a '1' in the square alongside it to show that it is his first over. When Koertzen calls 'Play', I enter the time in the first column and start my three stopwatches – one for each batsman and one for the England innings as a whole.

I am now ready to record the first ball. It is faced by Trescothick and called wide by Koertzen. Wides are recorded in the batsman's column as ✝ just as in the standard system. Four wides would be shown as ✣ . It does not count as a ball received because the batsman cannot score from it. The likelihood of a batsman being stumped off a wide the first ball he receives is more remote than his being run out without facing a ball. Wides are marked as W in the Notes column.

Lee bowls the next five balls outside the off stump and Trescothick either ignores them or plays his characteristic sham defensive stroke inside their line. As no run has been scored, these are entered as dots just as in the standard system. Had the batsman blocked them, I would have put a dot above the first dot. The final ball he pushes to mid-off and I put a 4 above the dot to denote that he has hit it some distance towards mid-off. I use a cryptic code to chart the area of the field in which non-scoring hits are played and runs are scored. My code is based on the following key, which, as in Trescothick's case, is reversed for left-handed batsmen:

This method is approximate but it does show if a batsman has a favourite scoring area and can reveal if a bowler is prone to conceding runs to a particular stroke. My radial scoring charts are constructed from these little numerals.

After Viv Richards had scored 232 against England at Trent Bridge in 1976, the England captain, Tony Greig, asked me for a set of charts showing the batsman's scoring strokes against each of the six bowlers he faced. I was able to construct these from my sheets and I also separated the 313 balls received

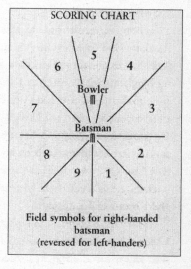

by Richards to show his scoring rate against each bowler. After Richards had amassed 291 in the final Test at The Oval, then the highest innings I had scored at any level of cricket, Greig publicly destroyed my charts!

At the end of the over, 6 is entered in the Balls Received column for Trescothick, while that for Strauss, who has yet to face a ball, is left blank. I enter W1 in the Notes column to show that a wide has been bowled, and put 1 in the Overs, Runs and Extras spaces. Although no runs were scored from the bat, because of the wide it is not a maiden over.

At 10.34 a.m. Jason Gillespie begins his first over from the City End. I note the time and enter his name in the other bowling column. It is Strauss's turn to take strike and the scoring is done in his column.

He steers a boundary past the slip cordon off his fourth ball and I enter 4 with a 1 above it to denote the area in which he scored it. Strauss plays at the sixth ball and misses it, his error being recorded by putting an X above the dot. At the end of this over, any totals that have changed are updated, i.e. the Balls Received column for Strauss and the totals for Overs, Runs and Extras for Strauss. Trescothick's spaces are left blank.

I then record the time at which Lee starts his second over (10.39). As he bowled the previous one from the same end there is no need to write his name, ditto marks are sufficient. He is hit for three boundaries by Trescothick, the first through mid-off (4), the second through wide mid-off (4/3) and the third through extra-cover (3/4). At the end of that over he has faced 12 balls and hit 3 fours, which are entered in his boundaries column. All run fours are included in this tally but not scoring strokes that have been boosted to four or more by overthrows. The End-of-Over columns show that England have scored 17 for 0 wickets off 3 overs with Trescothick contributing 12, Strauss 4 and there is one extra, a wide.

Strauss is dropped at first slip by Shane Warne off the third ball of Gillespie's second over. I enter E1 above the dot to show that the ball was edged into the slip area, and add a red dot. This links to a red dot in the Notes column, where I record 'Dr [dropped] Warne 1st slip (low to left)'.

I prefix the direction of all edged strokes with a small e. For routine scoring, such elaborate refinements are obviously superfluous, but for Test match broadcasts I need to record many minor details in order to answer the commentators' diverse questions. First Brian Johnston and more recently Jonathan Agnew have relished setting me such posers as, 'How many times did Trescothick play and miss against McGrath?' or 'How many of Bell's runs have come from edged strokes?'

The over is a maiden so the six dots are underlined and M1 is annotated in the Notes column to show that it is the first maiden of the innings and to facilitate a check with the bowling figures. The End-of-Over Totals require entries only when they have changed during that particular over so only the number of that over (4) needs entering.

The third ball of Lee's third over is called a no-ball by umpire Koertzen. This is recorded as ⊙ , just as in the traditional system of scoring. If the no-ball had been hit for four runs it would have been shown as ④ in the batsman's section – similarly with any other number of runs scored off a no-ball. A no-ball counts as a ball received because, unlike a wide, which is not included, the batsman can score off it. As with wides, one run is added to the total runs conceded by that bowler for each no-ball from which no score results.

Like other extras, no-balls are itemised in the Notes column (NB) and a tally is kept of them immediately alongside. NB1 denotes the first no-ball call of the innings.

Strauss hits the first ball of Gillespie's third over towards the square-cover (3/2) boundary. Damien Martyn chases and appears to make a spectacular diving save on the boundary. However, the third umpire consults slow-motion replays that reveal the fielder was in contact with the ball when part of his body touched or crossed the boundary marker and four runs are signalled. I put a dagger above the 4 and add '† TV (Martyn save)' to the Notes column.

I use the Notes column to record the weather at the start of each day's play, the daily attendance figures, substitution of fielders (this became slightly congested during the 2005 Ashes series with the unfortunately named Pratt appearing rather a lot!), dropped catches, unsuccessful appeals for anything except lbw, injuries, bowlers changing from over to round the wicket, any exceptional pieces of fielding, five and seven-ball overs and unusual incidents. Even the most obscure and apparently useless piece of data can prove invaluable.

Two overs later, Trescothick calls for a run for a prod that carries only a few feet – 4VS above the run denotes a 'very short' single towards mid-off.

The first ball of Lee's fifth over was a bouncer ↑ . Shooters are shown as arrows pointing downwards. Two balls later, Trescothick hits a no-ball to the boundary backward of point (2/3). A circle round the 4 denotes the no-ball and NB is added to the Notes column. At the end of the over, one run is added to the Extras column in addition to the four put on the batsman's tally. Trescothick edges the fifth ball of the 10th over into his pad and I put EP above the dot.

When Michael Kasprowicz replaces Lee at the Pavilion End, his name is entered in that bowling column and Lee's bowling figures (5-1-24-0, denoting 5 overs, 1 maiden, 24 runs and 0 wickets) are underlined in red on *Sheet 3* to indicate the end of his spell.

During that over, Strauss brings up the 50 with a cover-driven boundary and I enter the partnership details (48 minutes, 68 balls) in the Notes column. Those partnership details, as well as minutes for batsmen, are annotated for all multiples of 50.

Trescothick edges the second ball of Kasprowicz's second over and is caught by Matthew Hayden at gully, but Koertzen has called 'no-ball' and the batsman cannot be out caught off it. E2 above the no-ball symbol denotes the edge and its direction. A † links it to the Notes column where I put 'ct' Hayden.

At the end of that over the first hour of the innings is a minute short of being completed, so I note 1 HR in the Notes column and record 13 overs/56 runs in the appropriate section on *Sheet 2*.

Shane Warne replaces Gillespie at the City End. His name is entered in that bowling column and Gillespie's bowling figures (6-1-24-0) are underlined in red on *Sheet 3* to indicate the end of his spell.

Warne's first and third balls hit Strauss's pads and I record this by putting a P above those dots. His fourth ball is driven first bounce into the sightscreen. While the damaged ball is being changed, the umpires call for drinks. I always record the time of the start and finish of such intervals (11.31 to 11.34 a.m. in this instance) but, by tradition, this counts as playing time and cannot be deducted from the individual batting times. This came about because of the difficulty in noting such things in a normal scorebook. It has always seemed nonsensical and has convinced me that the only accurate and logical measurement of the duration of an innings is the number of balls received. This scoring system makes such a calculation extremely simple.

Trescothick hits the last ball of Warne's third over above the sightscreen for the first six of the match. I record this in blue in the top diagonal half of his boundaries space and in Warne's appropriate column on *Sheet 3*.

Overs 21 to 23 include examples of an unsuccessful appeal for a catch by the wicket-keeper, Warne changing from over to around the wicket and the hundred partnership. The fourth ball of the 24th over hits Strauss's pad and Warne appeals unsuccessfully for lbw. This is shown by putting an L above the dot. If there had been no appeal, the fact that the ball had struck the batsman's pad would have been recorded with a P.

The third ball of Warne's seventh over produces the first wicket, Strauss being bowled through the gate by a quicker ball. The fall of a wicket produces a pressure point in any scoring system, but practice soon helps to evolve the best sequence of action and there is normally a period of two minutes in which to complete it before the new batsman starts his innings.

First, I stop the watch recording Strauss's batting time. It shows 113 minutes and this is recorded on *Sheet 2*, together with the other essential details and statistics – b Warne 48, Fall of Wicket 1-112, Boundaries 10, Balls Received 76, and a note of how he was out. A red W with EX above it (to denote that he played on via an edge) is entered in Strauss's batting column on *Sheet 1*.

All the totals are completed in the End-of-Over Totals section. Strauss's column in that section and his own batting column are ruled off in red, and his Balls Received and sixes/fours columns are carried down. The time of Strauss's dismissal (12.23) is entered on both sheets.

The name of the new batsman (Michael Vaughan) is entered on the next line of the vacant batting column. Warne's over is continued on the line below Vaughan's name, together with the time it restarted. The time at which Vaughan stepped on to the field of play is entered alongside his name on *Sheet 2*, and the right-hand stopwatch is set to zero and restarted.

Hat-tricks are a scorer's nightmare. Beware any commentator foolish enough to utter that ridiculous cliché 'he failed to trouble the scorers' within my hearing! The secret is to keep calm and establish an order of action. Scoring relies on rhythm.

So the process continues. It quickly becomes routine with a logical sequence of recording, adding and checking. Reduced to its bare essentials, the system requires just one digit to record each scoring stroke. Less recording is necessary while the over is in progress than with the traditional scoring method. Instead of marking each run in the batting, bowling and innings tally sections of the standard scorebook, my method requires just one entry. It is also immediately possible to tell exactly what has happened to each ball – who bowled it to whom, from which end, at what time and how the batsman reacted. Unless a wicket falls, all the totalling is done at the end of the over while the fielders are changing positions and when there is no action to record.

At lunch, as at the end of any session, or at a stoppage for rain or bad light, the three watches are stopped and all the totals on *Sheet 1* are carried down. The lunch score and not-out batsmen's details are entered in the largest box on *Sheet 2*.

The End-of-Over Totals facilitate a check of the number of balls received by each batsman. I usually do this during drinks intervals, at the end of each session of play, or when I am bored. The total number of overs is multiplied by six and the number of no-balls is added to that total. If there have been any five or seven-ball overs (Billy Bowden rarely completes a match without transgressing), these have to be taken into account, too. That tally is then compared with the total number of balls received by the dismissed and not-out batsmen.

When lunch is taken at 12.30 p.m., 27 overs have been bowled, including 5 no-balls – 27 x 6 + 5 no-balls = 167. Trescothick (89) + Strauss (76) + Vaughan (2) = 167.

Before we leave *Sheet 1*, here is a full list of the symbols that I use in the batting columns:

B	Bye
E	Edged stroke
EP	Edged ball into pads
F	Full toss
G	Hit on glove
L	Hit on pad – lbw appeal
LB	Leg-bye
P	Hit on pad – no appeal
S	Sprinted run
T	Hit on thigh pad
VS	Very short single
X	Played and missed
Y	Yorker
•	Blocked
↑	Bouncer
↓	Shooter
U	Bowler used shortened run-up

The last of those symbols was introduced in Australia in 1979–80 when Rodney Hogg, suffering from heat exhaustion, frequently bowled *à la* Keith Miller off only five or six paces. I employed the same symbol in February 1988 when, after straining his calf muscle during the last over before tea on the first day of the Christchurch Test, Richard Hadlee delivered what were to be his last two balls of that series from a mini run.

Sheet 2, the innings scorecard, is the commentator's main source of reference. It records the starting and finishing times of each batsman's innings and its length in terms of balls and minutes, his score and number of boundaries, the total at which his wicket fell and the manner of his dismissal.

The lower part of the sheet shows the final bowling analyses, the hourly run and over rates, the time taken for each fifty runs scored by the team, the full details of each wicket partnership, the total and individual scores at the end of each session of play, details of when a new ball was taken, and notes of any records set during the innings.

Coloured inks are used to highlight the more important entries and to make it easier for the commentator to select essential items from a sheet containing so much data. Names and run totals are shown in blue, as is the close of play, or stumps, score. Red is used for hundred partnerships, lunch and team totals, and any other data of special interest.

Sheet 3, the cumulative record of bowling analyses and extras, is essential only to radio and television commentators. Spaces for cumulative bowling figures are incorporated in the bowling columns of the ball-by-ball pages of the sheets that I market.

Entries are made only at the end of each over or at the completion of a session of play. A red line is ruled under a bowler's figures when he is taken off. Intervals, close of play and interruptions for rain and bad light are also shown, thus enabling the commentator to calculate quickly the length of each individual bowling spell. The number of boundaries conceded by each bowler is shown cumulatively, the result of my pandering to a special plea from Brian Johnston.

Extras are recorded in separate columns on the right-hand side of the sheet. No-balls and wides are also recorded against the name of each bowler.

This sheet facilitates a number of cross-checks. The total of the overs delivered by each bowler should equal the number bowled so far in the innings ($7 + 6 + 7 + 7 = 27$ at lunch). The total of maidens, runs conceded, wickets, no-balls and boundaries can be checked in the same way.

Over the years, various publications have held competitions in which entrants were asked to score 50 consecutive overs of a current Test match using my scoring method. Usually their only guidance was an illustration of part of a *Sheet 1* accompanied by a very brief explanation of the system. Most of the entries were of a very high standard and many came from the 12 to 16 age group. One even typed his entire 50 overs. As a school scorer confirmed, 'the method is easier to use and to check, it can generate excessive statistics, and it confuses those who look over my shoulder!'

JOHN ARLOTT

J OHN ARLOTT was the 'Voice of Cricket' from 1946 until 1980. No voice can have given greater pleasure to more people throughout the English-speaking world than the splendid Hampshire burr of Doctor Leslie Thomas John Arlott, OBE. His retirement after the 1980 season left a void in broadcasting that will never be filled. A sensitive, sympathetic and humane man, he was exceptionally good company and it was a real delight and privilege to work with him for fifteen summers.

From our first meeting he treated me like a son. My father had died two years earlier and John became very much a father figure to me. We were both Pisceans and both only children. Apart from our mutual love of cricket, women and wine – note the order – the similarities probably ended there. He had helped me through my introduction to Test match broadcasting and done everything to build my confidence. He didn't need to, but perhaps he recognised something of himself in me. I was by no means the only young scorer, broadcaster or journalist to have been immensely boosted by John's encouragement. David Frith, now one of cricket's leading historians and writers, was another to benefit tremendously from John's kindness.

I was soon introduced to his family, his library, his cellar and the overwhelming hospitality of his vast dining table at The Old Sun in Alresford. His claret raids on Bordeaux had hooked him on the splendid local custom that encourages families to congregate each evening around a dining table rather than a television screen. During mammoth evening meals, stimulating conversation was fuelled by prolific quantities of food and wine. Those scenes were later recaptured at The Vines when he moved with his third wife, Pat, to his final resting place, Alderney in the Channel Islands.

No broadcaster can have been more delightful to work with or commanded more love and respect from his colleagues, his listeners or the players themselves. A singular man, he has always cared passionately for those close to him. In his final, bedridden days he insisted on his set of *Wisden Cricketers' Almanack* being brought to him in batches, so that he could painfully add the signature that would substantially increase their value to his estate. The death of his eldest son, Jimmy, in a motoring accident was a tragedy that affected John for the rest of his life and, apart from the first days of Test matches when he bowed to the traditions of the Test Match Broadcasters' Club, the only tie he ever wore was a black one.

The most vital contribution that John made to my career was to inspire me with confidence. He had a caring mentality. No one entering the cricket broadcasting circuit could have received more consideration. He was extremely thoughtful, supportive and encouraging, quick to praise on air and to give thanks for my help at the end of each broadcast. 'Are you enjoying it?' he would ask frequently. It took me a season before I could truthfully answer in the affirmative.

John Arlott was, by some distance, the greatest radio commentator that cricket has ever produced, his fruity tones as integral a part of the summer game as the sound of bat on ball or the scent of newly mown grass. His commentary technique developed directly from his years as a policeman, mainly with the Southampton CID, where his police training enhanced his powers of observation. During his spare time he began to compose verse. By the time his work was brought to the attention of the BBC he had become known as 'The Policeman Poet'. Now he had a poet's flair for description and language to add to his extended powers of observation and analysis. What better training for a sports commentator?

When commentating on radio, John tried to imagine that he was addressing one person. Adopting the technique of a landscape painter, first he would sketch the scene with broad strokes and reveal the state of the match with its latest score. Using this backcloth, he would build up the action, frequently spicing it with the personal characteristics of the combatants involved. He would need to watch an individual for only a few moments to conjure up the appropriate Arlottism – umpire Dickie Bird's cap 'jutting like a beak', Lillee's thunderbolt breaching a batsman's defence 'like a hole in a Henry Moore statue', fast bowler Asif Masood starting his approach to the wicket with a nervous backward chasse 'like Groucho Marx stalking a pretty waitress'. Fuelled by a vat of his excellent wine, I once asked him what single aspect of his technique had made him the supreme commentator. He looked quite shocked at my question, thought for a few moments, then replied, 'It's not because I'm so good, Frindalius, it's because the others are so bad.'

John's beginnings approached the humble and he never abandoned them. He never trusted the Establishment and had many battles with it. He stood for Parliament as a Liberal candidate and never abandoned those principles. He would always champion the underdog, the professional against the amateur and, in the case of apartheid, the blacks and coloureds against a hideous regime. On his only visit to South Africa in 1948–49, he was asked to complete an emigration form on his departure. His replies were splendidly terse: 'Religion – occasionally; Sex – frequently, but never after a heavy meal; Race – human.' 'Don't you come back to South Africa, Mr Arlott,' warned the official. 'Don't worry, I won't,' he replied, and he didn't. He was instrumental in getting Basil D'Oliveira to England and thus played a part in the Union's excommunication from the Test arena from 1970 until 1992.

John was at his happiest in the company of professional cricketers. This helped him considerably with his commentaries because he knew of their personal feuds. Without bringing attention to any rivalries he could emphasise the efforts of a certain bowler to dismiss a batsman whom John knew he detested. Since John's retirement, only the former players who have joined *TMS* would have had an inkling of those personal relationships that often explain actions on the field. The essence of his commentary style depended upon his knowledge of the personalities of the players batting and bowling against each other. He understood how they inter-related. I suspect that, apart from the more obvious examples, few subsequent commentators, Trevor Bailey being a notable exception, have considered this aspect of the action they are describing. They see the basic picture and are blissfully unaware of the hidden agendas of the protagonists.

John's gifts of description as a cricket commentator flowered on the basis of his unusual background and detailed knowledge of an extremely wide range of subjects. Self acquired, his education was more rounded than that of most university graduates and enabled him to take a long, detached view of any match. His favourite quote was a remark made by C.L.R. James, the Trinidadian writer: 'What do they know of cricket who only cricket know?' He stretched the term 'mul-titalented' beyond any previously known boundaries, bestowing a Bradmanesque intensity upon whatever interest he pursued. Besides cricket, John was an authority on several other sports, Victorian aquat-ints, engraved glass, pottery, Thomas Hardy, Dylan Thomas, garden-ing, cheese and wine, especially wine. While he was the *Guardian*'s correspondent for both cricket and wine, two of the major attractions of his life, the line of demarcation between them was so narrow that no one ever discovered it.

His knowledge of wine had grown steadily from the end of the MCC's 1948–49 tour of South Africa. Someone remarked that his heavy social life had taken its toll of his appearance and if he wanted to preserve domestic harmony when he returned to England he ought to replace his thirst for beer with a moderate intake of wine. His total conversion was completed long before our first meeting in 1966 and I cannot recall him drinking beer ever – brandy, certainly, but never the hop. His knowledge earned him the role, unprecedented for an Englishman, of Selector of Wines for the SNCF. Chooser of the wine list for the French national railway was an accolade that gave John immense pleasure and no one has ever researched that list with greater enthusiasm. Knowing his subject inside and out, he was often invited to judge his beloved subject at French wine-fests and his reward was always taken in kind.

In the mid-eighties I flew to Alderney with *Wisden*'s Editor, Graeme Wright, to spend a few days as willing victims of John's bounteous hospitality. On our journey from the island's tiny airfield I offered to do some work in the garden. I enjoy mowing lawns and needed the exercise after a season of sitting in commentary boxes. 'Hell's teeth, no! If you start gardening, my old retainer will either think I'm going to sack him or that he's about to die! Never fear, I have a little task for you in the cellar, Frindalius.'

John's house, one of the largest on the island, had originally been called Balmoral. He had swiftly amended that to The Vines. Richie Benaud had presented him with a few suitable Australian specimens, which were making their way tentatively up a distant perimeter wall. Our arrival coincided with the delivery of forty-eight cases from a recent wine-fest. The cellar was vast. When the Germans invaded Alderney, their commandant had seized Balmoral as his headquarters and converted its cellar into his communications room. Old wiring from those days of occupation still clung to the walls.

We squeezed past the cases stacked in the passage outside the cellar door and climbed down into the musty room.

'Now, Sir William, you are familiar with organising libraries so you're the very man to re-rack this cellar. Everything's mixed up. I want all the reds in this area and all the whites over here. Please sort them out and then perhaps you would like to start unloading the new visitors.'

And that was it. He vanished up the stairs clutching a bottle and, frustratingly, the only corkscrew. After an hour I had rearranged the existing stock and began racking the new arrivals. Graeme had been allotted the cushy task of loading the empty cartons and cases into John's automatic Maxi and accompanying him on a winding single-track road to 'Hades', a cliff-side cave where the islanders incinerated their rubbish. I continued the unpacking and had reached the last few cases when John's wife, Pat, called down. She sounded rather flustered.

'Bill, can you find a bottle of brandy and join us in the kitchen, please?'

The three of them were sat around the large wooden table. Graeme looked ashen. John had his head in his hands. Pat looked slightly amused. She explained that John had confused the controls on his automatic car and charged into an approaching van on the cliff-top path. Luckily, there had been no injuries – except to John's pride.

'Hell's teeth!' he snarled. 'First accident I've ever had!' Pat looked amazed.

'But, John, we've only just had the car repaired from when you drove it into the post office wall.'

'First accident involving another vehicle,' fumed John.

Even though he was indisputably one of the thirstiest souls to inhabit this planet I cannot recall seeing him drunk. Of course, that may have been because he had got me too legless to notice. He certainly commentated and wrote more lucidly when he had drunk a glass of wine. I remember him being genuinely horrified when a new house-guest refused a drink, admitting to being teetotal. John's eyebrows shot up. 'Hell's teeth! Do you realise that when you wake up in the morning that's the best you're going to feel all day?'

On the memorable morning of our first meeting, he had plucked from his battered old leather briefcase two bottles of claret, a gnarled vine-root corkscrew and two large chunky wine glasses. When he travelled by car, the boot always housed a case of claret. 'Nothing too special – it gets shaken up too much on the journey.' When he moved most of his cellar stock from Alresford to Alderney in 1980, the cheaper bottles went as air cargo while his valued stock enjoyed a luxurious sea voyage.

In the early seventies, John invited me to help him check proofs and research the cricket section of the *Oxford Companion to Sports and Games*. I spent several memorable days at The Old Sun in Alresford, an hour's drive from north London. I always arrived on the stroke of 9 a.m. to be welcomed by John proffering a mammoth glass of white wine. 'Just a freshener, William.' It was always essential to complete most of the day's tasks before lunch. During one visit he took me for a tour outside. A dustbin was crammed full of bottles with others stacked on the ground around it.

'The dustmen don't call very often,' I remarked.

'They were here three days ago', corrected John.

When we reached the garage, I saw an old desk lying on a sea of discarded books.

'Would you like that desk?' asked John. 'I don't use it any more now that I work on that large table.' I accepted it eagerly, restored it and it has been an essential part of my study for nearly forty years.

Before he began his commentary on the opening morning of the Centenary Test against Australia at Lord's in 1980, he decided to fortify himself with a double brandy. He had decided that it was to be his final Test and, just before the scheduled start of play, he followed it with another. I must have instinctively raised my eyebrows in surprise. He nodded reassuringly. 'Purely medicinal, Frindalius. I promise I'm not enjoying it.'

When John started cracking jokes, producer Peter Baxter became a tad alarmed, too. Heavy drizzle combined with the presence of Dickie Bird guaranteed a delayed start and he didn't want his team roaring with laughter when we went on air. John waited until ten seconds before the announcer handed over to us before asking, 'What do you do if an Irishman throws a pin at you? Run like hell. He's got a ruddy handgrenade in his mouth.' The world was welcomed with unrestrained guffaws.

In the mid-eighties, when John was flown from Alderney to Oxford's Radcliffe Infirmary for some surgery, Pat phoned to tell me about it and I asked if I could visit him. 'He'd love to see you tomorrow, if you can manage it,' she said. I had started loading some bottles into the pilot's case that carried my larger books and files to broadcasts when the phone rang. It was John. 'Could you bring a couple of bottles of Médoc, please? That's M E D ...' I irritably assured him that it was a claret I was familiar with and hurried to the off-licence. Next day

I lugged the case with its six bottles of wine up the long run of steps from the car park and joined a crowd of visitors waiting for the lifts. Arriving on John's floor, I asked a nurse where Mr Arlott's room was. She glanced at the bulging case, grinned and pointed to a distant door. It had a large and unique label that read: 'John Arlott, OBE. ONLY ONE GLASS OF WINE PER DAY.' I knocked. 'Come in,' came the familiar burr. I did and was faced with a smirking Arlott clutching a pint glass. I revealed the contents of my case. 'Quick! The vultures will have spotted you. Put one behind my pillow, two behind the wardrobe, one behind that curtain, one in the back of that locker and open the last one.' Mission completed, I had just taken a sip from a wine glass and John had drunk a quarter of a pint when the senior nurse arrived with Pat. They glowered at me and found four of the bottles in no time. As I was leaving the ward, Pat told me that John had got the shakes when he had come round from the anaesthetic and they had had to put brandy in his drip. I suspect he considered that an accolade.

I was a supreme admirer of John's radio commentaries long before I ever entertained hopes of joining the radio commentary team. His voice was distinctive and never grated. His use of language and avoidance of clichés was special. He was never boring. Rarely would a twenty-minute commentary session pass without him contributing a memorable phrase or description. One of his reasons for deciding to retire from cricket broadcasting after the 1980 season was that he feared he was not thinking of anything new to say. He felt the old magic had gone. 'I'm not getting any better at it,' he said.

He disproved this dramatically during his final commentary for the BBC. Just four days after his final Test, John returned to Lord's for the last Gillette Cup final. Surrey were playing Middlesex, badly. Mike Brearley had put Surrey in and they struggled to 201 in their full 60 overs, a target their opponents overhauled with seven wickets and more than six overs to spare. Earlier that week they had clinched the county championship, mainly because of 85 wickets at 14.72 runs apiece taken by their tall, balding, world-class South African seam bowler fearsomely named Vintcent van der Bijl. As that giant assassin returned to his mark at the far end, John, who had not seen him before, began his stunning description.

'Van der Bijl walks back to his mark at the Nursery End. He turns, the sun glinting on his high, domed forehead. He runs in now, looking like a taller, younger, more expansive and exuberant version of Lord Longford [pause] ... but not nearly so tolerant!'

John was certainly the easiest commentator to work with. He rarely required me to pass him anything except the bowling figures or another bottle. Others have compelled me to lug around bus and train timetables, helicopter charts and tomes on British wildlife. He did startle me once during an Ashes Test but it was after he had lunched well. 'What I really want to know, Bill, is if England bowl their overs at the same rate as Australia did, and Brearley and Boycott survive the opening spell, and there are not more than ten no-balls in the innings, and assuming that my car does 33.8 miles per gallon and my home is 67.3 miles from here, what time does my wife have to put the casserole in?'

I can only remember John losing his temper twice and both times he was commendably restrained. The first happened in 1975 when we were broadcasting a county championship match at Lord's between Middlesex and Glamorgan. This was a three-day county fixture that we broadcast, along with two other matches, on the Light Programme (Radio 2) on Saturday and continued on World Service on the Monday and Tuesday. John relished his twenty-minute commentary slots on *Test Match Special*. Sharing a county match with two other commentary positions was not something he enjoyed. He would have at best three or four five-minute commentary slots and a brief close of play summary. By the time six o'clock approached he had exhausted his wine supply and was looking forward to doing his summary and catching the train home to dinner at Alresford. That Saturday there was a new announcer in the sports room and he was eager to make an impression. Instead of a swift handover to John, he intoned, 'And now we are going over to John Arlott at Lord's where Glamorgan won the toss, batted and collapsed from 70 for 1 to 159 all out. Fred Titmus took 4 for 40 and Phil Edmonds scythed through the middle order with his left-arm spin to take 5 for 54. Alan Jones and Roger Davis were the joint top-scorers for Glamorgan with 37. In reply, Middlesex have scored 197 for 3 from 52 overs with Mike Smith 81 and Mike Brearley 48 putting on 124 for the first wicket. Now over to John Arlott.'

John looked absolutely livid. I never saw him look so furious. His eyebrows rose swiftly up his forehead as he put down his glass and picked up the microphone. 'That's right,' he growled. 'Back to the studio.'

The other instance that caused John to be visibly upset occurred at Headingley and the culprits were Fred Trueman and me. Unlike Brian Johnston who used me as his compliant stooge, John did not involve me in his commentaries unless something major occurred. To some extent I could relax as I scored, enjoy the cricket and occasionally chat to other members of the team who were off duty. On this occasion I was discussing dinner arrangements with Brian Johnston and was scoring on automatic pilot. Suddenly I realised that John had stopped commentating and was looking expectantly at me. I mimed that I had not been listening. Mime is rarely used on radio but can be useful sometimes. John made it obvious that he was not going to co-operate. I hunted for my lip-mike, found it under some papers and mumbled apologetically, 'I'm sorry, John. I didn't hear what you said. I was discussing something with Brian.'

John frowned at me, muttered, 'Doesn't matter, doesn't matter,' and returned to the action. 'Boycott waits tensely as Lillee runs in, bowls and beats him with a superb outswinger. My word, that moved late. You would have been proud to have bowled that, Fred.'

Absolute silence. Fred, having just been handed a pile of post, had savaged his way into a small jiffy bag and extracted a tiny limp-covered book entitled *Carr's Dictionary of Extraordinary Cricketers*. He had opened it at a page about a sheikh who had his own cricket team. Whenever the sheikh's team won he used to burn the loser's tents and abduct their wives. Fred was fantasising about introducing this custom to the Old England XI as John questioned him. Flustered, Fred said, 'I'm sorry, John. I wasn't listening. I was reading a book someone very kindly sent me ...'

John cut him short with, 'Well, as everyone's hanging on my every word, I'll continue with the commentary.'

In fifteen summers we had only one serious disagreement. We were broadcasting a championship match from within the pavilion at Bradford. Just as we were about to go on air in the final session, we lost both cue programme and John's talkback link to our engineer, who was housed in a BBC van outside.

'Bill, will you go down and find out what's wrong, please?' asked John.

'But, John, if I stop scoring, we won't have any current bowling figures or batsmen's stats. I can't leave here.' I had put three days of concentration and effort into compiling my detailed scoresheets and was naturally reluctant to abandon them like an unfinished symphony.

John was most unhappy but luckily the cue returned in the nick of time and my scoresheets were duly completed. Afterwards we discussed the *impasse* over a glass. I apologised for not obeying his instruction and he apologised for putting me in such an invidious position. He knew that I regarded the scoresheets as an art form. We debated over several other glasses whether a perfect broadcast should take precedence over a perfect set of scoresheets. Next day neither of us could remember how that debate ended. It certainly did not affect our friendship.

It is impossible for me to think of the Derby ground without remembering John Arlott. John was revered at every ground, none more so than at Derby, where we operated from an Outside Broadcasts truck, which was parked beside the sightscreen across the racecourse from the grandstand. I was given the driving seat and the engineers provided a wooden lectern that fitted neatly over the steering wheel to house my scoresheets and other paraphernalia. We had a perfect view of the game, looking straight down the pitch and, as John was required to commentate, from the passenger seat, for three twenty-minute spells only each day, our box attracted visits from his many Derbyshire friends, most of them former players.

Our first visitor was always Eddie Gothard, then the club's treasurer.

Eddie was hospitality personified and he never greeted John without being in possession of wine and glasses. An amateur, he had skippered the county in 1947 and 1948 with great enthusiasm, once creating a sensation by slipping himself into the attack when Cliff Gladwin, Bill Copson, Dusty Rhodes and George Pope were resting, and taking a hat-trick against the eventual champions, Middlesex. The scalps of Alan Fairbairn, Bill Edrich and Walter Robins had brought his career tally of wickets to four.

No sooner had we finished our pre-lunch broadcast at the Derbyshire v. Hampshire match in 1968, than the chef, white-hatted and in full regalia, with John's wine, salad, Ryvita and glasses on a silver salver, marched solemnly out of the grandstand restaurant and around the boundary to our vehicle. 'Arlow' did full justice to this bounty before settling down to his customary nap, confident that I would wake him five minutes before we were scheduled to broadcast.

He had barely nodded off before the batsman moved away from his stumps and pointed at us. The umpire turned to see what was wrong and immediately waved and shouted in our direction. It was Cec Pepper, an Australian with a typically colourful vocabulary. 'Get those fucking lights off,' he boomed. I was totally bewildered. I had not switched any lights on, nor had my snoozing companion. 'The fucking fog light's on,' roared Pepper. As I started trying various switches, John woke up.

'What have you done now, Frindalius?' he asked blearily.

'I think I've put the fog lights on.'

'Oh, Christ!' he muttered and started turning on switches, too. Soon we were lit up like Blackpool Tower. Pepper was beside himself with fury and most of the players were writhing on the ground in hysterics. The crowd was laughing. None of our engineers knew where the fog-light switch was and the vehicle's driver was not due back for another two days.

Eventually, a spectator who had once driven a similar lorry when they had been used as field ambulances during the war, shouted up to my window, 'It's on the steering column.' I had knocked it with my knee without realising.

After a delay of four minutes, order was restored, play was restarted and John resumed his nap. I was so unnerved that I forgot to wake him until a few seconds before the studio came over to us. He asked me for the scoresheet and the score. Blinking his eyes into focus he began his commentary precisely on cue. Unfortunately, I was the only one who heard his first sentence. He had picked up his glass instead of the lip-mike.

Like Johnners, Arlow enjoyed a good *double entendre*. Throughout the first two post-war seasons, Billy Neale and Jack Crapp batted first and second wicket down for Gloucestershire. As they resumed their partnership after an interval, John couldn't resist informing his listeners that 'the Gloucestershire batsmen are taking the field. It's Neale and Crapp.'

It was never apparent to the public, both men were far too professional, but it was no secret to their friends and colleagues that John and Brian Johnston were not close. Brian admired John and would have been very happy to socialise with him, but their backgrounds and outlooks were very dissimilar. Luckily, I got on with both equally well. Including the county matches prior to Brian joining *TMS* from television in 1980, I enjoyed twenty-eight seasons working alongside him and many of those seasons had passed before John confessed to me that he resented Brian's adopting me as his stooge during the commentaries. It was not jealousy that inspired his resentment but the feeling that Brian was lowering the tone of the broadcasts. Brian's approach to commentary was totally different from John's. He did not have the latter's brilliant capacity to paint word pictures and relied on creating an atmosphere of bonhomie and making listeners feel that they were eavesdropping on the conversations of a friend. For my part, I unashamedly enjoyed being cast as Brian's straight man. As well as being great fun, it expanded my role in the *TMS* team and did my career no harm at all. The more that I was heard the better. My speaking engagements increased dramatically.

Brian used listeners' letters as a commentary tool, a ploy that Jonathan Agnew has subsequently employed to great effect. John Arlott rarely introduced any communications with the public into his commentaries. John would tease Brian on air by encouraging people 'to keep on writing to him because he loves it'.

John became increasingly irritated by Brian's obsession with cakes and his enticing listeners to part with an increasing variety of produce. One Saturday at Lord's there had been an almost non-stop delivery service of cakes and assorted comestibles. During a suitable break in the action below him, John gave a large sigh and, referring to Brian, said, 'He was a little upset on Friday because he didn't get anything, which means that a lot of you are actually eating your own food. This simply won't do. In case you have missed those three wickets that fell during the catalogue of groceries … And Mrs Matthews of Penge, I'm afraid he doesn't think much of your nut brittle. That's been left forlornly by his microphone. He's just gone off with a wheelbarrow full of produce to take home to his freezer so he can squirrel it through the winter. All I can say is that if you've got any old, musty, dirty bottles of red or white liquid, just stick a label on them and send them to Fred or me.'

Often it was hard to find the microphone or an empty space on the desk because of a vast array of cakes, toffees and other goodies. 'All we need now is a toothbrush,' snarled John. One arrived next day.

With one dramatic exception, John's few gifts from listeners took the form of poems, cricket photos and the occasional cricket book. At Headingley in the early seventies, he received a small jiffy bag from a suspiciously named 'J. Lord'. It definitely did not contain a bottle and it felt squelchy. Fearing it might be an explosive device, he handed it to a policeman who took it to the middle of the rugby field behind our box. In case of the presence of gelignite, the policeman avoided the opening flap and made a careful incision in the side of the bag. We stared from the safety of the top of the stand. There was no explosion, just relieved laughter as the copper held up a large bag of jelly babies.

Like Trevor Bailey, John was not overly fond of Australians. Unlike

Trevor, he did not like the country either. For one thing, it was far too hot. We shared a loathing for heat. Immediately upon entering any commentary box, both of us would set about opening all unsealed windows. I had done so in the overheated NATO offices at Fontainebleau and driven the Americans to distraction. Like a witch confronted by water, they appeared terrified of fresh air. John made just two trips to Oz. 'Thankfully, they were both return journeys,' he growled. The first was with Len Hutton's tour in 1954–55. They sailed from Tilbury on the SS *Orsova* early in September. By the time they reached Colombo some four weeks later, John had enthusiastically helped drink the ship dry. The remainder of the voyage was fairly dismal. Eventually, they disembarked at Fremantle and stood on the quay with their luggage, awaiting interrogation by the immigration officials. John seemed to have attracted a rather unsympathetic one. After a ten-minute grilling, the unsmiling official demanded, 'Tell me, Mr Arlott, do you have a criminal record?' 'Hell's teeth,' responded John. 'I didn't know it was still compulsory.'

He was whisked away to Perth by some local journalists, who had booked a table for lunch at the Hilton. A keen young wine waiter had been warned that their guest was an expert on wines and to search out his best stock. The waiter approached their table festooned in bottles and nervously assured them, 'G'day, gentlemen. I've searched out four of my best reds, and when you've finished them, I've got six more in the freezer.'

One reason for John's dislike of Australians stemmed from his feud with Alan McGilvray. A redhead with a fiery temper, no great sense of humour, a love of whisky and no great regard for Poms, Alan had greatly upset John early in their working relationship. Following immediately upon one of John's twenty-minute commentary stints, Alan had contradicted just about everything John had said. Arlott was incensed and demanded that never again would McGilvray follow him in the commentary roster, and he never did.

I had one spectacular row with Alan. It took place after play in a bar below the stands at the Sydney Cricket Ground in 1983. Alan was drinking with Keith Miller when I arrived and it was Keith who invited me to join them. The electronic scoreboard had been congratulating McGilvray on broadcasting his 200th Test match. I had mischievously checked this meticulously and could find only 194. I suspected that he had included the 1938 Ashes series, which he broadcast from a studio in Australia using cables from England. The subject cropped up and, for a start, I asked him if he counted the 1970–71 Melbourne Test that had been abandoned without a ball being bowled. Alan went berserk with rage. Having obviously touched a raw nerve, I decided it would be prudent to make my excuses and leave. I dreaded having to work with him on what proved to be his final visit to England but throughout that 1985 tour he could not have been friendlier, and for the first time he complimented my work on air. He even inscribed a generous message in a copy of his autobiography, *The Game is not the Same*. Many years later I often chatted to Keith Miller at Paul Getty's ground and he still remembered Alan's amazing tirade with great amusement.

After his escape to Alderney, John was reluctantly persuaded by the lure of vast royalties to write his autobiography, *Basingstoke Boy*. The task, which he began too late, weighed heavily upon him and, one memorable phase apart, he did not enjoy it. I rang him during that phase and my enquiry about the great work's progress, after two years' toil, produced an unexpectedly gleeful response. 'Exceedingly slowly, Frindalius. I've just reached puberty.' Pause, then that wicked chuckle. 'Christ, it's good!'

As a commentator, he eschewed the personal pronoun and loathed writing about himself. Throughout *Basingstoke Boy* he refers to himself in the third person. He was highly unusual in never introducing his personal life into his commentaries. The listener would have no idea who John had dined with the previous evening, what he had watched on television, what appalling traffic chaos he had encountered on his journey to the ground or what his dog had eaten for breakfast.

John began work on his autobiography while continuing to write articles for the *Guardian* and *Wisden Cricket Monthly*. Once Ian Botham began to bludgeon and blast the 1981 Australians, John bitterly regretted having retired at the end of the previous year. As the miraculous recovery began at Headingley, the television set was moved into his Long Room study so that he could watch the action unfold as he pounded his typewriter. By the time Bob Willis had routed the Aussies with his 8 for 43, John was physically exhausted by the tension and not a word had been typed. For the remainder of that extraordinary series, the television was moved into Pat's office next door. When a wicket fell, she used to call John in to watch the replays. 'Yes,' said John, 'and if it was one of England's, she used to knock first.'

Asked why he had chosen the remote Channel Island of Alderney, he would always reply, 'I wanted to join two thousand other drunks clinging to a rock.' In fact, he had fallen in love with it many years before and spent a number of holidays there. He soon became president of the island's cricket club and took a great interest in its matches. He even managed to persuade the *Guardian's* sports desk to include the occasional snippet of a match report. At this time I was responsible for the cricket section of the *Guinness Book of Records*. One Monday, John's report leapt off the page at me. 'Batting for Alderney against Pearl Assurance, David Whatmore scored 210 off only 61 balls.' This sensational innings had to qualify for inclusion if it were genuine and I phoned John at The Vines.

'Ah, I hoped you'd notice it, Frindalius,' greeted John.

'Did he really score 210, John?' I queried.

'Absolutely authentic. His wife was scoring.'

'Um,' I replied dubiously, 'and what about the 61 balls? Was she using the linear method?' I asked.

'No, nor the rhythm method, Bill, but I knew you would query it, so at the end of his innings I took two members of my committee down to the bottom of the cliff and we counted them.'

Needless to say, I added it to the *GBR's* cricket pages.

John's primary education, from 1920 until 1926, took place at Fairfields, the oldest school in Basingstoke, a large Victorian building that backed on to May's Bounty, Hampshire's most northerly county ground. John's first sight of cricket was through the railings then separating the school land from the cricket ground, which was the home of North Hants and Basingstoke Cricket Club. Confused by this title, John told me that for several years he enthusiastically supported Northants, believing that it was the Northamptonshire team who played the other side of his school fence. On 28 June 1994, some sixty-eight years after he had moved on to Queen Mary's, the local grammar school, I was privileged to be invited to attend the unveiling of a plaque on the wall of Fairfields facing May's Bounty to celebrate John's attendance.

It was typical that John should complete his final session of Test match commentary with the minimum of fuss. After giving the scores for England and the two current batsmen, he said simply, 'And after Trevor Bailey it will be Christopher Martin-Jenkins.'

At the end of the next over, prompted by a public address announcement from Alan Curtis, the entire attendance at Lord's, led by the players and umpires, rose and applauded our commentary eyrie atop the pavilion. Standing behind me, armed with an appropriate 'freshener', John tapped me on the shoulder and burred, 'Damned glad to see me go, aren't they.'

As an early member of the Lord's Taverners (No. 19), it was appropriate that John should make his very last cricket commentary at a Taverners match. Seizing the microphone immediately after celebrated cartoonist Bill Tidy had clean-bowled a well-sponsored batsman, John wheezed, 'The perfect cartoonist's dismissal. He drew him forward, crossed him off and rubbed him out.' Bill has decreed that those lines should appear as his epitaph.

John died at The Vines on Saturday, 14 December 1991 at the age of 77. I flew to Alderney, with Mike Brearley and Ian Botham as co-passengers in a tiny plane, for his funeral and attended his memorial service in Alresford. It was a most tremendous privilege to have known and worked with him. We shall never see his like again.

SEVEN

JOHNNERS

Brian Johnston swiftly transformed the *Test Match Special* box from a fairly dour and disciplined broadcasting studio into a haven of cakes and comedy when he joined us in 1970. Miraculously, he did this without missing a ball or interrupting the flow of play. When I first joined the team in 1966, I wasn't allowed to say a word and all communications had to be written on small cards. Brian's arrival changed all that. He had commentated for BBC Television since 1946 but his jovial style did not fit in with a new regime and he was banished after the 1969 season. This proved to be a giant blessing in disguise for him and for *TMS*. He had been installed as the BBC's first cricket correspondent in 1963, a role he relished until his enforced retirement from the BBC TV staff in 1972. Before joining us he had occasionally broadcast Test matches for radio.

At heart, Johnners was a frustrated music-hall comedian. After spending World War Two as a technical adjutant of a tank regiment, and winning the MC, he had escaped the family coffee business, been invited to join the BBC staff and made his name in a variety of radio roles ranging from *In Town Tonight*'s roving reporter to succeeding Franklin Englemann in *Down Your Way*. His happiest moments occurred when the former programme visited the Victoria Palace theatre and he was invited to take part in the Crazy Gang's show. He became a great friend of Bud Flanagan, Naughton and Gold, Nervo and Knox and

'Monsewer' Eddie Gray. Frequently, he was the willingly hapless victim of their sketches because he loved being on stage. Probably the highlight of his entire career was singing 'Underneath the Arches' with Bud Flanagan.

His immense love of cricket and incredible sense of fun ensured that he made no enemies and was welcomed wherever he went. He was a highly professional broadcaster whose unique skills were honed on interviewing unsuspecting citizens on those two classic radio programmes. He was genuinely interested in people of all walks of life, which is one reason why he inevitably got the best out of his subjects. His *A View from the Boundary* interviews with famous names devoted to cricket include many classics.

Brian's final guest in that *TMS* Saturday lunch-interval feature was Roy Hudd. Johnners was Roy's greatest admirer and would have loved to swap roles. They got on like a house on fire. When play resumed and CMJ was commentating, they sat behind us in the cramped old box at The Oval and Roy told a succession of jokes. Johnners was enthralled and during his next piece of commentary he told all eight tales. His skill in interweaving a description of the cricket with a well-honed music-hall routine was unrivalled. Paul Reiffel was bowling and CMJ happened to end one sentence and start the next with 'Reiffel'. Brian and Hudd immediately started singing the line from 'Strawberry Fair' – 'Reiffel, Reiffel, fol-di-diddle eyeful!'

Brian loved practical jokes and visiting overseas commentators were his favourite prey. During one commentary stint he persuaded Alan McGilvray, doyen of the Australian Broadcasting Commission, to tuck in to a large slice of cake before gleefully saying, 'I think that's a question for Alan to answer.' Sounds of choking were followed by a squall of crumbs and currants. Alan's successor, Neville Oliver, was tricked into reading a note announcing that the draw for the NatWest Trophy final would be made during the tea interval. When we all guffawed, Neville turned scarlet, screwed up the note and hurled it behind him.

Many times when we had handed over to the studio during rain breaks, Brian got the rest of us to pretend we were on air when a colleague returned unwittingly to the box. Tony Cozier was the most memorable victim of this favourite prank. As he came into the box I was showing Brian the up-to-date England averages for the series so far. 'Thank you, Bearders. Well, those are England's batting and bowling averages so far. Bill hasn't had time to work out the West Indies ones yet but Tony Cozier has just joined us and I know he has them at his fingertips.' Tony picked up the microphone and made some plaintive excuse. 'No, Tony. The listeners have been waiting for those figures. I'm sure you have them prepared.' Only after more desperate pleas did Johnners put down his mike and say, 'Well done, boys. Very good rehearsal.'

In stage parlance, Johnners was a great 'corpser' and his fits of the giggles, some lasting several minutes, caused several listeners to have road accidents or burn their ironing. His reaction to Aggers describing Botham's hit-wicket dismissal as failing to 'get his leg over' ended with him trying to finish reading the scorecard in a Michael Bentine falsetto.

I was responsible for another hiatus in commentary. It happened during a Lord's Test involving India. Don Mosey was commentating. I sat at his left side and summariser Trevor Bailey was on his right. To my left was the former Indian captain the Nawab of Pataudi, known to us as 'Tiger'. A steward brought in the day's post. Brian was sitting behind us reading his when I opened a packet containing the *Israeli Cricket Association's Book of Records*. A fast bowler with a long run was taking ages to bowl his over and I had time to flick through its pages. Unfortunately, when I came to the Partnership Records, I spotted that the one for the tenth wicket was 69 between Benny Wadwacker and Solly Katz. I showed this gem to Johnners who turned puce, started baying like a hyena and had to leave the box. Don Mosey, an inveterate giggler, had no idea what the joke was but began chortling as he commentated. Tiger asked to see the booklet, read the offending entry, stuffed a large handkerchief into his mouth and swiftly joined Johnners outside the box. That did for Don, who still had no idea what we were laughing about. Tears streamed down his face as he too left the sinking ship. Trevor and I continued with the commentary until Don had recovered.

Johnners revelled in spoonerisms, named after the splendid Reverend William Archibald Spooner (1844–1930) who memorably proposed a loyal toast to 'the Queer Old Dean'. Intriguingly, he was Dean and Warden of New College, Oxford, where Brian played cricket four days a week but still managed to fool the examiners. I suspect that he may have hissed a few mystery lectures. No one, probably not even their perpetrator, knows whether Brian's spoonerisms were accidental or rehearsed, but many have deservedly gained a place in cricket folklore. 'Henry Horton crouches low over his bat as he waits for the bowler. He looks like an old man shitting on a suiting stick,' is a favourite. One that was definitely accidental, because he always denied it, but which I remember vividly, involved Asif Masood, a young Pakistan fast bowler who toured England in 1974. 'And now we're ready for the first ball of England's innings,' Brian announced. 'Massive Arsood runs in from the Nursery End ...'

Johnners had an inexhaustible fund of stories and could recite Max Miller's complete act without a note. He loved to pose daft questions. 'Now, Bearders, you've studied the Good Book. Which two ice-cream sellers are mentioned in the Bible?' When I failed to guess them, his face would light up gleefully as he trumpeted, 'Lyons of Judea and Walls of Jericho!' He would then give his victim a second chance by asking, 'What high-jump record appears in the Bible?' No one has ever guessed 'and the Lord cleared the temple'.

One morning I entered the cramped dark old box at Headingley to find Johnners sat with his head in his hands.

'What's the matter, Brian?' I asked.

'Nothing, Bearders. I don't want to talk about it.' Increasingly worried and alarmed when he didn't sit up, I persisted.

'Anything I can do to help?'

'Oh, well, if you must know, it's the three Ms.'

'The three Ms?' I asked, totally mystified.

'Yes, Bearders, the three Ms. The missus, the maid and the mortgage – they're all overdue.'

Brian carried on working into his eighties to help fund the private education of his ever-increasing brood of grandchildren. On one occasion he showed me what turned out to be a perfectly genuine letter from the bursar of one grandson's school. A new typist must have been responsible because it read 'Dear Mr Johnston, we regret to inform you that your grandson's fees have been increased to £3500 per anum.'

'What do you think I should do, Bearders?' asked granddad. Before I could answer, Fred Trueman snatched it from me, read it and said, 'Johnners, if I were you I'd write back and tell them you'd sooner go on paying through the nose.'

News of the arrival of his first grandchild came soon after tea on the second day of the Sydney Test of January 1983 and a suitable bottle or two was broached in celebration. The notes column of my scoresheet records 'BJ heard his first grandson had been born an hour ago. Grandfather doing well.'

One of BJ's favourite tricks was to release the seat mechanism on his colleagues' chairs, a ruse usually carried out with impeccable timing as they were in mid prattle. I have a similar chair at home in my study. Occasionally the seat drops a foot and I still berate Johnners.

Talking of chairs, Brian holds one bizarre *TMS* record. He is the only member of the team to have wrecked two chairs in the same over. This drama occurred in our old box over the Ladies Stand at Old Trafford soon after lunch. Behind the commentary area there were three velvet covered chairs that must have been acquired from a theatre or cinema, the sort that you push down the seat to sit on. When Johnners came in and sat on the first there was a splendid Goon Show sound effect of rending material and collapsing chair. We all laughed and so did he. He removed the wreckage and sat in the next one – with exactly the same result. Rather than risk a hat-trick, he stood up until it was his turn to commentate.

He had a favourite cartoon that featured two dogs meeting:

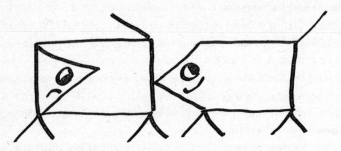

Rex Alston was the hapless victim of Brian's most famous prank. This happened in 1962 when Pakistan were playing the MCC at Lord's and the BBC broadcasting boxes were situated alongside the press box at the top of the Warner Stand. The Pakistanis had brought two Hussains on that tour, Mahmood Hussain and Afaq Hussain. It was the second one that aroused Brian's interest, especially when he saw how the BBC Pronunciation Unit had decreed his first name should be pronounced. Triumphantly, he entered the radio box brandishing a scorecard. 'Morning, Ballston,' he trumpeted. Rex had acquired that nickname after an unfortunate comment he made at a county match at Canterbury when he had reported that the players had taken tea early but that there was plenty of action because 'all over the lovely St Lawrence Ground small boys were playing with their balls.' Johnners pointed to Afaq Hussain's name on the scorecard.

'Look, old man, he's playing. We can say it on the air at last. You can't just call him Hussain because of the other one. I'm going to use both names and run them together quickly. Very risky just to call him by his first name. You'd better practice. Afaqhussain. Afaqhussain. Afaqhussain. Good luck, old man. I'm off to do telly!' Rex was speechless.

Pakistan fielded first, Ted Dexter scored a magnificent 79 and Afaq never even fielded the ball. Playing hours were 11.30 a.m. to 6.30 p.m. in those days. At 6.10 p.m. the announcer handed over to Rex just as acting captain Hanif Mohammed brought on a new bowler with Barry

Knight facing, 50 not out, at the Pavilion End. Rex peered through his glasses and his worst fears were confirmed by Brian, who, having finished his TV duties, was prodding at Hussain's name on the score-card. Rex took a deep breadth and announced, 'Well, Hanif's made a bowling change and it's a fuck tonight at the Nursery End.' Scorer Michael Fordham nearly fell off his chair and Johnners chortled as he corrected Rex in a loud stage whisper.

'Sorry, old man, I got mixed up. That's not him. That's Mahmood Hussain. Afaq's twelfth man.'

The leg-pulling reached a crescendo in 1993, Brian's final season, with Aggers and Neville Oliver teaming up with spoof letters from Ivor Biggun and Mrs Tess Tickle. Unlike some of his victims, Brian never minded being the subject of a merry prank. When Cornhill introduced prize-giving ceremonies at the end of Test matches, BJ would usually be brought to the microphone and given a sponsor's handout listing the platform party. On one occasion this had been doctored so that Brian's opening sentence was, 'And heading the platform party is the Chairman of Cornhill, Mr Hugh Jarce. Next to him ...' Amazingly, Johnners had not realised what he had said. In fact, he had read out the rest of the list before he reacted to the uncontrolled merriment behind him.

At Headingley that summer, Peter Baxter and Jon Agnew combined to trick Brian into recording a twenty-second trail to the day's play for Radio Five Live. Aggers normally did this but pretended that he had a domestic crisis and couldn't get to the ground in time. I wasn't in on the jape and helped Brian draft the text and time it. Being a consummate professional, he didn't really need a stopwatch to do twenty seconds on the dot and achieved the task first time. 'Sorry, Brian,' came Peter's voice over headphones, 'two seconds too long.' Johnners looked puzzled, deleted a couple of words and tried again. 'Sorry, Brian, that's two seconds too short.' Back went the deleted words. Take three. 'That's fine, Brian. Well done!' announced Peter – followed by roars of laughter and a dramatic entrance by the missing Agnew.

Johnners was soon plotting a fiendish payback. With the aid of

Steve Pearson, television's master floor manager, the stage was set for Aggers to do a television interview during a lunch break in the next Test at Edgbaston. The interview platform was on the flat roof above our main radio box and several of us climbed up the ladder with our heads just poking over the edge of the roof to watch the fun. Jon had to ask Fred Trueman and Jack Bannister about the dearth of fast bowlers in England.

'Well, Jonathan, I don't know about that. What worries me is the rising damp in my kitchen. Just can't get rid of it.' Fred kept his vast meerschaum pipe in place as he spoke and blew clouds of acrid smoke into Jon's face. Aggers coughed and turned hopefully to Jack.

'I agree with Fred,' came the broad Brummie accent. The producer yelled into Jon's earpiece 'Get them to answer the question!' Poor Aggers soldiered on as Fred and Jack stonewalled with silences and unrelated waffle. Finally, the unmistakable voice of Johnners burst into Jon's earpiece. 'Has the long-nosed commentator exacted his revenge?' The tape is now a collector's item.

BJ was commentating at The Oval when we heard a loud rasping noise behind us. It was coming from Fred. Continuing to describe the action, Johnners asked, 'What are you doing, Fred?'

'Er, er, I'm filing my nails, Brian,' Fred replied, somewhat baffled to be asked.

'That's an odd thing to do, Fred. I always throw mine away.'

Like Raleigh flooding Britain with tobacco, Brian Johnston was solely responsible for inundating our pokey little commentary boxes with an avalanche of cake. His plaintive SOS for fodder when, in 1970, Nancy forgot to send up tea to our Lord's eyrie, was heard by alert cooks throughout the realm. The first offering was brought in by a lady resident of St John's Wood, one Aileen Cohen, the very next day. She arrived at the Grace Gates and told the steward, 'I've got a cake for Brian Johnston.' He welcomed her warmly. 'Seems a fair swap, missus! Come in.' The cake worked as a password and she was allowed through all the checkpoints and into our box, then sited in the Warner Stand. Once she had been warmly thanked by Johnners, the floodgates were opened to any listener craving a mention on *Test Match Special*. Soon anyone bearing a cake for BJ was granted free entry not only to our box but also to the ground. Rarely have I arrived at the Lord's pavilion during a Test match without a steward thrusting a cake into my already laden arms. Brian always insisted that the produce was equally distributed among broadcasters, engineers and guests.

Cakes have come in all shapes, sizes and substances. We let Mushtaq Mohammed devour the carrot cake that smelt of wacky backy. Few of us dared take too much of the large tray of crumbs floating on rum donated by a Barbados hotel. Peter Baxter often delivers any unconsumed offerings to a local children's hospital. The inmates should have slept well after being let loose on that one. Then there was the cake bearing two enormous and very lifelike female breasts that Fred threatened to take a large bite out of until someone produced a camera. Amazingly, Johnners managed to describe the cake without resorting to the obvious. On one of his birthdays an ace cake-maker presented him with a pair of his trademark co-respondent's white and tan shoes made out of cake and icing. They would be displayed at his famous garden parties on the Friday evenings of Lord's Tests. Pauline, his widow, still has them in the freezer.

A chocolate-covered cake in the shape of a cricket bat arrived at Lord's one hot Saturday. It had been placed in direct sunlight on top of a heated television monitor in front of Fred. A message was inscribed in white icing across the front of its blade. Johnners began the commentary that session.

'Well, the players are just taking the field after tea. We've been sent a wonderful chocolate cake in the shape of a cricket bat. Something's printed in white icing on the front. What's it say, Fred?'

'Don't know, Johnners — I can't find my reading glasses.'

'Well pass it over here then.'

Fred lifted it off the monitor and the message vanished as melted chocolate cascaded over the sleeve of Fred's smart tan jacket. Brian ignored his victim's protests. 'Oh, Fred! Now we'll never know who sent it.'

One morning the door of our box at The Oval opened to reveal someone dressed as a chicken and carrying an enormous tray about five inches deep. She (I assume it was a female because of the thin legs encased in wrinkled yellow Nora Batty stockings) clucked through her chicken's head and placed the tray near Trevor Bailey. Trevor was a champion cake consumer, definitely in the gannet class. He left his seat and examined the label. 'It's from the Egg Marketing Board,' he announced. Henry Blofeld duly thanked the Milk Marketing Board. As Trevor leant over to get a closer look at the 'cake', his spectacles fell off. To his horror, the cake consumed them like quicksand. Only the earpieces remained visible, sticking above the surface like periscopes. Trevor regarded them with horror, paused and then, like Basil Fawlty searching for the missing roast duck, scooped them out of the goo. He quickly cleaned the lenses with his fingers and put them on with lemon goo still clinging to the frames. For the remainder of his stint he looked remarkably like Biggles wearing goggles.

When Brian attended my wedding to Debbie in 1992, we had to cut two cakes – the official one and one presented to Brian from a fellow guest who heard he was going to be there.

We all live in fear of some lunatic cricket-loathing chemist sending a cake with special ingredients designed to remove *TMS* from the airwaves. Whenever Rory Bremner, a superb impressionist and very handy cricketer, impersonates Brian, he has him asking, 'If there's a cake on the ground, will it please report to the commentary box.'

Johnners also flooded the box with nicknames that were to echo around the world's airwaves, probably because he couldn't remember our real ones. He was solely responsible for my being dubbed the Bearded Wonder and it was Brian who then reduced that epithet to Bearders. It led to Debbie being called Mrs Bearders, something she has never enjoyed. Don Mosey used to call her the Hand Maiden because she used to bring in my lunch, with wine, and phone my copy through to various publications. Brian soon reduced this to Handers. His nickname for Don was probably his most curious concoction – the

Alderman. Brian said it was because Don reminded him of a very pompous Yorkshire alderman whose company he had once had to endure at a function.

The others were either derived from surnames, such as Blowers (Blofeld), Backers (Baxter), Cozers (Cozier) and Jenkers (Martin-Jenkins), or had been established before their arrival in the *TMS* box. Tony Lewis was known as ARL from his initials. Trevor Bailey had been named the Boil by Doug Insole after a Swiss PA announcer had pronounced the name 'Boiley' when listing the players at a European soccer match.

Neville Oliver, Alan McGilvray's successor as the visiting ABC commentator, was energetic, flame-haired and ruddy complexioned. He was very entertaining with his lively vocabulary and eye for the absurd and unusual. Possibly because his main sport was rowing, he viewed and described cricket without inhibitions. I first heard him when the Adelaide Test of Mike Gatting's 1986–87 Ashes tour was doomed to a dead draw. Neville enlivened an especially dull phase by describing a female television technician ironing various interesting personal garments beside a TV van. As he appeared as 'NO' on Peter Baxter's commentators' duty schedule, Neville was inevitably christened the Doctor by Johnners. At the end of his third, and final, tour of the UK, Neville received a letter from a GP in Scotland inviting him to be his locum while he took a fortnight's holiday. Soon after we began referring to him as the Doctor, we had an interesting call from one of his colleagues in Hobart. His buddy revealed that they called him Bubbles. Apparently, the Hobart boss had bestowed this name at his job interview. 'Neville Oliver! Neville Oliver! Sounds like a fart in a bath. I'm going to call you Bubbles.'

Brian delighted in trying to catch me out by asking near impossible questions and setting a challenge that he knew needed a massive amount of research. He could then prolong the by-play by describing my progress. 'The Bearded Wonder's on his third volume of scores now and has got as far as 1928,' he would comment gleefully. He often pretended that he had calculated the answers himself by sneaking a look at my scoresheet and saying, 'I'll take a guess. I think Gooch has hit thirteen fours.'

'Yes, you read the sheet correctly, Brian,' was as close as I could get to a payback. His questions about the number of boundaries conceded by various bowlers made me redesign the cumulative bowling sheet to add two extra columns for each bowler. There were very few chances for me to exact my revenge. Occasionally, I would take advantage of his colour blindness when he asked me what colour Bishan Bedi's patka was and tell him blue when it was green.

He enjoyed umpiring but he twice stuffed me in that role. Once, when I was walking back to the end of my twenty-yard run and he was at square-leg, he quietly convinced a fielder placed just in front of square that I wanted him to move just backward. As soon as I delivered the ball, he yelled, 'No-ball. Too many legside fielders behind square.'

At 3.58 p.m. during a charity match at Fenner's, I had scored 49 when he called tea.

'But there's still two minutes to go,' I protested, knowing that I had to declare at the interval.

'I'm not having you boasting you scored a fifty at Fenner's. That's tea!' And off I had to trudge.

Johnners had never been to India. During his time as the BBC's cricket correspondent it was impossible to broadcast commentary from India. Since it was a country he had always wanted to visit, he decided to join *The Cricketer* tour in time for England's second and third Tests in February 1993. The tour leader was Trevor Bailey so the social element was in excellent and very experienced hands. Brian had no interest in foreign food and seldom ventured beyond basic home fare. His GP had advised him to keep clear of local water and anything, such as salad, that had been washed in it. He was also advised to have a glass of whisky as a nightcap. Like me, Johnners detested whisky, and for a similar reason – it was the first alcohol that had caused both of us to keel over – but he obeyed instructions and took the prescribed medicine.

The second Test was played in Madras, a sweltering, humid city.

Our walk from the coach took us across a small bridge over an extremely unpleasant brown stream. 'Oh, Bearders! How wise to double a river with a sewer!' was his most memorable comment of the tour. Thankfully, he survived the dangers of the M.A. Chidambaram Stadium and we enjoyed a few very pleasant days at Fisherman's Cove, an hour's drive south. In Bombay we stayed at the famous Taj Mahal Hotel overlooking the Gateway of India. This is the cleanest and most westernised of Indian hotels and the Johnstons were staying in the modern wing. On the third day Brian came into the commentary box looking distinctly green and unhappy.

'Are you OK?' I asked.

'No, Bearders. The medicine didn't work. There were a few very loose deliveries this morning!'

When John Arlott decided to retire, he announced it at the start of the summer and was feted wherever he worked throughout that 1980 season. Brian decided then that he would not announce his retirement in advance but he confided in me that he wanted to finish after an Ashes summer and preferably when we had won. The Great Scorer must have been listening because his final Test match was against Australia at The Oval in 1993 and, although Australia had won four and drawn one of the rubber's previous five games, England won this encounter by 161 runs to end an unprecedented run of eighteen matches since their last victory against the old enemy. It also marked the end of forty-eight summers of humour and fun from Johnners.

At tea I had packed up most of my books and Debbie had loaded most of my gear into the car parked in the playground of Archbishop Tenison's School across the Harleyford Road. I had already photocopied the summary sheets of the first three innings and as soon as the game ended I used the fax machine to copy the Australian second innings. Johnners was in full spate as I put the copy in front of him, bade a quick farewell and left. I was driving along the Embankment listening to the summaries when Johnners asked for that final scoresheet. 'It's in front of you,' I yelled at the car radio. 'Oh, this really is too bad of him,' said Brian. 'The Bearded Wonder's bolted.'

Soon after that season, Debbie and I visited Johnners and Pauline at their holiday home in Swanage. We had a drink at his local golf club, Pauline cooked an excellent lunch and then we walked along the front and enjoyed an ice cream. 'Three things happen when you reach my age, Bearders. The first thing is you lose your memory.' Pause for effect. 'Can't remember what the other two are!'

Johnners was so exuberant and zestful to the end that we all overlooked his age. Physically, he looked in his early sixties, mentally he had never left his teens. The only reason that he had a twenty-minute break in the middle of his two-hour one-man show was so that the audience could have a rest.

We shook hands and he waved from the gate as we drove off. A few weeks later he collapsed in a taxi taking him to catch a train to speak at a lunch in the West Country. He died on 5 January 1994. Now that he has gone, I know exactly how Ernie Wise must have felt when he lost the great Eric Morecambe. Johnners was 81 years young and very, very special.

EIGHT

MORE COMMENTATORS

I HAVE BEEN privileged to work alongside many outstanding commentators and expert summarisers. While John Arlott and Brian Johnston were the pioneers of post-war cricket broadcasting, and two of its greatest exponents, other notable contributors were also key players in the *TMS* commentary box.

Over four decades, the host of talented visitors from overseas include Tony Cozier. He first appeared at Headingley in 1966 when Roy Lawrence returned to Jamaica to cover the Commonwealth Games. Tony is a vastly experienced broadcaster and writer. For more than two decades he edited the *West Indies Cricket Annual*. A great party animal with enormous zest for life, he has accepted the considerable highs and current lows of Caribbean cricket with great equanimity. Tim Lane, Australia's multisports commentator, liked to spice his commentaries with some colour. His best effort involved 'a lady whose bikini top has a red cross on each ... section!' India's ebullient wicket-keeper-batsman Farokh Engineer made one of the most memorable comments, sadly off air. Looking out of the rear window of our box at Edgbaston, he spotted a crowd of art students. One of the girls was extremely well endowed and Rookie's eyes nearly left their sockets. 'My God!' he exclaimed. 'All that body on one woman!'

JONATHAN AGNEW

Aggers joined *TMS* after being appointed BBC cricket correspondent in 1991, initially in the role of summariser for the five-Test series against West Indies. He was already an experienced broadcaster, having worked at Radio Leicester since 1987 and become their sports producer two years later. Articulate and humorous, he immediately absorbed the informal atmosphere created by Brian Johnston. Like Johnners, Jon is a compulsive giggler and it took him barely five Test matches before he contributed a major part to one of the most hilarious episodes in broadcasting history. The close of play summaries by Jim Swanton and, more recently, Don Mosey had been replaced with a discussion of the day's events by a commentator and a summariser. The combination of Johnners and Aggers after the second day of The Oval Test on Friday, 9 August 1991 proved lethal and was never to be repeated. England had taken their overnight total of 231 for 4 to 419 all out, with Robin Smith contributing 109. West Indies were 90 for 1 at stumps. Seated in the front of our cramped box on the pavilion roof were Tony Cozier, who was composing his report for a Caribbean paper, Jon, Brian and me. All went well until Brian tried to describe Ian Botham's bizarre dismissal. Recalled for his 98th Test after a two-year absence, he had withstood the missiles of a four-strong pace battery comprising Ambrose, Patterson, Walsh and Marshall for 131 minutes. At 2.32 p.m., with his score 31, he faced his 82nd ball. It was a searing bouncer. He attempted to hook it on to the Harleyford Road, missed, was struck on the helmet, staggered back, realised one leg was about to demolish his stumps, lifted it as he spun round but just dislodged a bail. For the only time in 161 Test innings, Botham was out hit wicket.

It was later, when Brian and Jon attempted to analyse the dismissal, that the broadcast disintegrated. At the back of Jon's mind was a conversation he had had in the press box with John Etheridge, cricket correspondent of the *Sun*. Etheridge had told Aggers that he reckoned his paper's headline the following day would be 'Botham cocks it up by not getting his leg over'. Totally unaware of Jon's desperate battle to ignore this tantalising morsel that was threatening to become a sound bite, Brian waffled a little before probing for a more graphic description of the Botham demise. 'His inside thigh must have just removed a bail,' Brian suggested with a mischievous twinkle. It was a great mistake. Compelled to go one better, Aggers released the Etheridge demon – 'Yes, he didn't quite get his leg over.'

I was quietly packing up my scoring paraphernalia and dropped a stopwatch. Fearing that I would snort or burst into laughter, I froze with my back turned. Brian soldiered on bravely, desperately trying not to giggle. 'He did very well indeed,' he managed. Then he saw Aggers, hands over face, trying to suppress tears of laughter. 'Do stop it, Aggers!' Johnners struggled on, describing a stand of 35 between Chris Lewis and Phil DeFreitas. He had just begun to mention David Lawrence's contribution when I failed to control a fairly vicious snort. It was the coup de grace. Johnners collapsed, reddened and could only offer some odd squeaks of suppressed hysterics. Aggers pulled himself together, mumbled 'Lawrence …' and collapsed again. There was a long silence. Peter Baxter suggested that someone said something. We looked at Tony Cozier. He smiled, winked and continued with his typing. Johnners eventually recovered, said 'I'm all right now,' completed the day's scorecard and handed back. He was obviously very angry with himself for being so unprofessional and I cannot recall a more miserable end to a day's broadcasting.

Next morning one of the engineers told us to put our headphones on and played us a recording of what is now universally known as 'The Leg Over'. I must have heard it fifty times and it still has me crying with laughter. Johnners immediately realised its value and, for the remaining two years of his public life, always had a cassette recording of it in his pocket to play at functions he attended.

West Indies collapsed that day, losing their last seven wickets for 18 runs as Phil Tufnell took 6 for 4 in 33 balls. They followed on against England for the first time since 1969 and lost by five wickets. Fittingly, it was Ian Botham who struck the boundary that gave the hosts their first drawn series against West Indies since 1973–74.

The previous summer had been the last of Jon's thirteen seasons as a professional fast bowler with Leicestershire. Lack of financial security and the responsibility of a young family had been major factors in his decision to retire from playing at the age of 30, but his success as both a local radio broadcaster and writer had prepared him for his next career. Two years earlier, *8 days a Week*, his playing journal of a season, had been highly praised and he had become a regular contributor to the *Today* newspaper. One early season phone call to *Today*'s sports editor proved to be as spectacular a key moment for him as my letter to the BBC in 1965 was for me. Aggers was offered the post of cricket correspondent and a few weeks after bowling his final ball in first-class cricket, he flew to Australia to cover Graham Gooch's ill-fated tour. Although he achieved a number of memorable scoops, he didn't enjoy being a 'Beastie' on a tabloid paper. Christopher Martin-Jenkins had just relinquished his role as BBC cricket correspondent to take up a similar post with the *Daily Telegraph* and Aggers enquired about the vacancy. Apparently, David Gower, still smarting from the 'Tiger Moth Incident' and a major falling-out with Graham Gooch, had also shown an interest. Aggers was offered the job and he has carried it out supremely well.

Besides being extremely hard working and conscientious, he has the same infectious schoolboy humour as Johnners and has continued to enliven the *TMS* box since the great man departed. Perhaps he grumbles a great deal more than Brian did, but possibly he has a great deal more to grumble about. While respecting the traditions of the programme, he has been determined to shape it in his own image. He rarely, if ever, observes the ritual of wearing the Test Match Broadcasters' Club tie, now known as the *TMS* tie and awarded to newcomers on their first day with the programme. Until the last decade, we all wore the tie on the first day of a Test match and anyone who didn't could be compelled to buy a drink for all his colleagues. Now only the old brigade of Peter Baxter, CMJ and myself uphold that tradition, which is sad.

I have managed to make Aggers corpse on air a few times, most notably when I passed him a totally genuine *Guardian* article on paedophiles written by Roger Boyes.

Jon was not given the warmest of welcomes by Fred Trueman, who had obviously prepared his greeting. 'Hello, Jonathan. Good to see you, son. Nice to have another fast bowler in here. I think between us we took 311 Test wickets!' It would be surprising if Aggers relished being reminded that his three Test matches produced a grand haul of four wickets costing 93 runs apiece. To balance the statistical scales, it should be recorded that in 1987 he achieved an extremely rare feat in modern times by taking 101 first-class wickets in a season. He was one of *Wisden*'s five cricketers of that year. His first-class career bests were equally impressive – 90 and 9 for 70.

Like Johnners, Aggers relishes props such as listeners' letters, emails and faxes. He is the first to welcome a cake. His advertising is more discreet than that of Blowers (not difficult) but he has formed a splendid alliance with a pork-pie manufacturer in Melton Mowbray. One mention of the company secures a hamper of pies for each Test. He is also one of the untidiest members of the team, leaving piles of paper and post to be tidied away.

He will not thank me for destroying one myth. The Agnew family are not denizens of his much-vaunted Vale of Belvoir, which he correctly, but with a gleam in his eye, pronounces Beaver. 'It was a bit moist in the Beaver this morning,' he will announce with a wicked grin, hoping to corpse all those within earshot. I have stayed at a B&B farm in the Vale and its owners, plus those in many hostelries in the region, which I felt compelled to visit in the interests of research, have assured me that the hamlet in which Aggers resides is some distance beyond its limits.

HENRY BLOFELD

I was the scorer when Henry did his first cricket commentary for the BBC at a county championship match between Essex and Warwickshire at Chelmsford in 1972, two years prior to making his

TMS debut. We were precariously perched in a tiny hut on the roof of an ancient BBC Outside Broadcasts van. I liked his refreshingly different style of commentary and we enjoyed each other's company. His rich plummy tones may have set a few listeners' nerves on end over the intervening years but I find them a bonus. If you are listening to three or four commentators over a period of six or seven hours, a contrast in accents and style is essential. Henry Calthorpe Blofeld has become an engaging eccentric, famous for his bow ties, love of wine, fondness for P.G. Wodehouse and his catchphrase 'My dear old thing!' Like John Arlott, Henry is a hard-working *bon viveur*. The most colourful character in the current *Test Match Special* team, he is also one of the most energetic, his entire working day divided between the microphone, his laptop or, more than likely, the only outside telephone line in the commentary box.

When Blowers began his *TMS* career, he played it with a very straight bat, sticking to the action and paying little attention to extraneous details. Peter Baxter, to his subsequent deepest remorse, encouraged him to add a touch of colour to the picture by introducing passing traffic and unusual spectators. Henry has never been one to do things by halves and there have been many times when the buses, helicopters, pigeons and wandering or wayward spectators have demoted the cricketers to minor roles in a rich but often confused tapestry. It has all added to the fun as far as I am concerned. Our old commentary position at The Oval provided him with the biggest range of material. Overlooking the busy Harleyford Road towards Vauxhall on our left, it was often on the flight path to Heathrow and offered an unparalled skyline of historic buildings. Once I kept a separate score of the interlopers he described and a formidable list it was. Henry was very proud of it and during his next period of commentary he read it out. He kept my list and it may have featured in one of his several extremely successful volumes of autobiography.

Like John Arlott, Henry has been able to offer descriptions that stick in the memory, whether one wants them to or not. 'I can see a lady with the most enormous pair of binoculars!' is my favourite.

There have been good-looking dustbins in MCC colours, butterflies with a limp and a vast array of birds and insects, not all of them confirmed sightings. In Pakistan he had a bizarre altercation with Don Mosey about the identification of a building that Blowers insisted was a toothpaste factory.

His obsession with buses was unfortunate because he almost died as a result of an accident featuring one when he cycled under it during his days at Eton. He was an exceptionally promising right-handed opening batsman and wicket-keeper whom many contemporaries expected to play for England. Unconscious for more than three weeks, he did well subsequently to represent Cambridge University, where he gained a blue in 1959, MCC, Norfolk (1956–65, making his debut when 16) and the Free Foresters. He scored two hundreds at Lord's. The first was a remarkable innings for the Public Schools against the Combined Services in 1956. Following a batsman with the unfortunate name of Duck, he took the score from 71 for 6 to 214 all out, finishing with an undefeated 104. *Wisden* records: 'Among several splendid batting displays the century on the first day of Blofeld, the 16-year-old wicket-keeper, was notable. For one so young, he showed remarkable confidence against experienced bowlers, and employed a wide range of strokes which brought him thirteen fours and one five, all run, in his not-out 104 made in two and a quarter hours. Blofeld's aggregate for three innings in Schools' matches at Lord's during the week was 179 for once out.' His other Lord's hundred was in a first-class match for Cambridge University against the MCC in 1959. Opening the second innings he scored 138 against an attack that included the spin of Gamini Goonesena and Denis Compton. His attacking innings enabled Cambridge to declare and win the match.

Since Brian Johnston's death, Henry has adopted me as his stooge and we have enjoyed a double act where I am able to delight in pointing out any errors involving the score or identification of players. There have been one or two. Ours has probably developed into a love-hate relationship but it appears to have added a bit of spice to the commentaries and we both enjoy it. We are now comfortably the oldest members of the *TMS* team, Henry being about six months younger than I am. He has become an accomplished journalist and the author of several books, most notably *The Packer Affair*, which is the definitive account of that sensational episode of cricket history. During seven weeks early in 1978 he watched Test matches involving all six current Test-playing countries. In the late seventies and early eighties he gained icon status in Australia when a floodlighting pylon on the famous 'Hill' at Sydney Cricket Ground was proclaimed the Henry Blofly Stand.

For several seasons Blowers relied on me to scrutinise any notes or emails that were passed to him. In effect I became his censor. Brian Johnston, David Lloyd, Jon Agnew and even our producer have competed in a prolonged campaign to get him to read out the most blatant *double entendres*. Frequently they have succeeded in bypassing me by slipping them under his pile of post from the far side hidden under *bona fide* notes instructing him to hand over for the shipping forecast. One slipped through the net just before lunch on a Saturday at Edgbaston and involved Evesham Cricket Club. The club needed to pass an urgent message to its scorer, who was sitting in the Eric Hollies stand. Apparently, his deputy had been taken ill and they needed him back. The note advised that the scorer, Richard Head, would be listening to *TMS*. 'Dick's a shy man,' the note continued, 'and he wouldn't want to hear his name read out over the ground's public address system. Please help us get him back for our afternoon match.' Blowers dutifully read out the note and added, 'So, if you are listening Dick Head, please hurry back to Evesham.' Collapse of *TMS* team.

At the start of the Lord's Test against Bangladesh in 2005, Javed Omar, their opening batsman, having played international cricket for ten years, decided he wanted to be known as Javed Belim. It gave Aggers a cunning idea. I provided him with the Bangladesh official letter heading and he printed a bogus letter from the team manager advising us that their wicket-keeper, Khaled Masud, wanted to be known as Khaled Bernard. He was going to use 'Cyril' but I thought that even Henry might spot that. The letter was printed, a signature forged and Peter Baxter inserted it among some emails for Blowers to answer on air. He came to it and duly announced the name change. I expressed extreme surprise and annoyance. We were occasionally using the Bangladesh coach, Dav Whatmore, for comments. He gave these from outside the pavilion with Shilpa Patel, the BBC's cricket organiser, holding his mike and cueing him in. Chance had it that he came on air soon after Henry had revealed the latest name change.

'What do think of Khaled Masud changing his name to Bernard, Dav?' asked Blowers.

There was a dramatic pause, Dav having been in on the jape. 'I think you've been had, Henry,' came the broad Aussie accent.

Then there was the spoof fax concocted by my wife, Debbie. She is a teacher and never short of conversation. I have never been forgiven for once confusing her flow of chat with a car radio broadcast and trying to turn down the volume. During breakfast at Langar Hall, where we all stay for Trent Bridge Tests, Henry became increasingly irritated by Debbie's incessant chanter. Eventually, he lost patience and asked her to pipe down in fairly brusque terms. Debbie is the elder sister of Ian Brown, a very successful television comedy writer whose shows have included *Drop the Dead Donkey* and *My Family*, and she shares some of his skills. By way of revenge, she fabricated the following fax, which Henry dutifully read out in full:

Fax to

Mr. Henry Blofeld,
c/o BBC Commentary Box,
Surrey CCC,
The Oval,
Kennington,
London

From: Dorothy Manners,
Honey Cottage,
Towcester,
Northants.

Dear Mr Blofeld,

I hope you will forgive me for writing to you at your place of work, but I do not have any other way of making contact with you.

I am sure you receive many requests for your services which are consigned to the wastepaper bin, but I would be grateful if you could give this one consideration.

I am the Secretary of a newly-formed association, The Radio and Television Commentators Appreciation Society (RATCAPS) and my committee has asked me to approach you with a view to becoming our President.

This is merely a titular position, requiring no effort on your part, except the occasional personal appearance.

We have decided to hold some informal get-togethers at various times throughout the year and would be very grateful if you would be able to attend one of them. We have discussed the arrangements for the meetings and have come to the conclusion that, since many of our members are rather elderly and cannot cope with late nights, we should hold them at a more suitable time of day i.e. at breakfast. We understand that this will be a departure from the norm, but we know that you are the most adaptable of Commentators and will readily rise to the occasion with your notable wit and good-humoured banter, especially early in the day.

I await your decision with interest, and have enclosed my address but would appreciate an early response (perhaps over the air on Test Match Special!), however if you answer thus, please would you speak up because many of our members are somewhat hard of hearing.

Yours in anticipation,

Dorothy Manners (Colonel)

'Ah! Wonderful. You're a colonel, Mrs Manners,' cooed Blowers having missed all the breakfast hints. Fearing that the entire point of this exercise would be lost, I had to intervene.

'Henry,' I interrupted. Blowers dreads these interventions because he knows I am about to deliver a killer punch.

'Yes, Bill?' he replied with just a hint of irritation.

'Did you say that fax came from Towcester?' I asked, innocently.

'That's what it says,' responded Henry, looking increasingly apprehensive.

'That's odd,' I said, 'the phone prefix is the same for Devizes.'

'Oh! Did you send this, Bill?'

'No, but I'm married to the lady who did and you were rude to her at breakfast.'

On a hot afternoon when we were in our old box in a pavilion turret at Lord's, Henry spotted yet another butterfly passing our window. 'Oh, look! There's a cabbage white!' A few moments later, he saw another one. 'Look, Bill. There's another cabbage white!'

Bored with his butterflies, I decided that it was time for the stooge to move in.

'It's the same one, Henry. One of its wings has a dirty mark on it.' Henry grunted and was about to continue with the cricket when I added, 'Isn't it odd that we've only seen cabbage whites today, no exciting coloured one like Painted Ladies and Red Admirals …'

'Thank you, Bill,' interrupted Henry, perhaps not feigning his irritation.

Later in the afternoon an email arrived from a lady who was listening to us beside a buddleia bush in her garden. 'I've got a lot of colourful butterflies in my garden,' she wrote and listed them. Jon Agnew was on email watch and saw his chance. He quickly copied her message, adding a few exotic butterfly breeds to her list, before passing it to Henry.

'Ah, Bill, look at this. One of our listeners has a garden full of colourful butterflies. She can see a Green Hairstreak, a Yellow Brimstone, a Norwegian Blue, a Painted Lady and a Three-winged Green.'

'A Three-winged Green?' I asked in mock innocence, having been privy to the Agnew additions. 'Wouldn't that fly round in ever-decreasing circles …?'

'Yes, and disappear up its own … Aaagh!' cried Henry, realising too late where he had been led.

Henry is a master at semi-disguised advertising. The BBC is understandably strict about advertising on the air. Many years ago a commentator, bereft of material during a stoppage of play, read out all the advertising banners he could see. It proved to be his final broadcast. Henry is only a tad more subtle. 'Thank you Lay and Wheeler for that excellent case of wine you sent me. Quite magnificent! Is that a British Airways plane, Bill? Could you look through your binoculars? It looks like one from the tail markings. Have you seen my phone anywhere – it's a Vodafone …' and so on. Hotels, restaurants, purveyors of fine wines and delicacies and airlines have all featured. Amazingly, producer Peter Baxter has retained a robust head of hair although it has turned prematurely white.

Henry's most dramatic *faux pas* occurred at Headingley when he referred to the balcony of a house overlooking the Kirkstall Lane, from which a score of spectators had a free view of the action, as the Jewish Stand. He meant to call it the Scottish Stand after a similar property in Auckland overlooking the Eden Park Stadium. Unfortunately, his remark was heard by members of the local Jewish community, whose synagogue was sited nearby. He spent an uncomfortable afternoon apologising both in writing and on air. His mood was not best helped by a spectator who presented him with a litre bottle of kosher Coca-Cola.

Sometimes Blowers gets carried away and overruns his twenty-minute slot. At Bulawayo in December 1996, when England, chasing a target of 205, fell a run short thus producing the first drawn Test with the scores level, Henry was off his long run and in terrific form. He remained at the microphone in full flow for more than thirty minutes. No one wanted to follow that performance so he was encouraged to go on until the finish. Once, at Lord's, he overran by ten minutes after tea when Brian Johnston, who should have taken over, passed him a note saying 'PLEASE KEEP GOING UNTIL SIX O'CLOCK.'

Henry usually hits top gear when the action peaks. He increases volume alarmingly and hardly draws breath. He has an excellent vocabulary and is never at a loss for words. Perhaps his most memorable effort coincided with a monumental storm that ended the Brisbane Test in November 1998. Bad light and lightning had ended play an hour earlier with 30 overs unbowled and just four wickets separating England from defeat in the first Test. Blowers was in magnificent form as the skies blackened and vast bolts of lighting illuminated the ground. Within eight minutes the ground was totally under water and England were saved. He described the dramatic scene in splendid detail and we all applauded him when he finished – a rare accolade indeed.

ALAN GIBSON

Yorkshire-born, in 1923, but reared in London, Alan was an erudite scholar with an extensive vocabulary, and a former president of the Oxford Union. Like John Arlott, he had stood for Parliament as a Liberal. He had also scripted many broadcasts, made regular appearances on a variety of discussion and quiz programmes, and was an authority on English hymn-writers. Above all, he was an extremely thirsty man. Unlike John, he slaked his thirst with beer from the barrel and seldom ate in daylight hours.

We first met at Trent Bridge in 1966 on the occasion of my third Test match with the BBC. It was Derek Underwood's first Test. He had been given just two overs as John Snow and Ken Higgs bundled out West Indies for 235. Coming to the wicket as England's last man with the total at 260, he had been hit in the face by a Charlie Griffith bouncer that provoked a shocked John Arlott to say, 'No! No! No! It can't have happened!' John turned away from the microphone and for ten seconds no listener knew what had happened. Then, controlling his emotions, he said calmly, 'Griffith chucked a bouncer and hit Underwood in the teeth.' 'Deadly' escaped with a cut and bruised lip and battled on while Basil D'Oliveira, in only his second Test, carefully extended the hosts' lead. England's record last-wicket partnership against West Indies was 56 between Jim Laker and Harold Butler at Port-of-Spain in 1947–48. Eager to contribute, I passed Alan a card revealing this information when the current stand reached 27. Alan introduced it with relish. 'Bill Frindall, in a fit of optimism, has passed me a card telling me that England's record tenth wicket stand for this series is 56. Well, they're almost halfway there!'

He returned to the microphone forty minutes later with the stand worth 47. D'Oliveira drove and pulled boundaries off Sobers before Underwood heaved Gibbs past long-on to break the record. I handed Alan my card again. He read it out and added, 'We now have a phrase meaning the opposite to putting the mouth on it – putting a Frindall on it!' At that moment a fire engine raced down the Bridgford Road with its siren wailing. I handed Alan another card. In those early days I was kept well away from the mike. Communication was by card only. Those in black were for revealing on air. Ones in red were for the commentator's amusement only. I must have forgotten to explain this code to Alan because he read out my message. 'Bill has just handed me another card. It's printed in red so it must be urgent. It says that Sobers has just sent for the fire brigade to put out Underwood!'

Three years later, when England were hosting New Zealand at Lord's, Alan was in devastating form at my expense. A wicket fell and I wrote the dismissal against the wrong batsman. Correction aids such as self-adhesive white strips weren't available. The only correction fluid on the market involved two phials of chemicals and a lengthy drying process. In dire cases such as that one, when an eight-inch strip needed replacing, I resorted to cutting out the offending segment with a scalpel and replacing it with a blank section from a cannibalised virgin sheet, sticking the new section to the back of the scoresheet with sellotape. I had just cut out my error when Alan noticed what I had done. Seizing the foolscap page from me he revealed to the listening world, 'Bill Frindall has just indulged in some major surgery on his scoresheet. Using a scalpel, he has savaged a swathe from it. In fact, the hole is sufficiently large for me to be able to look through it and commentate on the next ball. And Taylor runs away from us, bowls to Underwood, and he pushes that for a single to midwicket. England move on to 285 for 8 and Underwood is off the mark.'

Retrieving the sheet, I quickly finished my repair. My hand was shaking when I refastened it to its hardboard base. One of the bulldog clips flew off and hit Alan's microphone with a loud metallic noise. 'Do not be alarmed, dear listener. That was only Frindall moving on to the heavy artillery.'

I was now acutely embarrassed. A head-down period of silent scoring was required but the gods were determined to give me a hard time that evening. The bowling figures were secured to their board with two elastic bands. When I routinely passed them to Alan at the end of the over, one band shot off, flew past his nose and hit Freddie Brown in the left ear. Listeners would have picked up his muffled scream before Alan explained. 'Ah! Bill Frindall's campaign continues. He's moved on to the role of sniper and fired an elastic band into Freddie's ear.'

After we had broadcast a match at Bristol, Alan invited me back to his apartment for supper. I was introduced to toad-in-the hole and his library.

'I want to show you the game of card cricket I invented, Bill. I'm very proud of it. You would love playing it because it differentiates between types of bowler and all nine forms of dismissal. You can even locate the part of the field in which a catch has been taken.'

'That's amazing. How many packs of cards does it need?'

'Only thirty-six,' he replied, without a trace of humour. 'I used to keep our scores in an old book. Should be over here. Have you seen it, dear?' His wife looked a tad guilty, made her excuses and left.

His final broadcast for *TMS* was at Headingley in August 1975. Alan's great beer-drinking partner Don Mosey was producing the programme and on the first morning he ordained that no pints of beer were to be brought into the commentary box. Alan was stunned that his mate should deprive him of his brew. He obeyed the command for the first three days, consuming his liquid lunch on the rugby terracing behind our box, but when he entered the box for his final stint on the fourth evening, he was carrying a pint of amber liquid. Don was furious. 'Don't worry, dear boy, it isn't beer,' said Alan, and nor was it. It was whisky. During his twenty-minute spell of commentary Alan consumed half his glass and became a little slurred. When he started declining Latin nouns, alarm bells began to ring and edicts were passed from London. Sadly, it was his finale. The following day's play was abandoned after the supporters of a convicted criminal vandalised the pitch with knives and oil during the night .

Our last meeting was even sadder. He had moved to Taunton after his wife left him and, glass in hand, he would watch all Somerset's home games. I asked him how he was. 'I'm just waiting to die, Bill.'

TONY LEWIS

ARL, who had written and presented a variety of programmes on Radio Wales, was a highly experienced broadcaster long before he joined *TMS*. His relaxed style of writing and broadcasting, allied to the pleasant lilt of his Welsh accent, made him instantly popular with the listeners. A former captain of Glamorgan and England, he arrived with an abundance of tactical knowledge and anecdotes. With the possible exception of Vic Marks, Tony was the only one of our many summarisers who was equally adept at commentary.

Sadly for *TMS*, he was snapped up by BBC television as soon as Peter West retired, but we worked together for the *Sunday Telegraph* for many years when I provided their detailed scoreboards and statistics. It was Debbie Brown's Saturday task to phone our respective copy through to the sports copytakers. Struggling both to meet his various copy deadlines and to comply with Peter Baxter's roster of summarising duties resulted in many minor panics. Most of his copy would be typed but often he had to scribble the final sentences as he dashed to the microphone. As Debbie was a primary school teacher, she was used to small children not finishing their work properly and she was able to correct the more blatant errors. Also, as a member of Kent and Surrey, she knew her cricket. Tony quickly learned to trust her judgement but there was one hilarious cock-up. Bob Taylor, England's popular wicket-keeper, had started to grow prematurely grey. As he always wore a sunhat when keeping and a cap or helmet when he batted, his grey hair was never visible on the field. But once, when he dived to retrieve a wild throw, his hat fell off revealing his grey locks. Tony seized on this just before he had to dash to our box and scrawled '… it was a p..gnant moment'. Debbie couldn't make out the second and third letters but guessed 'pregnant' and that appeared in his report the next day. When they met the following Saturday, Tony astonished Debbers by asking her if she was feeling pregnant. He had actually written 'poignant'!

Another memorable slip-up was the copytaker's fault. Bowling against New Zealand at Lord's in 1986, Neal Radford, Worcestershire's right-arm fast-medium seam bowler, was making no impression against Martin Crowe and Jeremy Coney. Then Radford bowled a bouncer to Coney who pulled it to midwicket where Graham Gooch brought off a superb diving catch. In his copy, Tony introduced the dismissal with '… and mercy came to the aid of the toiling Radford'. Unfortunately, this appeared in the following day's report as '… and Murphy came to the aid of the toiling Radford', opening up a surprise career for an unknown Irish physiotherapist.

CHRISTOPHER MARTIN-JENKINS

We first met when Christopher was assistant editor of *The Cricketer* and I delivered a statistical contribution to his office. He made his *TMS* debut in 1972 and is alone in having enjoyed two terms as the BBC's cricket correspondent (1973–81 and 1984–91). An elegant batsman and an off-spinner who makes the most of his height (6ft 3in), he captained Marlborough College, had three seasons with the Cambridge University Crusaders, appeared for Surrey second eleven, and among other notable clubs has appeared for the MCC, Free Foresters, the Arabs, Sir Paul Getty's XI and Horsham.

I played under his captaincy for the MCC at Charterhouse in 1973 (16-6-43-4) and in charity matches on a Surrey heath at Albury. He has played under mine for the Maltamaniacs at Farnham and we have appeared together for the Gettymen at Wormsley. His sons, James and Robin, are both keen and able cricketers, Robin having established himself as a key all-rounder for Sussex. CMJ won two half-blues for Rugby Fives and is an enthusiastic golfer who sometimes plays nine holes before breakfast on Test match days.

He has a wonderfully clear and authoritative voice, interspersing a fairly schoolmasterly approach of the Rex Alston genre with splashes of humour and impersonation. He is an excellent mimic and an outstanding guest speaker. When, during a lunch interval at Old Trafford, Buckingham Palace announced that the firstborn of Prince Charles and Princess Diana was to be called William, CMJ began the post-lunch session with, 'Welcome back to Old Trafford where the news from the Palace has brought immense joy to our scorer and to Fred Trueman's Old English Sheepdog.'

Even after more than three decades of broadcasting around the world, CMJ is in the same category as I am when it comes to technical know-how, i.e. hopeless. He has been known to start broadcasting with his microphone fastened behind his head. In the West Indies he was spotted on the press coach trying to dial a number on his hotel room's television remote control.

Immensely thin, in spite of a hearty appetite, and with very long legs, CMJ can be somewhat accident prone. He is at his most lethal in commentary boxes where cables seem to leap up and entwine themselves around his ankles, while various pieces of broadcasting equipment and even the occasional coffee cup will hurl themselves to the floor as he lurches past. Frequently, he will leave the commentary position with his headphones, plugged into their appointed desk socket, still clinging to his head. He has demolished an entire rack of my books trying to extricate the bottom one without lifting the others.

(*Above*) South Africa's team for the timeless Test, 3–14 March 1939. I was just three and a half hours old when it began; appropriately enough, many records were set during the longest first-class match ever played.

(*Below left*) Aged eight, not long before my parents decided to move to Canada in search of a better life.

(*Below right*) At the 1951 Festival of Britain with Aunt Jean, who had taught me to read, tell the time and, most importantly, how to catch a ball.

(*Top*) The Primary Club, captained by their patron, Derek Underwood (seated, centre), take on Beckenham in 2002, fifty-five years after my previous visit.

(*Above*) Jack Parker's benefit brochure, bought on my first trip to see a first-class game, at The Oval in 1951, when I watched Denis Compton play.

(*Left*) Peter May in action for Surrey against Derbyshire; he was another of my early heroes.

The beardless wonder has a blazer full of pens, standing alongside the Temple Bar second eleven, 1954. This photo was presented to me on *TMS* at The Oval in 1993.

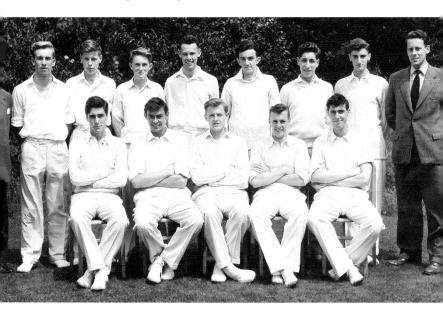

The Reigate Grammar School first eleven, 1957 (I am standing, fourth from right). Used as a batsman in those days, my only bowling spell came in my last game when I took 2 for 7.

My parents, Howard and Evie, with their grandson Raymond, in 1960.

Corporal Frindall on duty in Fontainebleau, 1962. Despite the location, I was still able to continue playing cricket.

The Moustachioed Wonder relaxes after taking his hundredth wicket of the season while playing for Grantham in 1964.

Maltamaniacs: (*Top right*) The first official touring team, in Marsa, Malta, 1975, included Khan Mohammad, Frank Keating and Phil Gould; (*Centre right*) a damp day in East Grinstead with Alan Dixon, 'Butch' White, Ken Suttle, Duncan Preston, Richard Stilgoe and Johnny Dennis; (*below*) signing off in 2003 where I managed to share in the highest stand of the innings, batting at No 11.

Guernsey 2003
Maltamaniacs

Debbie and me on our wedding day, 29 February 1992, with Trevor Bailey and Brian Johnston.

With Debbie and Aunt Jean on gaining an Honorary Doctorate in Technology from Staffordshire University in 1998.

Daughter Alice gets in some early training as a commentator.

With Debbie and Alice after receiving my MBE in 2004, thus becoming only the second scorer ever to be honoured.

In action on the cricket
field: (*above*) bowling for
the Lord's Taverners at
Canterbury in 1985
(*Tom Morris*);
(*left*) Mark Coombs's
painting of me batting.

The sight of him clutching a container bearing liquid fills every scorer with dread and demands the immediate removal of any scoresheets within his range. If you are familiar with the Mister Men books, CMJ is most definitely Mr Clumsy.

He is also Mr Disorganised. Because of his dual role as a chief cricket correspondent, first for the *Daily Telegraph* and now for *The Times*, rarely is he in the box in time for his appointed commentary stint. Peter Baxter often has had to phone or visit the press box to extract him. Johnners used to refer to him as the late CMJ. He is alone in having to be airbrushed into a *TMS* team photo. The only time he was on time for this annual event, he turned up a day early. He once covered an entire day's Test cricket at Lord's wearing one brown shoe and one black one. 'Have you got another pair like that at home?' asked Johnners.

DON MOSEY

Like Fred Trueman, Don was the epitome of the archetypal Yorkshireman. Fittingly, they made their *TMS* debuts together at Headingley in 1974. He came into broadcasting late after a longish stint with the *Daily Mail* covering Yorkshire's matches. I first met him when he was Tony Preston's second-in-command in the Outside Broadcasts department of the BBC's North Region in Manchester, and he subsequently succeeded him as senior producer. I always found him fun to work with because he had a good sense of humour and an extensive vocabulary. Beneath a prickly exterior lurked a heart of gold but he kept it well hidden from anyone who had enjoyed a privileged upbringing, attended a fee-paying school or inherited a double-barrelled name. An old boy of Keighley Grammar School, Don was always relaxed with Tony Lewis and me, both fellow grammar school lads. For the others he revelled in his role of irascible northerner.

Curiously, Don and Brian Johnston appeared to get on extremely well. When they both had a break in commentary they would play the Word Game. This involved each player drawing up five-letter squares and alternately giving a letter to his partner. The object was to form complete words, five-letter ones scoring more points than four, three or two-letter ones. It was a primitive form of palindrome. Johnners was the undisputed champion and their scores at the end of a season were usually on the scale of Brian 80, Don 22. The wily Johnners would overcome Don's superior vocabulary by giving him a succession of Ss and Zs. Few of Brian's completed squares omitted the words TRUSS and SCREW. When CMJ or Blowers were commentating, I would often hear in the background, 'I'll give you a Z, Alderman,' followed by a bleat of frustration from Don.

Don's personal life hit a low in the early 1970s, his wife divorced him and he had a nervous breakdown. To pass the time while he was recovering in hospital, he would watch cricket on television, turning down the sound and providing his own commentary. Restored to health, he covered a few county matches on radio before being elevated to the *TMS* team. He later remarried his wife.

Don had been a handy all-rounder in league cricket. I played alongside him once when he invited me to join his XI for a charity game at a holiday camp. All I can recall of the cricket was that we played on a small and very rough field where they had held a donkey derby the previous week. One of Don's cronies was accompanied by an extremely attractive young lady with exceptionally long finger nails. When the poor chap changed his shirt it looked as though his back had been lashed by a cat-o'-nine-tails. What I do remember is the camp, which reminded me of my national service square-bashing nightmares. Holiday makers were prevented from escaping by sentries at the guardroom beside the main entrance. Signs of tunnels and holes in hedges indicated where some had tried. Anti-social behaviour, such as failing to attend a camp concert, was punished by a dozen laps of the camp on a dual pedal-bike. There was a pond for children to fish. Both children and fish were removed at night and replaced the following morning. We dined in a small hangar at an extremely long table. Servers operated at one end at great speed and the plates had to be passed quickly down the sides. Spillages were dramatic. Big Brother boomed friendly messages over the public address – 'A child is crying in hut 457, please attend to it immediately.' I never went back.

Don enjoyed seventeen seasons with *TMS* before retiring in 1990 after the publication of his memoirs *The Alderman's Tale*. Allegedly, he had aired a few grievances and fired a few rounds at those who had crossed paths with him or were occupying jobs he reckoned he could have done better himself. I say 'allegedly' because I have not read the book. It caused a furore when it was brought into the box in Don's absence at the start of the season. Johnners was especially bitter because, apparently, his great Word Game partner had been less than generous in some of his comments about him.

'Have you seen what the Alderman has written, Bearders?'

'No, Brian, I haven't seen the book.'

'Well, borrow this copy and tell me what you think.'

I took the book back to my hotel but didn't have time to read it. I did look up my name in the index, though. There was a single reference. I turned to it and read, 'Bill Frindall is an absolute genius.' I closed the book with some relief because he had often referred to me as Rasputin. I handed it back to Johnners the next morning.

'What do you think about it, Bearders? Isn't it disgraceful?'

'He says I'm a genius. I think it's a wonderful book.'

'You rotter, Bearders!'

ORGANISERS AND SUMMARISERS

PETER BAXTER

Test Match Special owes a tremendous debt to Peter Alastair St John Baxter. He has fought our corner in numerous battles with programmers and management since taking over the reins from Michael Tuke-Hastings in March 1973. Since the departures of John Arlott and Brian Johnston he has ensured that the programme's traditions have been upheld. He is immensely hard working and well organised. On the eve of every major cricket outside broadcast he will have spent many hours on site, organising the rigging of commentary positions for not only the *TMS* box but also Radio Five Live, World Service and numerous overseas broadcasting positions. Many of the latter are sited some distance from the main position. He personally transports much of the gear in enormous metal cases that dwarf my own collection of travelling luggage. It is rarely that Backers is not already at his desk when I arrive in the box two hours before the start of play on Test match days.

One of the most time-consuming of his multitude of chores involves dealing with masses of correspondence from listeners of all ages. He also has to decide which ones are spoof. Aggers thought that one had slipped through the Baxter net when he handed it to Johnners during a letter answering session in a rainy interval. 'Here's one from, eh, Berkshire,' said Aggers. Brian looked at and stammered, 'Ah, yes, it's from William H. Titt and …' Johnners corpsed and it was never answered but it turned out to be genuine. Brian spent most of the following day drafting a letter of apology but eventually gave up. His first effort, 'I'm sorry I laughed at your name, Mr Titt,' wouldn't have helped matters, even if he could have completed it without dissolving in fits of giggles.

With the splendidly mischievous and sensuous Shilpa Patel as his most capable assistant producer, Peter organises the broadcasting schedules for the entire season. A glance at the double-elephant sized wall chart listing the broadcasting and engineering personnel required for each match reveals the depth of planning required to achieve a summer's commentaries. He masterminded the entire radio coverage of the 1999 World Cup. Even more complex are the logistical arrangements needed for overseas tours, particularly those involving Asia.

Born in Derby in the harsh winter of 1947, Peter was educated at Wellington College and was expected to follow most of his ancestors into the Army. He began his broadcasting career with BFBS (British Forces Broadcasting Service) in Aden in 1965 and joined the BBC's Outside Broadcasts department that year. We first met at The Oval the following August at the fifth and final Test of my first season with *TMS*. He was a willing dogsbody during Brian Close's debut as England captain and saw the host team regain much lost pride with an astonishing innings victory. His 33-year reign as cricket producer is a BBC record by a considerable distance and may well be the world record for any broadcasting company.

He is also a vastly experienced broadcaster, at his best when compiling and presenting feature programmes on tours, Test series and star players. Peter has written and edited more than a dozen books involving *TMS* and his overseas tours. He is also a very popular and amusing guest speaker.

Possibly the most valuable of Peter's many contributions to cricket broadcasting is his creation of a substantial archive of the highlights of *TMS* commentaries and interviews. Very little survives of the years prior to his appointment. Whoever eventually succeeds him will have a very hard act to follow.

TREVOR BAILEY

For more than two decades Trevor's vast cricketing knowledge, astute assessment of players and situations, and his incisive comments were key features of *Test Match Special*. England's outstanding all-rounder of the 1950s, Trevor Bailey was the tenacious master of the forward defensive block. He revelled in his sobriquet, 'The Barnacle'. His massive concentration and astringent competitive spirit, allied to an excellent technique and keen appetite for a good crisis, rescued England from disaster on several occasions during Len Hutton's two successful Ashes campaigns. His 257-minute last-ditch stand with Willie Watson at Lord's in 1953 was one of Test cricket's most heroic feats. The pair survived from 12.42 until 5.50 p.m. – forty minutes before stumps – during which period Trevor ate Willie's lunch as well as his own. A high action allied bounce to his ability to swing and cut the ball at fast-medium pace, and his sharp brain outwitted many outstanding batsmen on flat pitches. He was also a brilliant close fielder and an astute captain of Essex.

I always enjoyed Trevor's company and we got on well. A great party animal, he loved organising them. He also possessed an acerbic wit and was fearless in its use. Fools were not suffered, gladly or otherwise. In addition to sharing *TMS* boxes for more than thirty summers, we worked together on nine cricket yearbooks.

Trevor could be splendidly vague and absent-minded at times. His unwitting theft of Jon Agnew's NatWest umbrella dominated an entire Test series. On the rest day of his debut Test in 1949 against New Zealand at Headingley, he took his wife on an unsuccessful trip to find the seaside at the spa town of Harrogate. On one memorable occasion, he entered the box, rubbed his hands with glee and announced that he had just bought a new car. 'What did you buy?' I asked. His reply was a classic – 'I'm not sure. It's a blue one.'

One evening at Trent Bridge he accused us all of hiding his car keys. When we had searched every bag and case in the box, I put forward the idea that he might have left them in the ignition. Sure enough, he had.

I suggested that we find a wire coathanger to unlock the driver's door. One was produced and, using the technique I had learnt in RAF and NATO motor pools, I swiftly opened the door. Far from being grateful, the Boil referred to me as 'Fingers' for the rest of the match.

No summariser has been more astute in spotting key moments of play or more frugal with his observations. In 2003 I lured him into the PA box at Bournemouth Sports Club during the final of the Portman Building Society Under-15 Club Championships. A tall, black Wanstead CC bowler looked distinctly handy and I asked Trevor for his comments. 'Nice approach, good action, pacy. They should sign him now.' Mervyn Westfield made his first-class debut for Essex two years later.

FREDDIE BROWN

Ebullient and ruddy faced, Freddie Brown was a complete contrast to Norman Yardley, his co-summariser when I joined *TMS*. Before lunch his comments would be restrained and, occasionally, sympathetic. After the interval he would play shots all round the wicket and give full vent to his opinions. I soon discovered that this change was not unrelated to his thirst for the heavier variety of falling-over water. Apart from the accidental firing of an elastic band into his left ear, as reported by Alan Gibson, I did nothing to incur his wrath.

His unique playing career spanned 24 years, encompassing just 355 first-class matches, 22 Tests and a ten-year hiatus. Those years also included his wartime experiences, first as an army officer in North Africa and later as a POW in Italy. He did the double in his first full season with Surrey (1932) and again in his first with Northamptonshire (1949). Having toured Australia with Douglas Jardine's 1932–33 'body-line' side, when he returned as captain of the MCC's 1950–51 expedition, he was frequently mistaken for the son of the earlier Freddie Brown. A late night drive back to his Melbourne hotel ended when he crashed his car into bollards sited in the middle of a wide boulevard. 'Damn things weren't there in 1932!' He proved an inspired captain, his team inflicting Australia's first post-war defeat in the final Test.

F.R. Brown's Fund for Blind Cricketers spawned the Primary Club, which celebrated its Golden Jubilee in 2005.

GRAEME FOWLER

Foxy was a dashing left-hander whose 21-Test career coincided exactly with Graham Gooch's ban for touring South Africa with a rebel England team. He scored 201 in his penultimate Test, and with Mike Gatting making 207, this remains the only instance of two England batsmen scoring double hundreds in the same Test innings. He is also proud of the fact that he is the only player to score 69 in his final Test innings.

Another 'only' against Graeme's name is that he scored a hundred in each innings of a first-class match with the aid of a runner. He strained a thigh muscle while fielding for Lancashire during Warwickshire's record fourth-wicket stand of 470 on the opening day of a championship match at Southport in July 1982. Opening the innings, he managed to score 26 and then a further 100 with David Lloyd as his runner. In the second innings, with Ian Folley doing the legwork, he took Lancashire to an amazing ten-wicket victory with an unbeaten 128. When Foxy completed his second hundred, Folley raised his bat to acknowledge the applause and had his hand shaken by a fielder.

Now coach at Durham University, Foxy has seen several of his protégés capped by England, most notably Andrew Strauss.

As a lively summariser, he is always entertaining and can be relied upon to wander into the surreal. His mode of dress varies considerably but is usually casual, bordering on weird. At Headingley a few seasons ago he arrived dressed as Henry Blofeld, complete with navy blazer, cravat and rat-catcher's cap. Incredibly, Blowers did not realise that he was being impersonated. A talented drummer who has appeared at the Royal Albert Hall, Graeme wore his drummer's vest when he interviewed John Keeble, of Spandau Ballet fame, for our *View from the*

Boundary feature. One more 'only' — Foxy is the only member of *Test Match Special* to have divorced one of his wives by fax.

JIM LAKER

James Charles Laker played against Middlesex at The Oval in 1951 in the first county match I ever saw. Tall and strongly built, he used to amble towards his bowling marker with the absent-minded air of a man who is wondering if he left a saucepan on the boil. Close fielders reckoned they could hear the ball whirl as it was in mid trajectory, so vicious was the spin imparted by his strong fingers. His periodic absences because of a callous splitting on his spinning finger were testament to the force of the Laker tweak.

We first worked together at Cheam Cricket Ground in 1965 when I made my scoring debut for television at one of the last of the Rothman's Cavaliers matches. Gary Sobers had just struck three balls from Surrey slow left-armer Roger Harman high over the line of poplar trees separating the ground from a railway line. Commentator Neil Durden-Smith asked Jim where he would bowl to Sobers in this form. Jim paused for ten seconds before growling, 'Three feet outside the off stump, turning sharply away!'

One of Trevor Bailey's more inspired ideas as secretary/captain of Essex was to acquire Jim's services for thirty matches (1962–64) three years after he had retired from first-class cricket. The Essex pitches were rather more heavily grassed than Bert Lock's dust bowls in Kennington. 'It took me three matches to spot little Gordon Barker's feet when he was batting,' was a typically laconic Laker remark. Before one match on a rarely used outground, Trevor, unsure what to do if he won the toss, sent Jim out to inspect the pitch. Jim shambled out, spent ten minutes wandering round the centre of the ground and reported back to the Boil, 'Sorry, Trevor. I couldn't find it.'

I worked for BBC Television for the first seven seasons of the John Player Sunday League, at first commanding the caption hut and feeding presenters Frank Bough and Peter Walker with the scores of the other matches being played that day, before succeeding Ross Salmon as scorer for Jim and John Arlott. If Jim made an error, he would never correct himself. At the start of one of these 40-over thrashes, he confused the identities of the two opening batsmen and wouldn't correct his error even when one of them was dismissed. The other opening partner survived and he still ignored my note pointing out the mistake. Not until John came on after 20 overs was the correction made.

On 2 August 1981, almost exactly twenty-five years after he had taken his outrageous 19 for 90 in the Old Trafford Ashes Test, I recorded a chat with Jim. Following major heart surgery, he had missed the first three current Ashes Tests, returning for the fourth at Edgbaston to commentate for BBC Television and write for the *Daily Express*. I began our chat by asking him how it felt to be back.

Jim: 'It's good to be back. Basically one is thankful to be here. Physically I feel fine.'

Bill: 'Did you miss being at the matches in person? Or was it a novelty to relax at home and watch them from a distance?'

Jim: 'It was interesting on one count. Of course, I'd never watched cricket on television for such a long time that it was nice to look at it from the other end. Probably the point that will amuse you is that my television set broke down on the final and great day of that Headingley Test match, and so I was listening to the radio boys all day.'

Bill: 'Can we ask what you thought of it?'

Jim: 'I enjoyed it. People ask me what I feel about radio commentary and I never know because you never hear it. Obviously, we're next door the whole time. I don't think I could do it for one thing. When you get some of these dull dreary days we can get away with it with a picture but you've got to talk the whole time and I don't think I'd go a lot for that.'

Bill: 'Your return has coincided with the twenty-fifth anniversary of what will always be known as Laker's match, England v.

Australia, fourth Test at Old Trafford on 26, 27, 28, 30, 31 July, when you became the first man to take all ten wickets in a Test match. In fact, you look rather like that slim-line Laker of 1956. How clear are the memories of that game?'

Jim: 'Well, I think they'll always stay pretty vividly in my memory, Bill. It was, as you say, a unique occasion and one is constantly reminded about it even twenty-five years on. I reckon I can get stopped perhaps twice a month by people in the street, often strangers, who still talk about it. All these reminders do keep it fairly fresh. I can remember most of the dismissals that took place.'

Bill: 'If my memory of it is correct, all the wickets fell from the Stretford End. Is that right?

Jim: 'No, Tony's wicket was taken from the other end, the Warwick Road End. Certainly all 19 of mine were taken from the Stretford End. The interesting thing was, of course, that we switched about continually, particularly in the second innings when I bowled 51 [*51.2*] overs. Tony in fact bowled 55 and I suppose he bowled 20 or 30 from that Stretford End. This is the most remarkable thing about that whole Test match. It was a freak. It could never happen again. There is no way that Lockie and I could bowl and share wickets like that. Couldn't happen in a million years.'

Bill: 'How long was it before he spoke to you after that game?'

Jim: 'He was a bit upset [*chuckle*]. I think possibly I would have been if I had been in his position. And I think one thing I never possibly will forgive myself for, because amidst all the glorification that was taking place afterwards, I possibly didn't spare enough time for Lockie. It was only in later years that I realised that he must have felt desperately unhappy. But fortunately, Tony and I, we were never very close in those days and it's only in later years, as we got older, that we became far more bosom pals than we were then.'

Bill: 'In fact, last year, during the Centenary Test [*at Lord's*] he stayed with you, didn't he?'

Jim: 'Yes, I was returning a bit of hospitality because I stayed with him the previous year in Australia.'

Bill: 'You also just managed to pip him for a monetary prize, the Brylcreem Awards. Were they worth £100 in those days?'

Jim: 'Yes. It was a little bit of a unique year, Bill, because that was the fourth time that year that somebody had taken ten wickets. They were coming down in ever-decreasing circles. I did it for Surrey against the Australians at a cost of 80-odd [88], then an off-spinner at Nottingham [Ken Smales – 10 for 66] did it, and then, of course, Tony did it against Kent when I had a bad finger and wasn't playing. He got 10 for 54 and I think this finally demoralised him at Manchester when they read out my figures of 10 for 53!'

DAVID LLOYD

Known as Bumble because his profile looks remarkably like one of Michael Bentine's television characters in *The Bumblies*, David could have made a living imitating George Formby. His dry laconic wit is akin to that of Jim Laker with a Lancashire accent. When he was coach to the Lancashire team, he was part of the assembly of club dignitaries who stood on the outfield at Old Trafford prior to the start of play in a Test match for the official opening of a new stand opposite the pavilion. We couldn't hear the public-address system and were all wondering after whom they had named the new stand. Johnners asked Bumble, when he came into the box, to do his summarising stint.

'We've called it F Stand,' replied David, managing to keep a straight face but with a twinkle in his eye.

'Why have you called it that?' asked a puzzled Johnners.

'Because it's between E and G Stands,' replied Bumble, maintaining his deadpan expression.

David had a remarkable career as a left-handed opening or middle-order batsman, handy left-arm slow bowler and athletic short-leg, playing for Lancashire for nineteen seasons (1965–83), including five as their captain. In 407 first-class matches he scored 19,269 runs at 33.33, including 38 hundreds, took 237 wickets at 30.26 and held 334 catches. He averaged 42.46 in his nine Tests but, curiously, exceeded 49 just once, when he made an undefeated 214 against India at Edgbaston in 1974. His career ended with a battering by Lillee and Thomson on England's 1974–75 tour of Australia. He was struck amidships by a ferocious ball from Thomson that shattered his pink plastic 'Litesome' box. As the physio extracted the fragments of plastic, Bumble memorably asked if they could take away the pain and leave the swelling.

He spent 1987 on the first-class umpires list before being appointed TCCB development officer for 'Kwik' cricket from its inception, promoting this packaged edition of the game around the schools with great success. Moving on to coach the England side, he motivated the players by introducing recordings and banners of Winston Churchill's wartime speeches. When Zimbabwe managed to draw a Test with the scores level, he exploded with the memorable comment, which he has now patented, 'We flipping murdered them!'

Many of the spoof mails delivered into our box are the creations of Bumble, one of the most notable being the 'Shy Ted' epic that was swallowed hook, line and sinker by Blowers in 2005. He has also helped with providing notes on our *A View from the Boundary* guests. Little unknown titbits featuring world famous collections of garden gnomes and running the London Marathon dressed as a parrot were added to letters sent by the subject's producers and agents. Sadly, Bumble was soon lured from *TMS* to Sky Television.

He is much sought after as an after-dinner speaker. I once worked with him on Guernsey when he devoted most of his speech to explaining in great detail how Fred Trueman devised his bowling run-up and delivery stride. According to David, it exactly equalled the distance between the backdoor and the end-of-garden privy at the home of Fred's parents, the final leap being necessary to navigate the privy doorstep if he left it a bit late!

VIC MARKS

Don't be fooled by Victor's modest and self-effacing mien. Beneath that casual bearing lies a dedicated and determined character whose perception and wry wit have made him a successful writer for the *Observer* and highly popular broadcaster for *TMS*. His relaxed Somerset accent is a welcome contrast to many now dominating radio sports programmes.

Vic was a resourceful middle-order batsman – his last three scores in Test cricket were 83, 74 and 55 – and an off-spinner whose variations of flight snared 859 victims in 342 first-class matches. He captained Oxford and Somerset with quiet authority. Sharing a dressing room with Ian Botham for a decade must have considerably developed his reflexes and sense of self-preservation.

I first encountered the Marks grin and snigger in Australia at a team-media reception on England's 1982–83 tour. A year later he returned an analysis of 5 for 20 in a limited-overs international in Wellington. It remained the record in such matches by an England bowler until Mark Ealham persuaded umpire Dave Orchard to give five lbw decisions 17 years later. I remember it especially because it enabled me to catch a significantly earlier flight back to a haven in Auckland. In 1989 we collaborated on *The Wisden Illustrated History of Cricket* without either of us realising that the other was involved.

Uniquely, Victor is Chairman of Somerset County Cricket Club's Cricket Committee and its sole member. Countless are the times when yet another disastrous performance by the Somerset team has prompted Aggers to suggest that the said Chairman falls on his sword.

He also unwittingly gave his name to the worst commentary box on the county circuit. A crumbling shed, it has been dubbed the 'Victor Marks Memorial Hut' ever since the Chairman of Cricket nearly perished falling through the open trapdoor that provides its only access. Annual coats of paint have shrunk its cramped interior even further since my first visit nearly forty years ago. It is the only blot on one of my favourite grounds but I have enjoyed recording some outstanding cricket from behind its grimy windows, particularly when working alongside those incredibly gifted commentators, John Arlott and Alan Gibson.

Although his limited wardrobe, featuring a few favourite creased shirts of colourful hue, has made him the butt of many unkind remarks by Aggers and Blowers, he has contemptuously flicked them to the boundary. He has a prolific memory and will counterpunch by revealing an embarrassing hidden misdemeanour when his victim least expects it.

SHILPA PATEL

Born in Mombasa, Shilpa was brought to England by her parents at an early age, so early that she cannot recall who was on the throne. After a stint at Lord's she joined the BBC in the mid-eighties and first appeared in the *TMS* box in 1993 during Brian Johnston's final summer. Officially, she is the BBC's cricket organiser but that title does scant justice to her many and varied talents. Besides being Peter Baxter's main production assistant, booking broadcasters and arranging accommodation, passes and parking, she is a Miss Fixit *par excellence*. Shilpa is supremely adept at arranging interviews with players, especially when they have to be grabbed from the clutches of other broadcasters immediately after a day's play. She also books and often chooses the guests for *A View from the Boundary*.

Shilpa is certainly the most attractive member of the *TMS* ensemble with a varied and fashionable wardrobe. Whereas many female broadcasters will slouch around in jeans and sweaters, Shilps usually looks as though she is about to attend a cocktail party. Her colourful vocabulary, unmatched by any other member of our team, made even Fred Trueman blanch, and no day is dull when she is around. Splendidly mischievous, she is great fun and a priceless addition to life in the box.

Four people have contributed most to transforming the atmosphere of the *TMS* box from its fairly dreary and formal state in 1966 to the lively, humorous one that we have now – Brian Johnston, Fred Trueman, Peter Baxter and Shilpa Patel.

MIKE SELVEY

I doubt if Mike Selvey is ever besieged by autograph hunters, because he is a master of disguise. Those who remember him from his playing days will recall his extremely long dark hair. He now looks like a cross between Kojak and Abel Magwitch. His mode of dress ranges from bohemian to aged rock, while his varied range of headgear includes fedoras and beanies. When the Lord's box was sited in a turret atop the pavilion, we were compelled to adhere to the MCC's dress code and don a jacket and tie. There was no code governing footwear, however, and Mike was the first to broadcast from there wearing sandals and no socks. Johnners, very much an establishment figure, was horrified and their partnership as commentator and summariser did not gel.

Mike's first-class career extended from 1968 to 1984 and encompassed, in chronological order, Surrey, Cambridge University, Middlesex, Orange Free State, Glamorgan and England. Tall and strongly built, he swung the ball late and his high action could produce alarming bounce. His peak seasons coincided with a wealth of English bowling talent but he enjoyed a sensational first session of Test cricket. On his Test debut against West Indies at Old Trafford in 1976, he dismissed Roy Fredericks with his sixth ball. He then swiftly added the scalps of Viv Richards and Alvin Kallicharran to claim 3 for 6 in his first 20 balls. Glamorgan headhunted his shrewd cricket brain and installed him as captain before a persistent knee injury in his second year ended his career.

Selve soon installed himself as a witty, perceptive and popular analyst both with the *Guardian* and *TMS*. Not surprisingly, he has great sympathy with bowlers and watching the winter toils of Flintoff, Harmison and Hoggard on Pakistan's moribund surfaces in 2005 must have made his legs ache. Like Trevor Bailey, he is quick to spot a shift of fortune in a match and assess the potential of new players. He can also claim a unique hat-trick – he is, to the best of my knowledge, the only *TMS* broadcaster to have fathered triplets.

FRED TRUEMAN

I was lucky enough to see Fred in his pomp and a magnificent sight he was running in at full throttle, black hair blowing, the powerful wheel of the right arm always hurling his rolled sleeve down to his wrist, the scowl and the aggressive follow through backed up by a few choice epithets. Barrel-chested and belligerent, he didn't scale down his attitude when he first joined *TMS* at Headingley in 1974.

Constantly perplexed by modern theories and field placings, 'I just do not know what is going off out there!' became his catchphrase. When he used it four times in one session, John Arlott admonished him with, 'But Fred, you're paid to tell us what is going off out there.'

FS certainly didn't know what was going on in 1977 when he arrived in the Lord's box in the middle of a discussion about E.W. (Tim) Padwick's monumental *Bibliography of Cricket*. 'What do you think of this bibliography, Fred? It's over eight hundred pages and was compiled by the Deputy Librarian of the City of London.' Fred looked flummoxed for a moment and then asked, 'Bibli… bibliography. What's it about?'

When Brian Johnston interviewed him during a break for rain and congratulated him on not missing many Test matches through injury, Fred was quick to remind him that he had missed a great many through the whims of England's selectors and Gubby Allen in particular.

'It's all right for you, Johnners, with a nice safe job interviewing people. The buggers didn't pick me for half the Test matches I should have played in. If I had played in all those, I'd have got four hundred and seven wickets, never mind three hundred and ruddy seven!'

'Well, you weren't always fit, Fred,' retorted Brian. 'I remember when you had back trouble in Melbourne and had to bowl in a corset.'

'I'm glad you remembered that,' fumed Fred.

'Well, you weren't always fit, Fred,' said Brian firmly, determined to make his point.

'Humph! I'm not the only one who's worn a corset on the field of play,' snarled Fred.

'Oh? Who else has worn one?' asked Brian quizzically.

'Brian Close,' replied Fred, with a gleam in his eye.

'Closey? Wore a corset, Fred? Never!' said Johnners, emphatically.

'Oh yes he has – ever since his wife Vivienne found it in boot of car!'

Fred and Veronica had a vast and very hairy Old English Sheepdog named William. He disgraced himself at Headingley on his one and only visit to a commentary box by munching on two of our microphones. When I spent a Leeds Test rest day at their wonderful house in the dales, Fred decided that William needed some exercise and sent me into the garden to play his favourite game. This was a sort of tug of war using an old car tyre. William was a strong and vicious opponent and he had tugged me about thirty yards across the lawn when we heard Veronica's call of 'William'. Simultaneously we both looked up at the house and let go of the tyre, which fell on my foot.

Perplexed one day by the news that someone had broken a record against Zimbabwe, Fred thundered, 'As far as I'm concerned, there should be two sets of records. One up to when I retired and one since!'

As I got older, I found myself agreeing more and more with him, which became a little worrying, but I did enjoy his comments and his stories. I did not enjoy his pipe. It wasn't a pipe full of tobacco, it was a teacup full of something smelling like rotting underwear and cordite. In our tiny eyries, often without windows or doors that opened, it could be a real menace. Someone sent me a joss stick to counteract it and I lit it during a Test match at Headingley. Johnners was very cross with me when I pretended I didn't know where the perfumed smell was coming from. I had hidden it on a ledge above the window.

Fred returned after lunch during a Lord's Test proudly brandishing a large pack of American tobacco. 'This is real shag,' exclaimed Fred proudly. Johnners suppressed a giggle. Fred crammed as much as he could into his vast pipe and set fire to it. Dark, acrid smoke filled the box and completely blocked out our side window. Johnners peered through the gathering murk.

'The light's getting worse. I think the umpires will have to bring them off in a minute,' he said. Then, pretending to notice the Trueman incinerator for the first time, he continued, 'Oh, Fred! It's your pipe!'

Feigning innocence, Fred asked, 'What's the matter, Johnners? Don't you like my new tobacco?'

'I don't mind tobacco, Fred, but I can't stand cordite,' admonished Johnners.

When it rained during a Lord's Test, BBC Television replayed some of the 1957 West Indies Test. Fred certainly wasn't bowling his much vaunted line and length and was getting clattered around St John's Wood by Sobers and Weekes. We chortled away, making some fairly uncomplimentary remarks, before we realised that Fred was standing behind us with a face like thunder. We braced ourselves for the onslaught. 'Isn't it astonishing,' he fumed, 'how much slower everything is in black and white.'

NORMAN YARDLEY

A former Cambridge University, Yorkshire and England captain, Norman was a very handy all-rounder who averaged 31 with the bat and 30 with the ball in first-class cricket. His canny medium-pace removed The Don in three successive innings. After he finished playing, he combined his business interests in the wine trade with the Yorkshire presidency, writing and broadcasting. His pairing with Freddie Brown for *TMS* preceded that of Trevor Bailey and Fred Trueman. A kind and friendly man, his comments were always constructive, well considered and fair.

During my first Test match at Trent Bridge, he arrived in the commentary box shortly before I did and was scanning the scene through a pair of powerful binoculars. Expecting an erudite comment on the prospects for that day's play, I was pleasantly surprised when he said,

'Eee, Bill, crumpet's not what it were in my day.' Apparently, according to Norman, in those days England players had access to windows at the rear of the pavilion through which girls could pass notes bearing their phone numbers. He certainly made me feel at home.

TEN

CAREER POT-POURRI

MY DAYS in BBC commentary boxes have provided a vital shop window for my career and have led to a great many sideline commissions. Contributions to newspapers preceded the advent of my broadcasting career and these have continued. In the course of four decades I must have contributed to all the major national papers. Apart from the weekly *Daily Express* column, at first my input consisted mainly of averages. Then came the 'All-in-a-Line' scoreboards for the *Sun* and *Sunday Telegraph* and, since 1994, my 'Billboards' for *The Times*. The latter are phoned through via a modem laptop connection but their predecessors had to be laboriously dictated, mostly by Debbie Brown, to copy typists at the newspaper's office. The *Sun*'s scoreboards included notes on dismissal and there was an occasion at Old Trafford when, before the days of slow-motion replays, it was impossible to tell whether the wicket-keeper's catch had come from the glove or the bat. I wrote 'Edged or gloved outswinger'. When Debbie phoned this through, she was asked to find out which one it was, a request followed by a curt 'the *Sun* is the paper that tells the truth!'

Both the *Sun* and *Sunday Telegraph* introduced sponsored cricket awards based on runs, sixes or wickets taken in first-class cricket through the season and I was heavily involved in those. When Trevor Bond resigned as sports editor of the *Sunday Telegraph* and moved to the *Mail on Sunday* as deputy to Ken Haskell, he commissioned me to report a few events as well as supplying stats. Alan Lee's move to *The Times* had left a vacancy that I was delighted to fill. Both Ken and Trevor were splendidly affable men who created a wonderfully relaxed working atmosphere. Trevor toured South Africa with my team in 1980 and has survived a few sorties to Guernsey and Alderney since then. For two years all went well and in addition to writing weekly articles and reporting a match every Saturday, I toured Sri Lanka, Australia and New Zealand for them. I arrived back barely a fortnight before the English season began to find that Ken had retired and I was now expected to be as enthusiastic to dish the dirt on players as I was to write about cricket. Life the following season was not enjoyable and it came as a relief in January 1989 when the paper terminated my contract. Under its terms they had to pay me a year's salary – a tax-free bronze handshake. They gave me a farewell lunch on a riverboat and we all parted amicably. It was an experience I wouldn't have missed but it had removed any urge to become a full-time cricket writer. Perhaps I should not have been so diligent in carrying out my duties for my other major contracted clients. I would be ever so happy if more of them paid me not to work for them.

In the 1980s I spent many Tuesday afternoons and evenings in the *Guardian*'s sports room compiling the leading first-class averages, which was always a challenge with little time between the arrival on tape of the final county scores and the paper's deadline. This was before the Internet or teletext and before I had been dragged reluctantly into the computer age. That event, very much a key moment in my career, occurred in November 1984 when Paula Dixon, a graphics editor whom I had met during my first stint with TVNZ, came to stay with me. Horrified at seeing me still using an Adler typewriter and carbon paper, she visited East Finchley's main stationery shop and enquired about computers. By a miraculous coincidence, three young graduates had just formed a company, Micrologic, and installed themselves in the room above the shop. They were all keen on cricket, Peter Thirlby especially so. He supplied us with a computer and software, taught Paula how to use it and she taught me. Pete then designed the program that I still use to record match and career records for Test cricket, limited-overs internationals and the English first-class season. Although he now lives in Buckinghamshire, we have kept in touch and he recently saved the day when a program crashed on the eve of a publication going to press.

Timing is everything and my new-found basic computer literacy was to prove a boon when I was invited to become editor of the *Playfair Cricket Annual* after Gordon Ross's sudden death in 1985. Founded in 1948 by Peter West, editor of its first six editions, it made its debut as Don Bradman was opening the Australians' tour with his customary hundred at Worcester. Named after Sir Nigel Playfair, an actor/manager between the wars, its only other editor, Gordon Ross, held sway for thirty-two years. A small, chirpy, immaculate figure, who always sported a carnation in his buttonhole, he had served in the RAF and toured Malta with me on my final visit there in 1978. I was invited to give the Address at a Service of Thanksgiving for him at St Bride's Church in Fleet Street. It was a nerve-racking ordeal and I awaited the verger's summons to the lectern with the same foreboding as standing behind the stage curtain before the opening of a show. I had bought new shoes and as I began the lengthy walk down the nave, the right one squeaked loudly. A hymn was being sung but the squeaks sounded deafening. I tried to put that foot down gently and my walk turned into a limp. The squeaks continued. The hymn ended. I was now almost hopping. The squeaks were muted but were now followed by a few titters. I tried not to bend my right knee and it turned into a goose step with ten yards to go before the left turn and a home run to the lectern. Memories of wrecking a commissioning parade at Feltwell returned. Mild laughter broke out now as some of the congregation thought I was trying to enlighten proceedings with an impersonation of John Cleese. Crouching seemed to help and I finally lurched to safety. It took several seconds before audience and speaker composed themselves. Gordon would have loved it.

I thoroughly enjoy editing *Playfair* but I'm still ten issues behind Gordon's monumental record. He also edited *The Cricketer Quarterly Facts and Feats*, an 80-page statistical journal, and I was invited to take over that, too. There was no way I could have coped with these extra tasks without a computer, which also enabled me to supply the *Guardian* with the full national averages for publication just one day after the season had ended.

Without the word-processing facility of a computer I could not have produced three books during the winter of 1988–89. In addition to *Playfair*, I compiled *Ten Tests for England*, my journal and scoresheets of England's 1988 disasters, and *England Test Cricketers*. The latter was a 518-page *magnum opus* that proved to be one of my most challenging projects. It covered each of the 536 cricketers who represented England from 1877 to 1988 with a profile, statistical highlights, match-by-match breakdown (compiled by Philip Bailey) and a photograph of every player except one that we couldn't find. I had to deliver it before I left for a month in South Africa. Only by working twenty-hour days for two months did I manage to complete it just twenty minutes before the taxi arrived to take me to Heathrow Airport. There, with tremendous relief, I handed it to the editor, watched by a smirking Trevor Bailey.

That South African trip was a marvellous treat as well as being a fact-finding mission. The first fortnight was spent as a guest of the South African Cricket Union (SACU) which was celebrating the centenary of Test and first-class cricket in the country. I made the trip at the personal invitation of Dr Ali Bacher, the SACU's managing director, and arrived in Johannesburg on my 50th birthday. My main present came in the form of a novelist and short-story writer from New Zealand. A splendidly erudite and witty companion, she kept me in mischief for the next month. After tours of Johannesburg and Pretoria, we visited several townships where we saw the incredible efforts made by Dr Bacher and his coaches to introduce cricket to the black population. Their progress has been phenomenal. Many changes were evident since my earlier visits as a player on tour in 1978 and 1980. The non-white population now lived in the cities and the general atmosphere was like walking round in any large multicultural city in

England. The English South Africans, outnumbered three to two by the Afrikaaners, would have accelerated the removal of apartheid but every white I spoke to was fearful of the dangers of removing all the barriers too quickly. That they were removed so soon after my visit and without the predicted bloodbath, was one of the twentieth century's major miracles.

During a coach journey to one township, I had the good fortune to be seated next to Bob Crisp, one of South Africa's most remarkable cricketers and men. Robert James Crisp (1911–94) is the only bowler to have taken four wickets with consecutive balls twice in first-class cricket. He is also alone in taking three hat-tricks in South African first-class matches. A right-arm fast-medium bowler, he achieved all three instances in Currie Cup games for Western Province.

Crisp's first two hat-tricks were taken during the 1931–32 season on the Wanderers' back ground in Johannesburg. He achieved the initial one against Griqualand West on Christmas Eve 1931 when his analysis of 8 for 31 included four wickets in successive balls. The second one occurred against Transvaal the following New Year's Day when he captured four wickets in the space of five balls. His third hat-trick was part of another four-in-four sequence, against Natal at Durban on 3 March 1934, when he recorded the best analysis of his career – 9 for 64.

Crisp played for Rhodesia (1929–30 to 1930–31), Western Province (1931–32 to 1935–36) and Worcestershire (1938). He took 107 wickets at 19.58 runs apiece for South Africa in 1935 on his only tour to England.

Bob led an action-filled life, revelling in his role of tank commander during the Second World War. Astonishingly brave, or incredibly foolhardy, he fought his own private war against the Germans in Greece and North Africa. During a single month, he had six tanks blasted from under him and was awarded the DSO 'for outstanding ability and great gallantry'. His reluctance to bow to authority led to General Montgomery personally preventing him from receiving a Bar to his DSO, the honour being downgraded to an MC. Crisp was mentioned in despatches four times and wounded on five occasions before being invalided out of the services.

Afterwards he founded the African magazine *Drum*, ran a mink farm, moved to Greece, and recovered from cancer by roaming around Crete with a donkey and a flagon of wine – 'I came back without any of them.' He told me that when he had received his decorations, the King asked if his bowling would be affected. 'I told him that it wouldn't because I had been hit in the head!'

Crisp is most certainly the only Test cricketer to have climbed Mount Kilimanjaro twice. The tallest mountain in Africa, the highest of its twin peaks towers over 19,000 feet. He played down this extraordinary feat. 'Well, it's not a difficult climb, more of a long stroll upwards. I had just completed my first climb when I met a friend whom I'd promised to take up it. So I just turned round and went back up again with him.'

Highlights of the centenary celebrations were banquets in Johannesburg and Port Elizabeth with over 1100 guests at each. The four major speeches at each event were televised and much was made of all the overseas cricketers and journalists. We watched the Nissan Cup final at the Wanderers and the five-day Currie Cup final at Port Elizabeth. A photo taken by me featuring a parade of vintage cars carrying a score of Test captains in procession around the ground at lunchtime was used on the cover of *Cricket World* magazine. The formalities over, I hired a car and drove from Port Elizabeth along the Garden Route to Cape Town. On the way, we stayed in a forest retreat and at a spectacular bay, spending a week over the journey. Cape Town is one of the world's most spectacular cities. I have many friends there and the week passed very blissfully. I was taken to another township by John Passmore, who cultivated a magnificent cricket ground there from a bare rugby field. The climax to the tour was my good fortune in getting the last compartment on the Blue Train from Cape Town to Johannesburg. The journey, lasting exactly twenty-four hours, is the epitome of luxury and is booked up for more than a year in advance. I had applied two months before and a lucky cancellation coincided with my visit to the booking desk.

Book royalties, fees from after-dinner speaking and contributions to *The Times* are my main sources of income during the winter. These have been supplemented in recent years by my BBC online contributions to *Stump the Bearded Wonder*. Johnners would probably have replaced the opening verb with 'stuff'. For many years I compiled the cricket records for *Wisden Cricketers' Almanack* and *The Guinness Book of Records*. Major works such as the three-volume *Wisden Book of Test Cricket* and *Cricket Records* tomes take many, many hours of preparation and proof checking. In the 1970s I was greatly assisted by Wendy Wimbush, who subsequently worked for the National Cricket Association, Ted Dexter, Jim Swanton, BBC Television and Channel Nine in Australia. Nowadays she scores in the press box at Test matches and for BBC Radio Kent's commentaries at Kent's home matches. She is also the main workhorse for the Cricket Writers' Club. Wendy, a cousin of the late actress, Mary Wimbush, became the first female to score in the BBC Radio box at Lord's when she recorded the Haig National Village Cricket Championship final between Astwood Bank and Troon on 9 September 1972 for the BBC's *Sport On 2*. The following year she scored the Benson & Hedges final between Kent and Worcestershire for Radio Medway.

I love commentating and thoroughly enjoyed my three seasons with *Cricket Call*, British Telecom's phone-in service that provided live ball-by-ball commentary on every county match throughout the season. It enabled me to watch about sixty days of county cricket each summer in addition to all the major matches broadcast by the BBC. Nowadays, my stints behind the microphone are limited to charity matches and the annual inter-county match on Guernsey. Occasionally, I have been invited to major games at Arundel, one of the world's most attractive cricket settings. It was during a memorial match for Peter May that I unintentionally stopped play. A policeman had discovered a dog in distress inside a parked car and handed me a scribbled note. Below the car's registration number was the printed word 'Rover'. I innocently remarked over the PA that I wasn't sure whether that was the make of the car or the name of the hound.

Peter May was very much my boyhood hero. He was a master of

that very tricky stroke, the on-drive, and I had the privilege of seeing him in his prime during the 1950s. On his only visit to South Africa, in 1956–57, Peter produced one of the most astonishing variations of batting fortune on record. After starting the tour with scores of 162, 108 not out, 124 not out and 206, he could muster just 6, 14, 8, 15, 2, 2, 61, 0, 24 and 21 in the Test series. As Fred Trueman often said, unless I managed to find the off switch on his microphone, 'This wonderful game of ours is a great leveller.'

Just once a statistical commission caused trouble and, sadly, it involved Geoffrey Boycott. I say sadly because Geoffrey blames me for something that was most definitely not my fault. Ahead of a vital meeting where the Yorkshire captaincy was going to be discussed, I received a phone call from one of the Yorkshire committee, Julian Vallance. He asked me if I could research the answers to a number of questions involving Geoffrey. I asked him what they were for and he told me. When I discovered that the questions included the number of times his hundreds had coincided with a Yorkshire victory and his average scoring rate in Test cricket, I could see the danger signs. I said that I would carry out the research as a statistical exercise but I did not want a fee and my name must not be mentioned. Vallance agreed. And what happened? Being Yorkshiremen, they eagerly accepted my no-fee offer but when the county's secretary, Joe Lister, despatched the condemning stats, my name was given as their compiler. Not surprisingly, Sir Geoffrey was not amused and has never forgiven me.

Perhaps it will cheer him to know that my scoring rate in Test cricket is even slower than his 15 runs per hour. Absolutely true. In over 350 Tests, I have scored only two runs for England. Both were no-balls missed by the official scorers and subsequently added after I had pointed out the omission to the umpires. Inevitably, Dickie Bird was involved in the first one. After consulting with his fellow umpire, he took me into the England dressing room and told the captain, Mike Brearley, that their total had been increased by one. Mike then announced, 'Bill Frindall has just scored his first run for England,' and led a round of applause.

I am often asked which was the most memorable Test that I have scored. It is a near impossible question to answer. Obviously, the Headingley and Edgbaston matches of Botham's Year, 1981, feature hugely, as does the nail-biter at Melbourne in 1982 when England scraped home by three runs. Then there were the three successive extraordinary cliffhangers in 2005's Ashes feast. My vote narrowly goes to the first Test between England and India at Lord's on 26–31 July 1990. For sheer weight of records it was by some distance the biggest statistical bonanza that I have recorded. Besides a host of individual, team and ground records, it provided a prolonged high level of drama and interest. Vic Marks wrote in the *Observer*, 'In the Radio 3 commentary box Bill Frindall seemed to be gleefully clutching his microphone every ten minutes to announce some new landmark'. Farokh Engineer, his fellow comments man, went so far as to suggest I should have been given the man of the match award!

It will always be remembered as Graham Gooch's match and his signature adorns its score page in my copy of *The Wisden Book of Test Cricket*. After setting the Test record for the highest match aggregate (456 – beating Greg Chappell's 380 at Wellington in 1973–74), becoming the first batsman in any first-class fixture to follow a triple hundred with a century, taking the vital wicket of Manjrekar, holding two catches and completing England's fourth victory in his last seven Tests as captain with a slick run out, Graham cannot have had too many challengers for that match award. Perhaps Angus Fraser came closest with match figures of 61.1-16-143-8. He played a major role in England's first victory at Lord's against any country other than Sri Lanka since 1983.

Gooch's 333 was then the sixth highest of Test cricket's twelve triple hundreds and it included the third highest tally of runs in boundaries in a Test innings. Only Hanif Mohammed (499) had then scored more runs in any first-class game. In a single contest, Gooch exceeded Ian Botham's record aggregate for a home series against India (403 in 1982). Long will Mohammad Azharuddin have nightmares about his decision to put England in. Their first-day total of 359 for 2 (the highest by any country since 29 August 1985 when England themselves, led by Gooch's 179 not out and David Gower's 157, scored 373 for 3 against Australia at The Oval) destroyed any fanciful theories involving helpful conditions for the swing bowling of Kapil Dev and Manoj Prabhakar. Certainly the bat was beaten several times early on, and Gooch was badly missed by wicket-keeper Kiran More when he had scored 36, but there was insufficient reason for India to opt to bat last on a dry pitch that was bound to take spin and become increasingly variable in bounce.

England's 653 for 4 declared was the highest total by any side put in to bat and their highest total against India. The partnership of 308 between Gooch and Allan Lamb, who also made his highest Test score, was England's highest against India for any wicket. Pilloried by the media and even by Bishan Bedi, his own cricket manager, Azharuddin retaliated with one of the most dazzling displays of strokeplay ever seen. The exquisite timing and accurate placement of his shots were quite astonishing, the product of perfect balance, footwork and powerful wrists. Then came Kapil Dev's sensational approach to the problem of scoring 24 runs to avert the follow-on with last man Narendra Hirwani as his bemused partner. Four consecutive sixes beyond straight long-on and into the hard hats and rubble of the building site awaiting the Compton and Edrich stands, off the hapless Eddie Hemmings, removed the problem. This burst also surpassed the Test record of three successive sixes shared by Walter Hammond and Sylvester Clarke.

Gooch and Mike Atherton took just 148 minutes to extend the lead by 204 in a record England opening stand against India, the captain becoming the first to score five Test hundreds at Lord's and extending the record aggregate in Tests at headquarters, which he had gained from Gower in the first innings. India failed to realise the immensity of their task in scoring 472 runs from a minimum of 110 overs. Just once had such a total then been reached in the fourth innings of a Test and even that was sufficient only to draw the freak timeless affair at Durban in 1939. Apparently unable to reset their sights on a defensive target, they batted like millionaires on a one-day binge and beat a hasty path to destruction against some accurate bowling and superb catching. Sanjeev Sharma compensated for bowling that can most charitably be described as user-friendly by top-scoring and taking the match aggregate to 1603 runs, thus setting a new record for any contest at Lord's.

The final official scorecard will become a collector's item with its unique quartet of hundreds involving both captains and their deputies (Lamb and Ravi Shastri). The return of Gower and the inclusion of John Morris enabled Hampshire and Derbyshire to contribute more than one current player to England's cause for the first time since 1922–23 and 1982–83 respectively. When the welter of statistics had subsided, my outstanding memory of the match was Sachin Tendulkar's astonishing one-handed catch taken at full tilt after a thirty-yard sprint to dismiss Lamb in the second innings.

In 2001 Peter Baxter invited me to join Blowers, Aggers, CMJ and himself to receive a cake from the Queen during the tea interval of the opening day of the Lord's Test against Australia. Rain had stopped play at 3.33 p.m. and tea had been taken early. It was quite a battle to get through the crowds around the ground and even to squeeze through the pavilion corridors to the Committee Room. It was my first view of Her Majesty at close quarters. Her eyes sparkled and she was in great form. After we had been introduced to her, she said that she felt very sorry for us when we had to keep talking when rain had stopped play. Blowers enlightened her that the listeners preferred that to us commentating. 'That's rather sad,' she said. When she looked expectantly at me I reminded her what a good wicket-taker her grandfather had been at Lord's. Whenever the teams were presented to George V, a wicket, usually one of the opposition's, fell immediately afterwards. 'He was rather frightening,' she revealed. The cake, a Dundee fruitcake, was summoned and presented to Peter. Aggers asked if it had been baked 'personally'. 'Not personally, especially,' she countered and we were dismissed.

Three years later I was shocked but immensely pleased to receive a letter from 10 Downing Street advising me that, subject to my agreement, my name would be submitted to the Queen with a recommendation that I be appointed a Member of the Order of the British Empire in the Birthday Honours for Services to Cricket and Broadcasting. I was delighted to accept. It was a tremendous honour not only for my family and me but also for scorers and statisticians throughout the cricketing world. Secrecy was essential until it was officially revealed during the Trent Bridge Test. Then I took a lot of stick. We had a special *TMS* dinner at Langar Hall in celebration that night and I wasn't at my most alert the next day.

Buckingham Palace organises its investitures quite brilliantly. Mine took place the following November. Debbie, Alice and Aunt Jean (who had taught me to read and catch) were given excellent seats in the ballroom and had a clear view of the hour-long ceremony involving just over 100 awards. One of the first was Clive Woodward's knighthood for services to rugby union and we met for a brief chat afterwards. Perched on a balcony opposite the stage where Her Majesty presented the honours was the Orchestra of the Grenadier Guards. I was concentrating so hard on bowing at the right times and saying the right things that I didn't notice the music they played when it was my turn. Debbie took great delight in revealing that it was 'There Once was an Ugly Duckling'. After the bow and handshake I was expecting Her Majesty to ask about cricket or broadcasting. Instead she asked, 'Where's my cake?'

My sister-in-law is Sioned Wiliam, ITV's comedy controller, and she managed to get a table for six at the prestigious Ivy restaurant. It lived up to expectations. We celebrated well and were thrilled to meet David Baddiel, celebrated writer and comedian. I then had to travel to Potters Bar and appear on stage with Aggers, Mike Gatting and Ralph Dellor in *Sticky Wicket*. It was great fun to startle my fellow artistes and the audience by walking on in my full Buck House regalia clutching the gong.

ELEVEN

ARAB INVASION

IT ALL BEGAN when I was introduced to a visitor from Saudi Arabia at a party in Hampstead held by Joanna Briffa, a Maltese friend. It was August 1977. I was fairly bronzed after many days playing and scoring cricket. The Arab guest, Sheikh Aziz, took one look at my longish hair and black beard and asked which part of Abu Dhabi I came from.

'You could pass as an Arab, Bill,' Joanna laughed.

'What?' I asked, immediately hoping that the *double entendre* would be missed.

'If we dressed you up as an Arab, no one would realise that you weren't one,' Joanna persisted. Then came her crunch line, 'I bet you wouldn't score for the BBC all day dressed as an Arab.'

'How much?' I asked recklessly.

'£25,' she offered.

Another friend added £20 and we eventually got to £62. After a few more glasses of falling-over water I accepted, saying, 'OK, I'll do it for charity. I'll do it for the Primary Club.'

'No, you won't,' rebuked a blonde. 'You'll do it for Cancer Research.'

'Why?' I asked.

'Because I'm the treasurer,' she replied.

So it was that on the Saturday of the fifth Ashes Test I drove my car past the sentinels of the Hobbs Gates to my allotted parking place at the rear of the pavilion. The car had a BBC RADIO sticker across the top of the windscreen on my side and the steward would have recognised the distinctive Bermuda Green Audi and my wife, Jacky. Certainly he took no notice of the driver who was in full Arab gear. I wore the long dishdash over my bathers, sandals, an Arab headdress and sunglasses. Bert, guardian of parking spaces, was not fooled. 'Sorry, your highness, you can't park here. This is Bill Frindall's space.' I wound down the window.

'But, my dear fellow,' I charmed in my best Peter Sellers Indian accent, 'I have been told that this is now my space.'

'No one's told me, sir. Bill's got a lot of heavy bags and a short temper. It'd be more than my job's worth to let you park here.'

I decided it was time to play my trump card, a Saudi Arabian chequebook that I had been lent for just such an emergency. I waved it out of the window. 'Now, dear fellow. I have just bought The Oval. Unless you let me park here, you will not be working here next season.'

He scratched his head and very reluctantly ushered me into the bay. I removed my sunglasses and, using my normal voice, said, 'Thanks, Bert. Lovely morning, isn't it.'

'Bill! You bastard!' Spotting a group of youngsters with autograph books, he called to them, 'Here! Lads! Come and get a genuine Sheikh's autograph! He's just bought The Oval!'

Bert gave a triumphant grin as my car was surrounded by small boys and one or two girls. For ten minutes I signed 'Sheikh Bill Frindall'. No doubt some of them will read this and realise that they have a collector's item. I shall watch eBay. Eventually, I was allowed to emerge from the car in my full Arab rig. It was only then, with increasing trepidation, that I realised what lay ahead of me. First, followed by Jacky and a friend, Maureen, who carried all my cases of books, I walked across the forecourt and into the members' pavilion. As I walked through the Long Room, I was greeted courteously by Surrey members who usually ignored me. I raised my hands with palms together and murmured a few 'salaams'. Then up two flights of stairs and on to the pavilion roof where our commentary box was perched. Peter Baxter was the only occupant and I shall never forget his look of abject horror when he saw me.

'Bill, why today?' he asked, slumping into his chair. He only calls me 'Bill' when he is displeased

'Why not?' I responded in genuine puzzlement.

'Because today the BBC Review Board will be listening to every word. They will then decide whether *TMS* is going to continue.'

'Ah,' was all I could offer, doing my best to look penitent. Brian Johnston arrived as I was unloading the cases and setting up the watches and scoresheets.

'Oh, my Crippen, Bearders! Wonderful! We'll play a little joke on Arlow.'

John Arlott arrived, breathing heavily and looking like a man who has just climbed the north face of something more testing than a staircase, in urgent need of brandy and oxygen.

'Morning, Arlow. I'd like to introduce you to our friend from World Service, Mustachio Kamal.'

John blinked at me wearily as though I had brought a herd of goats into the box, and grunted a welcome. It was several minutes before he realised that this Arab was writing on Bill Frindall's record sheets in a familiar italic script. 'Hell's teeth, Frindalius! What have you done now?'

Don Mosey arrived and was distinctly unimpressed. 'I'm coming as Wyatt Earp on Monday,' he said. A shocked Alan McGilvray waved dismissively and was not going to join in the fun. Trevor Bailey chortled, 'Fred's going to enjoy this.' Peter Baxter quickly took control of the situation and decided that my garb was to be ignored. Like the Emperor's New Clothes, the Arab was not to be mentioned but Fred Trueman arrived late and joined Brian at the microphones before anyone could warn him. As a result, *TMS* was included on *Pick of the Week* for the first time. It was considered a real honour to have an excerpt from your programme wittily introduced by Margaret Howard on her weekly show. Here is a transcript of our debut:

MH: Cricket has been taking quite a bashing from the rain recently [*the first day had been washed out*], but last Saturday morning there was some play between showers in the Test match between England and Australia at The Oval. The intervals between play gave the commentators a lot of work to do filling in time but then, they never seem to be short of words. Even when play was going on, they found plenty to say. Mind you, the way Bill Frindall, the scorer, was dressed gave Brian Johnston and Freddie Trueman quite a talking point as England came to the end of the first innings.

FST: Who's that sat at the side of you Johnners? Have you ever seen anything like that in your life?

BJ (*giggling*): No. Listeners would be rather amazed if they were to look in the box – they might be amazed any day! It really is rather extraordinary. On my right at the moment there's a gentleman in Arab dress. It looks like an old sheet he's got on …

Arab (*protesting*): It's a dishdash!

FST: It's a dish wash!

BJ: Anyhow, we'll explain about it in a minute, as Thomson comes in now to bowl to Willis. In he comes, bowling from the Vauxhall End, and Willis goes to turn this on the legside, misses it, and Marsh moves across. Now what is your headdress called – the Arab headdress, Bill?

Arab: I've got no idea. It was given to the gentleman I borrowed it from by King Hussain.

BJ: He was sitting in the box and all of us came in and sort of pointed at him. One or two said, 'Good morning' – like that [*at this point BJ unwisely attempted an Eastern accent*] – and he sort of muttered underneath his beard.

Peter Sellers (*alias Arab*): Good morneeng!

BJ: And it is, in fact, done for a very good purpose isn't it?

Arab: Yes, I've been sponsored to the tune of something like £62 for Cancer Research.

BJ: What, so long as you …

Arab: I've got to stay all day, scoring, throughout the six hours of play, and …

BJ: In your Arab dress?

Arab: That's right.

BJ: Careful we don't remove it from you!

Arab: Careful!

BJ: Now Thomson's coming in to bowl to Willis – and that one's another class stroke from Willis, this time, through the covers. Two runs there, as Hughes chases it down towards the gasholder. That one he played through cover and extra cover. And we're seeing some good strokes from these numbers ten and eleven. So there's some good stuff. It's double figures for Willis – he goes to 11. 191 for 9, and still 5 to Hendrick.

FST: I hope he doesn't come to our house dressed like that because my sheepdog William will attack him. He'll think it's a mate.

BJ: My terrier Minnie would have a go at him, too.

FST: No wonder King Hussain gave it away. Look at it!

Arab: You're only jealous.

FST: Jealous!

BJ: And in comes Thomson now, to bowl to Willis. He bowls this one outside the leg stump – and he's glided that one for four. A lovely stroke there; any batsman would have been proud of. It came down at a rate of knots here. No question of anybody stopping it from long-leg. Malone was down there but he couldn't get to it. So, that was a beautiful leg-glide by Willis, takes him to 15. England 195 for 9.

Arab: A partnership of 21 – the third highest of the innings.

BJ: The highest being 86, I can reveal to you, and the next one being 39 between Roope and Underwood. 86 for the first wicket by Brearley and Boycott.

FST: Reminds me of a story, seeing Frindall dressed like that.

BJ: Is it repeatable on the air?

FST: Oh, yeah. It's about the fastest thing on two wheels in London

— an Arab crossing Golders Green on a pushbike! [*Fades with Brian's laughter.*]

MH: Freddie Trueman, Brian Johnston and Bill Frindall in the commentary box at The Oval. And even the cricket was good.

The BBC Review Board must have been content. A few letters of complaint were received about Fred's joke, though.

Unknown to me, until he wrote an irate letter, a visiting Irishman was sitting at the Vauxhall End that morning with his eight-year-old son. It was their first Test match. Apparently, I was the young lad's hero and he borrowed his dad's binoculars to study the window of our box.

'He's not there, Dad.'

'Of course, he's there. He has to score all day. Look more carefully. He's the one with the beard.'

'No,' insisted the lad, 'he's not there. There's a bald one, one smoking a big pipe and an Arab.'

'Don't be stupid, son,' said his dad, snatching the glasses off him. 'Begorrah, you're right!'

He spent the rest of the day trying to win back his son's respect and affection by buying him crisps and pop.

The Arab made his second, and positively final, appearance the next day. My accountant, Chris Warne, had invited me to play for his local side, Poynings from Sussex, against West Wycombe. Chris had heard the previous day's commentary and asked me to play a joke on the rest of his team. He made sure that the opposition were in on the act and they agreed that Poynings would bat first. I arrived at the ground wearing my cricket gear and already padded up. Over it I wore the Arab costume with a rug hiding my boots and pads. When they arrived from the pub I was sitting on a bench near the pavilion. While our openers were piling on the runs I got some of the team to explain cricket to me. They were very polite and totally taken in. Chris had asked me to bat at number three and told the others that I was going to be late. If I hadn't arrived everyone was to shift up one place in the order.

Eventually, a wicket fell. The number four batsman got up, collected his bat and gloves and made to walk to the middle.

'No, wait! I want to try this batting.' I shed the blanket, my dish-dash, headdress and sunglasses. To everyone's amazement I strode to the middle and took guard carefully. I was clean bowled second ball. My new team-mates were killing themselves when I returned.

'You didn't teach me very well, did you?' was all I could muster.

TWELVE

BBC COMPUTER TEST

I F VARIETY IS the spice of life, mine has been richly stimulated. Of the many varied projects with which I have been involved, the BBC's computer Test of 1972 between England and Australia was the most original, fascinating and daring. Billing it as the 'Test of All the Talents', the BBC used it to mark the twenty-fifth anniversary of the post-war resumption of Ashes Test matches and to demonstrate the use – or misuse – of computers. It was ideally timed to attract a large audience of cricket devotees, frustrated by England not being involved in an overseas tour that winter. In fact, the winter was entirely devoid of Test cricket in 1971–72, apart from the five-match rubber between West Indies and New Zealand played in the Caribbean from February to April. The *Sun* newspaper carried my daily match reports and full scores throughout the computer Test.

At this time, very few people could afford the cost or enormous space necessary for personal computers, and laptops remained a dream. Indeed, computers were restricted to major companies and it was in the offices of BP House in London that this simulated match was played on a couple of Univac 1108s costing £3 million and occupying a vast room. Once Steve Bonarjee, BBC Editor (Radio), General Current Affairs, had replaced his initial scepticism with infectious enthusiasm, he quickly convinced his non-technical colleagues that this odd project could be transferred into radio. So successful was the 'conversion' achieved by this ebullient Alastair Sim look-alike that, for five successive evenings, a half-hour programme of commentary and narrative was followed by fifteen minutes of analysis and interviews on Radio 4.

First, two selection panels were chosen, England's pairing of John Arlott and Brian Johnston being chaired by Sir Neville Cardus, while Australia's panel comprised Bernard Kerr (ABC Director of Sport – chairman), Alan McGilvray and doyen cricket writer Ray Robinson.

Bearing in mind that the match was to be played at Lord's in early June and that eligibility was confined to those who had played in post-war Ashes Tests, they selected the following teams:

ENGLAND	AUSTRALIA
L. Hutton (Yorkshire)	A.R. Morris (NSW)
G. Boycott (Yorkshire)	R.B. Simpson (NSW)
P.B.H. May (Surrey)	* D.G. Bradman (S. Australia)
D.C.S. Compton (Middlesex)	R.N. Harvey (Victoria)
M.C. Cowdrey (Kent)	A.L. Hassett (Victoria)
* T.E. Bailey (Essex)	K.R. Miller (NSW)
†A.P.E. Knott (Kent)	R. Benaud (NSW)
J.H. Wardle (Yorkshire)	A.K. Davidson (NSW)
J.C. Laker (Surrey)	R.R. Lindwall (NSW)
F.S. Trueman (Yorkshire)	†A.T.W. Grout (Queensland)
A.V. Bedser (Surrey)	W.A. Johnston (Victoria)

* Captain † Wicket-keeper

The selectors met over dinner and their discussions continued well into the night as they considered the post-1945 form of everyone who had appeared in Anglo-Australian Tests. Although Walter Hammond had averaged 58.45 in an outstanding 85 Test career, his post-war average (eight Tests) was only 30.50 and did not justify his inclusion. Their decision to give the England captaincy to Trevor Bailey was a surprise only because he had never captained his country. But for Gubby Allen, then chairman of selectors and supremo at Lord's, being offended by a ghosted newspaper article, Trevor would probably have succeeded Len Hutton. Listeners to *TMS* cannot fail to have been impressed by his supreme technical and tactical knowledge and his ability to assess players. Hutton himself rated the Barnacle as the best tactical brain in post-war English cricket.

Four omissions from the England computer Test side – Ken Barrington, Frank Tyson, Brian Statham and Tony Lock – attracted much criticism when the listening public were asked for their comments. Sid Barnes, Don Tallon and Gil Langley were Australian omissions that provided plenty of discussion. Both captains had to be present to control their teams on the computer and when the Don decided that, for personal reasons, he was unable to travel to England, he nominated Alan Davidson as his deputy.

Dr Maurice Kendall and John Poston of Scicon (Scientific Control Systems) were the statisticians who masterminded the programs that ran this match. Both were keen cricket enthusiasts. Poston was the consultant in charge of the operation of the program and he helped the two captains when necessary and laid down their guidelines. I was commissioned to supply him with England v. Australia Test statistics for the twenty-two selected players. As well as their basic tallies of runs, wickets and wicket-keeping or fielding dismissals, I was given a daunting shopping list for each player's dossier. The batsmen's analyses were split into their first and second innings performances, giving their distribution of scores in bands of ten, their mode of dismissal and the category of bowler by whom they were dismissed. The bowlers' economy rates, wicket-taking and maiden-over frequency, and mode of dismissals, were analysed in detail. My notes record that I spent 180 hours preparing that data.

Armed with these dossiers, Poston programmed a vast array of statistics into the computer. For batsmen they included their scoring rates, tendency to succeed in the first or second innings, main scoring strokes, vulnerable points and psychological qualities. For bowlers, the details involved their pace, degree of accuracy, break or swing, technical and temperamental strengths and weaknesses, and the climatical conditions in which they usually prospered. The Meteorological Office supplied an average schedule for five days of early June in London NW8.

Cricket is ideal for computerised representation because it depends on the result of many separate ball-by-ball conflicts between batsman and bowler. It has also been exceptionally well documented by its scorers and statisticians. The radio programmes required sections of ball-by-ball commentary, so the progress of this match had to be described by the computer in great detail. Each delivery, the batsman's attempted stroke and the outcome had be produced for each ball. Under a heading for the start of each over, giving the time, bowler, which end, his over and the total over numbers, a typical line of the print-out would read:

(Ball 1) TO COMPTON OFF-STUMP SHORT AWAY-SWING SQUARE-CUT 1 RUN.

Other factors had to be programmed to modify standard responses. A new ball would enhance the quicker bowlers' performances but a bowler's effectiveness would be reduced by the more overs he bowled. He was assumed to be slightly refreshed at the start of each spell. Both batsmen and bowlers could exceed the best performances they had actually achieved in Ashes Tests. The batting skipper could vary his batting order and instruct his batsmen to bat normally, take risks or block like Trevor himself. The captain could declare and could arrange for a tailender to be shielded. The bowling captain could change the bowling at any time, and deploy five variations of field placing to each batsman, ranging from the most aggressive to ultra-defensive. The computer generated a random number to determine which event occurred for each ball. It would record, print out and store this data before proceeding with the next ball. Play would continue for a set number of overs agreed by the captains but it ceased immediately a wicket fell. Both captains were completely absorbed by the computer's results and so was I.

The match, which ended in an Australian victory on the fourth day (the advertised fifth day was filled with a limited-overs match), was played out for twelve hours spread over two days. I compiled my usual full range of scoresheets (ball-by-ball, innings summary and bowling summary) from the computer print-outs. These formed the basis for the excerpts of commentary provided by John Arlott, Brian Johnston, Christopher Martin-Jenkins and Norman Yardley. The engineers added appropriate background effects such as bat striking ball, applause, cheers and, at the insistence of Johnners, an aircraft passing overhead.

Each day's play was analysed in the supplementary fifteen-minute programme by a panel chaired by John Arlott and including Neville Cardus and Brian Johnston. They were able to interview players who had played a key role that day. Ray Lindwall was the main architect of Australia's win with ten wickets in the match. By telephone from his florist's shop in Brisbane he was able to discuss the techniques of England's batsmen and I recall him saying, 'Boycott tended to commit himself into a stroke too early and, as I swung the ball away late, I would expect to have him caught behind or bowl him off stump.' I was lucky enough to see Ray bowl in 1953 and 1956. His sensational over against Peter May when the Aussies played Surrey on the earlier tour, kept my hero out of the England side until the final Test of that memorable series. Of all the outstanding fast bowlers I have seen, I rate Lindwall's run-up and action the smoothest and most impressive.

As far as the match itself was concerned, the Met Office's forecast played as big a part as my statistics. It caused Davidson seriously to consider putting England in, gave Bedser and Trueman ideal conditions for the new ball, freshened the pitch with a twenty-minute shower and enabled England to bowl Australia out relatively cheaply. This had frequently happened since the war. The same conditions prevailed the next day and, with the ball continuing to swing and seam in a heavy atmosphere on a green pitch, Lindwall and Miller scythed through the hosts' batting to gain a lead of 112 by early afternoon on the second day. As the pitch eased, a second-wicket partnership of 131 between Don Bradman and Bob Simpson took the game from England, who were eventually set 386 to win. Their record winning fourth innings score in

Ashes matches remains 332 for 7 at Melbourne in 1928–29, while their highest in England was then 263 for 9 at The Oval in 1902.

I was fascinated by the reality of several of the computer's individual results. It produced the shock of the match with its 44th delivery when Bradman was bowled by Bedser first ball. The machine had not gone berserk. Bedser had dismissed Bradman in five successive Test innings and twice had him out for a duck, at Adelaide in 1947 and at Trent Bridge in 1948. In fact, the Adelaide dismissal was also first ball and involved a similar delivery, which the victim rated as the best he ever received. A late inswinger, it pitched middle and leg before cutting away and bowling him off his pads. With his leg-cutters and late swing, The Don rated Alec the most difficult bowler he faced. The computer favoured England by restricting Bradman's match aggregate to 79 as he averaged nearly 85 per innings in his two post-war series. It also confirmed Compton's superior second innings records in post-war Ashes Tests as he averaged 36 in the first innings and 51 in the second. Even with his hand on the tiller, Trevor Bailey was unable to influence his own performance. His match return of 14 runs and no wickets bore scant resemblance to those he actually achieved at Lord's in 1953 and 1956.

Given their record in 66 post-war Tests to this point (Australia 23 wins, England 13 wins, 30 draws), a computer program would inevitably favour an Aussie victory. Bearing in mind that the pitch and overhead conditions favoured quicker bowlers, only rogue programming could have produced any other result. In Lindwall, Miller, Davidson and Johnston, Australia had one of the greatest attacks of all time, combining pace, swing and immaculate control. Their batting and fielding were fairly useful, too. Subsequent replays using more advanced technology have produced a similar result. The computer passed its own test with flying colours.

ENGLAND v. AUSTRALIA (Computer Test)

At Lord's Cricket Ground. Toss: Australia. Result: AUSTRALIA won by 142 runs.

AUSTRALIA

A.R.Morris	c Knott b Bedser	15		c and b Trueman	8
R.B.Simpson	b Bedser	5		c Hutton b Trueman	67
*D.G.Bradman	b Bedser	0		b Laker	79
A.L.Hassett	b Trueman	30	(5)	c Laker b Wardle	24
R.N.Harvey	c Compton b Trueman	37	(6)	b Laker	23
K.R.Miller	c Knott b Trueman	4	(7)	c Wardle b Laker	15
A.K.Davidson	b Laker	11	(9)	b Bedser	14
R.Benaud	b Trueman	53	(8)	b Laker	4
R.R.Lindwall	b Laker	4	(10)	c May b Bedser	12
†A.W.T.Grout	c Knott b Trueman	25	(11)	not out	7
W.A.Johnston	not out	1	(4)	c Knott b Trueman	10
Extras	(B 5, LB 2)	7		(B 6, LB 2, NB 2)	10
Total		192			273

ENGLAND

L.Hutton	c Johnston b Miller	11		c Simpson b Lindwall	26
G.Boycott	b Lindwall	0		c Harvey b Lindwall	14
P.B.H.May	c Morris b Davidson	13		b Davidson	2
D.C.S.Compton	b Lindwall	0		not out	95
M.C.Cowdrey	b Lindwall	0		c Simpson b Miller	13
*T.E.Bailey	b Miller	14		b Lindwall	0
†A.P.E.Knott	b Lindwall	2	(8)	c Harvey b Davidson	24
A.V.Bedser	lbw b Lindwall	7	(7)	b Miller	13
J.H.Wardle	not out	16		c Johnston b Miller	22
F.S.Trueman	c Morris b Miller	5		b Lindwall	2
J.C.Laker	b Miller	1		c Grout b Lindwall	20
Extras	(W 3, NB 8)	11		(B 1, LB 2, W 6, NB 4)	13
Total		80			244

ENGLAND	O	M	R	W		O	M	R	W	**FALL OF WICKETS**				
Trueman	22.5	4	61	5		25	4	84	4		A	E	A	E
Bedser	32	14	54	3		27.5	7	53	2	Wkt	1st	1st	2nd	2nd
Bailey	17	6	41	0		20	6	47	0	1st	14	14	10	37
Wardle	1	1	0	0	(5)	16	6	30	1	2nd	14	14	141	46
Laker	18	10	29	2	(4)	41	22	49	3	3rd	23	14	169	46
										4th	81	18	173	95
AUSTRALIA										5th	87	41	219	97
Lindwall	17	7	24	5		31.3	8	97	5	6th	102	47	219	126
Davidson	12	7	21	1	(3)	16	8	33	2	7th	122	52	236	165
Miller	17.2	8	24	4	(2)	23	8	53	3	8th	144	64	244	209
Johnston						12	6	13	0	9th	191	78	258	220
Benaud						16	4	35	0	10th	192	80	273	244

Umpires: C.S. Elliott and A.E. Fagg.

Close of play scores: 1st day – England (1st) 3-0 (11 overs; Hutton 3, Boycott 0); 2nd day – Australia (2nd) 142-2 (74 overs; Simpson 52, Johnston 0); 3rd day – England (2nd) 36-0 (17 overs; Hutton 26, Boycott 7).

* captain
† wicket-keeper

THIRTEEN

AUSTRALIA

H AVING NARROWLY failed to inflict myself upon Australia with the RAF in 1961, I had to wait another fifteen years before eventually heading Down Under. In 1975, two cricket nuts who ran Lonsdale Press decided to reproduce the England scorebook of that season's Ashes Tests, adding reports by various broadcasters and Patrick Eagar's photographs. They were staggered to discover that there had never been an England scorebook or, for home series, an England scorer. Official scores of Tests in England were kept by the respective scorers of MCC, Lancashire, Nottinghamshire, Surrey, Warwickshire and Yorkshire, usually at the back end of second eleven scorebooks. Luckily, the TCCB put Lonsdale on to me and they were relieved to find that my work was sufficiently neat to reproduce in colour. It may have helped that, around this time, David Benedictus wrote a feature on *TMS* in which he generously stated, 'If scoring is an art, Frindall is a Canaletto!' I'm not sure how delighted the eighteenth-century Venetian would have been but I was extremely chuffed. The first edition (1975) of *Frindall's Scorebook* sold out and I was commissioned to fly to Australia that winter for the host's long-awaited rubber against the West Indies. Unfortunately, work on three other publications prevented my covering the first four Tests but Geoffrey Saulez scored them on my sheets and I rewrote them for the book.

This was to be the first of a dozen highly enjoyable trips to Oz and

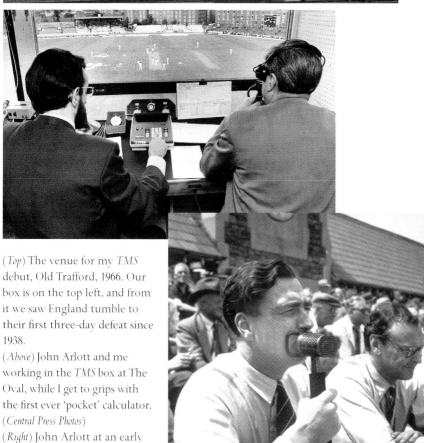

(*Top*) The venue for my *TMS* debut, Old Trafford, 1966. Our box is on the top left, and from it we saw England tumble to their first three-day defeat since 1938.

(*Above*) John Arlott and me working in the *TMS* box at The Oval, while I get to grips with the first ever 'pocket' calculator. (*Central Press Photos*)

(*Right*) John Arlott at an early post-war match.

Things don't always go according to plan in the commentary box, as Colin Whittock's cartoon shows.

"... And I'm sure then he's calmed down, Bill will tell us exactly when was the last time he had coffee spilled over his score cards and statistics ...!"

It's not just about the cakes, as this fine sunhat created by Johnners reveals.

Me dressed as an Arab at The Oval, August 1977. (*Patrick Eagar*)

The Queen presents the *TMS* team with a cake. From left to right: Baxter, Blofeld, M-Jenkins, Agnew and me. (*Patrick Eagar*)

The deadly duo of Lillee and Thomson join *TMS*.

The *TMS* team at Lord's, 2003. Back, left to right: Fred Trueman, Mike Selvey, Jonathan Agnew, Gerald de Kock, Chris Cowdrey, Barry Richards, Henry Blofeld; front: me, Vic Marks, Shilpa Patel, Peter Baxter and Eddie Barlow.

A portrait of Brian Johnston, presented to me by his widow Pauline. (*Brian Alexander-O'Neill*)

BRIAN JOHNSTON
CBE MC 1912 – 1994

To The Bearded Wonder with love from

Brian Johnston and Don Mosey playing the Word Game at Old Trafford in 1984. Johnners was undisputed champion.

My work space, Trent Bridge 2005, during the best Test series I have ever seen.

Hal Hooker displays the technique he had shown when he shared in the world record tenth-wicket partnership of 307. A month after achieving this, he became the only Australian to take four wickets in four balls.

Prince Leonard of Hutt River Province, 100km from Perth. He seceded from Australia in 1970, but his offer to play Ian Chappell's Australian side was declined.

The MCC at Brockton Point, Vancouver, in 1994. Don Bradman described it as the world's most beautifully situated cricket ground.

This photograph of a slumbering Glenn Turner during England's tour of New Zealand in 1983–84 became a regular picture onscreen when Turner came to commentate.

Bert Sutcliffe and John Sparling, who both played their last innings in a game against the Maltamaniacs in Auckland during the 1983–84 tour.

The Padang, Singapore, where I took 4 for 19 in my one international game – for Singapore.

With Sir Donald Bradman and Mike Carey of the *Daily Telegraph*. Bradman was a statistician's dream, and many of his records will surely never be beaten.

Brian Johnston with Paul Getty at the inaugural match at Wormsley, the stunning ground he built on his estate.

With Gary Sobers, who had scored 161 for West Indies on my *TMS* debut, at Marin, California in 1992.

is the one I remember most. On the outward flight I had the great good fortune to be sitting next to Les Ames, one of Kent's long succession of outstanding wicket-keeper batsmen, probably the greatest such all-rounder that the game has ever known. He made 102 first-class hundreds, including nine double centuries, 3058 runs in 1933 and over 2000 runs in five other seasons. Averaging 40 in Tests, he was the first England wicket-keeper to score a hundred, and his tally of 123 runs against South Africa at The Oval in 1935 remains the world record for any pre-lunch session of a Test. He twice won the Walter Lawrence Trophy for the fastest first-class hundred of the season. His keeping was of the highest class. He was equally adept against the leg-spin and googlies of Tich Freeman as he was against the fiery pace of Harold Larwood and Bill Voce. He still holds the world records for the most dismissals (128 in 1929) and most stumpings (64 in 1932) in a season. He was the first to achieve the wicket-keeper's double of 1000 runs and 100 dismissals in a first-class season, a feat he managed three times. He was the first professional to be appointed an England selector (1950–56 and 1958) and was manager on three MCC tours. After playing for Kent from 1926 until 1951, he was secretary/manager (1960–74) during their most triumphant years and president in 1976. A benign and friendly septuagenarian, he had much sage advice to offer to a novice visitor to Australia and some fascinating memories of the Bodyline Tour.

I was immediately taken by Adelaide's beauty. Laid out with military precision by Colonel Light, who performed a similar service across the Tasman at Christchurch, the city is a square block surrounded by parkland and the meandering River Torrens. The Adelaide Oval, even with the stands added since my first visit, remains one of the world's most attractive venues and has retained its old scoreboard. With St Peter's cathedral dominating one aspect and the Mount Lofty Ranges opposite, it has a fabulous setting and one of the best batting surfaces in the world. Ken Barrington's lowest score in ten first-class innings there was 51, his full sequence being (* = not out) 104, 52, 52*, 63, 132* (in 1962–63) and 69, 51, 63, 60, 102 (in 1965–66). I am amazed he didn't emigrate there and told him so.

In 1982, during my long hiatus between marriages, I met a senior high-school teacher during an Adelaide Test. We have remained close friends and she has been my mentor and guide throughout my many recent tours. Usually, I base myself in Adelaide and we share the driving to Brisbane, Sydney and Melbourne, lengthy journeys that take a dozen hours or more. The highways are good and traffic is light once you escape the cities, although other hazards have to be negotiated, such as stray kangaroos and koalas stoned on their eucalypt diet. Once we had to drive through a plague of locusts. It lasted for several minutes and we had to brake almost to a halt. The sound and sight of them colliding with the windscreen, leaving dismembered yellow remains, were a tad alarming – so was the stench of their carcasses. Perth, via the endless Nullabor Plain, is too far to drive – the flight takes nearly four hours – but the train journey sounds fun.

Adelaide's other serious attraction is its proximity to several of the world's most famous wine-growing areas. Over the years I have got to know them all pretty well. When Test matches had rest days both teams, together with broadcasters and journalists covering the match, were guests of Wyndham Hill-Smith, a nephew of Clem Hill, on his Yalumba Estate in the Barossa Valley. It was there that Richie Benaud introduced me to Sir Donald Bradman in 1976. Rest days could be a misnomer and several major injuries resulted from the Barossa Valley outings. Jeff Thomson seriously damaged his shoulder playing tennis there and his bowling was never quite as lethal afterwards. Usually, it was the journalists who came off worst and, in 1979, their injuries included a fractured shin and a gravel-grazed face.

It was during the 1976 Adelaide Test that I first saw Viv Richards at his imperious best, scoring 101 off 136 balls. My scoresheet shows that only two of his 17 boundaries were scored behind the wicket. Surprisingly, considering his later penchant for the on side, ten of those fours were gained on the off side.

During that first visit I scored the match from the old press area, close to the dressing rooms at midwicket. My sight of the centre of the pitch was obscured by a pillar, so I would see Lillee, Thomson, Roberts or Holding bowl, before looking past the pillar to see the batsman duck. Only when Richie Benaud arranged for me to demonstrate my scoring system on television in their commentary box at the Cathedral End did I briefly have a view down the pitch.

Sitting in the press box turned out to have considerable rewards. As well as meeting the legendary Clarrie Grimmett, I was placed next to Ray Robinson. He had become a regular correspondent almost from the day of my first broadcast, checking various facts and sending copies of his books. He invited me to stay at his house in Northbridge when I came to Sydney at the end of the series, which I was happy to do.

Melbourne, scene of the sixth Test, could not have been more of a contrast to Adelaide. A vast, sprawling city, its only saving graces are its large number of superb Victorian buildings, its parks and its profusion and variety of ethnic restaurants. Walking from the hotel through a wide park housing Captain James Cook's cottage, shipped from his native Yorkshire, was always a delight. The Melbourne Cricket Ground is the largest in the world with a capacity of 100,000. Rebuilt for the 1956 Olympics and subsequently totally restructured, it bears no resemblance to 'The Paddock That Grew', which staged the very first Test in March 1877. It does house one of cricket's finest libraries run by exceptionally knowledgeable staff. In 1976, the MCG was the scene of Lance Gibbs's 308th Test wicket (Ian Redpath caught at long-on for 101). When Fred Trueman was riskily awoken in the early hours of 31 January and asked for a comment, he responded with 'I'm not surprised. The bugger's been playing for twenty years.'

A year later, I was lucky enough to be invited, again by Lonsdale Press, to score the Centenary Test at the MCG. The brainchild of Hans Ebeling, who had opened Australia's bowling at The Oval in 1934 on his lone international appearance, it attracted the largest gathering of international cricketers in history. A grand total of 187 – 109 Australian and 78 English – they were photographed in three-tiered batches of thirty, Roy Swetman attempting to appear on either side of the same photograph by running around the back. That brought back memories for Charlie Barnett, who had managed to achieve that feat in a

school photo. By this time, Bill Edrich was sporting a black eye, inflicted by John Arlott when he unwisely awoke the latter from a heavy
slumber. Johnny Warr mischievously suggested that it might have
been inflicted by an enraged husband. It was JJ who, when attending
Edrich's fifth wedding in succession, was asked by an usher whether he
was with the bride or the groom. 'Season ticket!' replied Warr.

The match began on a damp pitch and provided five days of rich
entertainment. Australia, put in by Tony Greig, were dismissed for 138
but England could manage only a pathetic 95 in reply. When their
innings ended at 2.10 on the second afternoon, no one expected the
game to last until the fifth day – and the Queen was scheduled to
arrive at tea on the last afternoon. Australia declared at 419 for 9 in
their second innings after Rodney Marsh had scored Australia's first
hundred by a wicket-keeper against England. David Hookes scored a
spectacular 56 off 69 balls, five of his nine boundaries coming from successive balls off Greig. Rick McCosker, whose jaw had been fractured
when he mishooked a ball from Willis in the first innings, came in with
a runner and a heavily bandaged face at 353 for 8 and helped add 66 for
the last two wickets. Those runs were to prove vital as England were
dismissed for 417 at 5.12 on the final evening to lose by 45 runs, the
exact margin of their defeat in the inaugural Test 100 years earlier. The
highlight of that innings was a brilliant 174 by Derek Randall. He drove
Dennis Lillee to distraction with his antics, especially when he doffed
his cap after being hit on the head by him. When Randall fell while
avoiding another bouncer, he turned a somersault. At the end of his
446-minute epic, he lost his way back to the dressing room and found
himself facing the royal box. Reacting swiftly, he executed a swift bow
and disappeared through an adjacent window. His short speech after
clambering on to the rostrum to receive the Match Award was a classic. To the audience, 'Thank you for coming.' To Lillee, 'Thanks for the
bump on the head.' To the presenter of the award, 'Thanks for my
medal.'

That evening I went across to the Hilton to interview Randall and
Mike Brearley for BFBS. As I came out of the lift on the sixth floor,

I collided with Randall. Still wearing his cricket gear and blazer, he was playing imaginary strokes along the corridor. 'Did I really get 174, Bill?' he asked.

Back in 1976, I took Ray Robinson up on his kind invitation and spent the final week of the tour staying with him at his lofty house in Northbridge, a northern suburb of Sydney. His basement contained a vast library of his reporters' notebooks dating back to the mid-1920s and including the Bodyline Tests of 1932–33. He had developed a unique format for reporting a match by dividing each page of his note-book into four vertical sections, one for each current bowler and one for each current batsman. He would then make tiny, copious notes in each section and, like the linear scoring system, would use a line or two per over. From this it was amazingly easy to find the appropriate note when he wrote his press report. It was a system I adopted when I came to report matches for the *Mail on Sunday*.

One of Australia's greatest cricket writers, Ray overcame major surgery and poor eyesight to continue working until shortly before his death in 1982 two days before his 77th birthday, watching play through binoculars. He began his long career in journalism with the *Melbourne Herald* in 1925 and became chief cricket writer for the *Melbourne Star*. Moving to Sydney he worked for four major papers in addition to being Australian correspondent to the (London) *Daily Telegraph* and *Wisden* for three decades. A prolific author, he was a most concise writer who compressed more facts and figures into a page of copy than any writer before or since. He was one of the kindest, gentlest men you could ever meet, and was a wonderful host who taught me so much about Australia and its early cricketers.

While I was staying with Ray, I embarked on a search for my moth-er's godfather, her uncle David McNeill, who had emigrated to Australia shortly before the First World War and fought with the Australian forces (AIF) in France. In 1968 he had retired after nearly fifty years service with David Jones Ltd, one of Australia's major mul-tiple stores. As he was personnel director, no one in the company knew his date of birth and he was able to work full time until he was nearly 80. My mother hadn't spoken to him since 1945 and couldn't remember which city he lived in. I phoned the Sydney branch and was told that he had worked there but was now retired. They wouldn't give me his telephone number but offered to pass mine to him. A few minutes later he rang me. 'Where are you?' I told him and ten minutes later Great Uncle David and Great Aunt Eadith were outside the front door. They lived barely five minutes' walk away! That phone call proved to be another major key moment.

I visited them in their home overlooking Middle Harbour many times over the next decade. Even at the age of 90 David had immense energy and enthusiasm. I have recordings of our chats about his life and remember sharing his wine into the early hours. Eadith was twenty years his junior and struggled to keep up. Every Thursday she would drive him into Sydney and deliver him to David Jones. The staff, particularly its female members, relied on him to solve their personal problems. Eadith would lunch with her girlfriends and return around 4 p.m. to collect him. 'I used to go into the store and head for the centre of all the laughter. David never wanted to leave. I'd have to drag him away, kicking and screaming, covered in lipstick!' One day David had his lunch, told Eadith that he felt tired and was going to bed, and died in his sleep that afternoon. He was 93. Three years later my mobile rang when I was commentating for British Telecom at Taunton. It was Eadith's executor to tell me that she had passed away the previous night and that I was her sole beneficiary. News that I now owned property in Sydney was dwarfed by the realisation that I had lost two wonderful friends and an historic link with my ancestry. I flew to Australia and helped to sort out their affairs, bringing home many McNeill heirlooms.

While I was staying with Ray Robinson, I visited Hal Hooker at his home in the Mosman suburb of Sydney and interviewed him for BFBS. In the course of a first-class career of a mere 23 matches spanning just eight seasons (1924–25 to 1931–32), John Edward Halford ('Hal') Hooker (1898–1982) achieved a unique double. First he shared in a tenth-wicket partnership that remains the world record in all first-class cricket. Then, just a month later, he became the first and, so far, only Australian to take four wickets in four balls in Australia, achieving this feat in a Sheffield Shield match.

The last-wicket stand of 307 between Alan Kippax and Hooker is one of the most remarkable in the entire history of cricket. It began at 11.50 on Christmas morning in 1928 at the Melbourne Cricket Ground. New South Wales were 113 for 9 in reply to Victoria's first-innings total of 376. Their captain, Kippax, was 20 not out and, having failed in the first two Tests of that summer's series against England with scores of 16, 15, 9 and 10, he was under some pressure from the crowd. He cannot have dreamt that the 6ft 2in tall number 11 batsman, playing in only his sixth first-class match and about to join him in the middle, would still be batting with him twenty-four hours later. Hooker, then aged 30, was an extremely accurate fast-medium, right-arm bowler whose stock ball was the late inswinger. Although he had won batting awards at grade level with the Mosman Club, he was a natural tailender by first-class standards. His main assets were a calm temperament and a good defence, which he had cultivated by watching Jack Hobbs. Kippax was a year older. Known as 'Mr Elegant', he was an extremely graceful player who had to date made three of his 22 appearances for Australia.

Together they took the score to 170 at lunch (Kippax 60*, Hooker 18*). In the middle session they managed to negotiate the second new ball and add 100 runs. Of those, Hooker contributed 14 while Kippax made 85. After tea the Christmas Day crowd, which had built up as news of this gallant partnership spread, switched their allegiance and cheered every run. The pair continued to thwart the Victorian attack, which included four current or future Test bowlers, and were still there at stumps with the score 367 for 9 (Kippax 221*, Hooker 51*). Just ten runs were needed for the vital first-innings lead. Kippax accomplished it in the second over next day. Hooker then hit two successive boundaries off Ted a'Beckett. Attempting a third, he was caught high and one-handed by Jack Ryder at mid-off. It was 12.40 p.m. on Boxing Day. New South Wales had made 420 and neither batsman had given a chance prior to Hooker's aberration. Kippax, after a masterly exhibition in which he paraded his full range of strokes including many of his delightful trademark late-cuts and leg-glances, was left on 260 not out. The last of his six double centuries in Sheffield Shield matches took 387 minutes and included 30 fours. Three days later on the same ground, Kippax scored 100 in the third Ashes Test. Hooker, close to exhaustion after the longest innings of his life, hit just three boundaries in his career-best 62. For 304 minutes he had resisted an extremely strong attack without giving a chance. His abiding memory, though, was of his furious skipper racing down the pitch to reprimand him. 'You fool! You threw it away! Why didn't you get a hundred?' Hooker added, 'I hadn't missed a ball in two days and I went and did a silly thing like that. Fifty years later I still regret it.'

In his next first-class match a month later, also for New South Wales against Victoria but in Sydney, Hooker ended the visitors' first innings with a hat-trick. He then bowled the opening batsman with his first ball of the second innings. Three of his victims were clean bowled and he caught the fourth one himself. He told me that it should have been five in five. 'The next man, Jack Ryder, used to lift his head as he played the ball early in his innings. I bowled him a late outswinger, it took the edge but my slip dropped it.' His innings analyses were 6 for 42 and 2 for 94. Hooker's all-round performances in the two key matches against Victoria ensured that New South Wales regained the Sheffield Shield from them.

In spite of these two epic performances, Hal Hooker was destined never to catch the eye of the national selectors. After his retirement he continued to work for Alan Kippax in his sports stores in Sydney and Newcastle and, for nearly twenty years, he commentated on cricket for the ABC.

On Australia Day in 1988, I flew to Sydney to report on the Bicentenary Test for the *Mail on Sunday* and join the biggest party in Australia's brief history. The celebrations were for 200 years of white settlement, the First Fleet carrying Governor Phillip and Sydney's first enchained prospective residents having sailed into Botany Bay in

January 1788. It was nicely emphasised by a well-orchestrated but totally peaceful Aboriginal protest. One brilliant banner confirmed the original settlers' sense of humour by pointing out that the First Feet were Aboriginal!

As my plane approached Sydney airport, it passed directly over the harbour and provided a magnificent sunbathed view of the First Fleet re-enactment vessels surrounded by a 10,000-strong armada of small boats – a spectacular parade of sailing boats festooned with flags, balloons and bunting. That night's firework display, centred on the famous bridge, lasted over an hour and lit up the sky for miles. Dining in Rushcutters Bay with great aunt Eadith, I was treated to a grandstand view of this Star Wars extravaganza. As the first rocket exploded into a thousand cascading glow-worms I tried unsuccessfully to convince Eadith that I had arranged it all especially for her. The whole hype was put into perspective by Boris, a Russian taxi-driver who drove me into the city from the airport. He revealed that celebrating Bicentenary Day among the hundreds of boats in Sydney Harbour had completed a notable double for him. At the age of eight he had been in Moscow when that city had celebrated its 800th anniversary.

That tremendous piece of theatre was always going to be a hard act to follow but it was no fault of the cricketers that the Bicentenary Test failed to produce a pulsating finish. Even though the Ashes were not at stake, no one expected this Test match to be played as a celebration game with the festival atmosphere of the MCC Bicentenary match at Lord's the previous year. The New South Wales Cricket Association spared no effort in their presentation of the event, providing abundant hospitality for the teams and a galaxy of specially invited former Ashes players. For them, it was a superb five-day beano and a constant battle against overwhelming alcoholic temptation. The falling-over water won easily. Sadly, the media were not included on the party list. The English contingent did derive much satisfaction from seeing Australia compelled to follow on some 211 runs behind England's total of 425. It was an embarrassment that England were not to inflict upon them again until 2005 when Michael Vaughan's Ashes winning team enforced it at Trent Bridge. Australia amassed 328 for 2 in their second innings with David Boon making an undefeated 184 on a pitch that dried into a slow surface giving scant assistance to any bowler.

For Saturday's crowd of 27,164, the high point of the entertainment probably occurred during the lunch interval when a vintage open-topped Rolls-Royce transported Sir Donald Bradman at the head of a motorcade of veteran cars, which slowly lapped the SCG boundary. The Don, in his eightieth year, was at his most animated, waving vigorously to acknowledge a tumultuous reception on the ground where he had completed his hundredth first-class century. Geoffrey Boycott unwittingly stole the show when his car spluttered to a halt after a few yards. He briefly helped to push it before sneaking a lift on the running board of Ray Lindwall's vehicle. I wonder if some victims of his eccentric calling would have spotted an allegory there.

The match itself was dead from lunch on the fourth day and it was left to a commemorative computer Ashes Test to attract the spectators' interest. Its progress was displayed during intervals on the SCG's new computerised scoreboard. Programmed by a Sydney resident, it not surprisingly produced an Australian victory. Its star was legendary leg-spinner Bill O'Reilly, and it was appropriate that it should coincide with his being the central figure of a special press-box ceremony on that final afternoon. Attended only by the writers and broadcasters covering the Bicentenary Test, it marked Tiger's retirement from reporting Test cricket for the *Sydney Morning Herald*. Then 82, he was presented with a copy of David Frith's *Pageant of Cricket*. O'Reilly's trenchant comments attracted a vast readership and he made a typically entertaining and viperish speech of thanks. We had first met at Adelaide in 1978 when our identical tour holdalls became mixed up at the airport. He found himself with the weight of my mobile library and scoring paraphernalia while I became the confused guardian of four pairs of very large black shoes.

When I first worked at Brisbane's Woolloongabba Ground, it was a ramshackle affair of odd stands. Our broadcasting position was a bivouac on the roof of the press box. We were entirely at the mercy of the elements, which in Brisbane can be extremely vicious, ranging from scorching humidity to massive thunderstorms with hailstones the size of snooker balls. A sensational electrical storm rescued England from defeat in November 1998 when it flooded the ground in eight minutes. Henry Blofeld revels in such drama and was in virtuoso form. When Vic Marks was allowed to get a word in he said, 'What amazes me is that we've seen colossal bolts of lightning all round the ground but not a clap of...' At that precise moment the most monumental burst of thunder deafened everyone on the ground.

One day the wind was so strong that I had to use my left hand to batten down the scoresheets. It was impossible to let go and pick out of my case any of my reference tomes. The three commentators were aware of this problem and only one ignored it. No prizes for guessing which one!

Press and broadcasters were treated to an abundance of fresh fruit by the Queensland Cricket Association. Several trays bursting with pineapple, bananas, guavas, passion fruit and melon were placed in the press box every morning. We were also allowed access to the adjacent Cricketers' Club rooms. Sadly, all those, and the magnificent poinciana trees, have had to make way for a modern stadium that, from the air, looks like a Polo mint.

Brisbane is a small but exciting city sited on the bend of the Brisbane River. It has some of the best seafood restaurants in the world and transport across the river to the Gabba is by ferry or speedier craft called Fast Cats. A drive north up the Sunshine Coast introduced me to the top-heavy Sugarloaf Mountains, pelicans and fields of pineapples. Southwards lies the Gold Coast where high-rise buildings have put the beaches in shade for most of the day.

The WACA (Western Australia Cricket Association) Ground in Perth is closer to Singapore than it is to any of Australia's other major grounds. Like Brisbane, it has changed considerably since I first saw it in 1977. Then it was like a large English county ground but modern stands have totally changed its appearance. Access from the city's hotels is through a botanical garden where elegant black swans swim on large ponds full of giant water lilies. On the far side is the Swan River, gateway to some fabulous wineries. Western Australian wines feature among the world's best and were a great favourite of Sir Paul Getty. Shortly before Perth staged the America's Cup yacht race, the press and broadcasters were guests of the Royal Perth Yacht Club for a day. In the morning we were given a cruise up the Swan assisted by unlimited supplies of falling-over water. I was on the upper deck chatting to Lady Dorothy Hutton, Sir Len being absent at a business meeting in Perth. Dorothy had a penchant for gin and tonic, supplies of which were available on the lower deck. My journeys up and down the stairs improved my fitness for the afternoon when, to use the term loosely, we 'crewed' yachts over the America's Cup course.

I was at the ground in November 1982 when Terry Alderman chased, and brought down with a flying tackle, an intruder who had clobbered him from behind. Terry was stretchered off with a shoulder so badly dislocated that it required surgery and ended his first-class season. For club matches, the WACA ground is divided into two and, several weeks later, I guested there for the Incogniti while Alderman was trying out his shoulder in another match on the adjacent pitch. Three years earlier it had been the scene of a long-awaited dismissal once it was apparent that Peter Willey, Graham Dilley and Dennis Lillee were likely to play in the same match. At 4.08 p.m. on 18 December 1979, Lillee was caught Willey bowled Dilley for 19. It happened just once.

Perth is a favourite place, as is neighbouring Fremantle, which also has an abundance of seafood restaurants. The beaches are some of the finest in the world. One, a nudist beach, was the scene of one of my more embarrassing moments when I lost my car keys in the sand – but that story is for a different book! A thirty-minute ferry ride away is the island of Rottnest, which used to be a penal colony. After I had relayed this piece of information to Brian Johnston he revealed to his startled listeners that it had been a penile colony.

Standing in the bar of the England team's Perth hotel one evening in 1982 I was tapped on the shoulder by a slight, dark-haired, middle-aged man. 'G'day, Bill. I've declared war on Australia!' What might have been normal late-night banter in an Aussie bar assumed the significance of a real threat when I recognised this fellow as Prince Leonard George Casley, Administrator of Hutt River Province. Faced with a considerably reduced wheat quota in 1969 (it would have taken them 500 years to have cropped the average amount of wheat their 18,500 acre property had harvested in the previous two decades), Casley, a qualified accountant and lawyer, gave formal notice of his property's secession from Australia. As neither the State nor Federal Governments were able to contest this declaration, since 1 April 1970 Hutt River Province has been recognised as a Principality. HRH Prince Leonard's wife is HRH Princess Shirley, and their seven children, 24 grandchildren and 20 great-grandchildren all have royal titles. Although his original wheat quota has been restored by royal proclamation (his), he has supplemented his farming income with the sale of passports, stamps and coins. Coachloads of tourists travel 100km from Perth to view his gallery and museum.

Knowing that Prince Leonard, the epitome of an Aussie battler, had the power to declare war, I realised that standing next to him might not be the safest place to be. Spotting my nervousness, he quickly reassured me. 'Don't worry, Bill. I declared peace five days later. Now the bastards have got to recognise the Principality. I'm undefeated in war!'

We first met when I visited his Perth residence to interview him for BFBS. I had heard that he had his own cricket ground and team at Hutt River. After being introduced to Princess Shirley, who had interrupted her dusting to greet me, I asked him what sort of pitch he had.

'I don't want to get into technicalities,' he replied evasively.

'Is the surface grass or artificial?' I prompted.

'No.' Prince Len paused, then added, 'It's a little rough, but we've had some good games, not long ones, though. I challenged Ian Chappell to bring an Australian eleven to play my team.'

'What happened?' I asked, bemused.

'He declined. He asked me who I had playing for me and as soon as I mentioned Dennis Lillee he seemed to lose interest.'

I must have spent two years of my life in Australia, divided into a dozen instalments of various lengths. The natives have always been welcoming and tremendously friendly. The rivalry between Poms and Aussies, grossly exaggerated by the media, is usually good-natured and confined to cricket grounds. All the major cities have their attractions, although my favourite is Adelaide. With its abundance of sunshine and building space, Australia is an excellent country for young people.

FOURTEEN

BRADMAN AND LARWOOD

$\mathbf{A}$s a statistician I must have written or typed the name of Sir Donald Bradman more often than that of any other cricketer. During a career involving just fifty-two matches spanning twenty years, eight of which were lost to war, injury and illness, he almost totally rewrote the records of Test cricket. Such was his stature and influence on world cricket that in 1932–33, England, under Douglas Jardine's captaincy, felt compelled to resort to the infamous leg-theory 'bodyline' attack to curb his exceptional talents.

No other batsman approaches his Test career average of 99.94 (had he scored 4 and not 0 in his final innings at The Oval in 1948 he would have averaged 100), or his frequency of contributing a century every 2.75 innings. At the height of his career, newspaper vendors' posters regularly proclaimed 'HE'S OUT!', or 'BRADMAN VERSUS ENGLAND', or 'BRADMAN BATS AND BATS AND BATS'.

Although many of Bradman's records have been surpassed, several of those he set on his first tour of England in 1930 have proved unassailable. His aggregate for that five-match rubber was a mammoth 974, average 139.14, from just seven innings, including a record three double centuries – 8, 131, 254, 1, 334, 14 and 232. His 334, the first triple century in Test cricket, included a record 309 runs on the first day – 105 were gathered before lunch, 115 in the afternoon session, and another 89 after tea. No other batsman has scored 300 runs in a single day of

Test cricket. His time of 214 minutes remains the fastest in which a Test match double century has been achieved.

The Don is alone in holding the record scores for two batting positions in Test cricket with 304 at number 5 (v. England at Leeds in 1934) and 270 at number 7 (v. England at Melbourne in 1936–37). He is also the only batsman to score hundreds in six successive Test matches. No one has approached his tally of twelve Test double hundreds. His second-wicket partnership of 451 with Bill Ponsford at The Oval in 1934 remained unbeaten for any wicket until 1990–91. Although all his Test appearances were confined to Australia and England, no one has improved upon his record scores on three major grounds – Adelaide Oval (299 not out), Brisbane's 'Gabba' (226) and Headingley (334). His 299 was a unique score in all first-class cricket until 1990–91. Compiled against South Africa in 1932, his innings ended when he ran out the last of his partners while attempting a vital single off the final ball of an over.

He was captain of the Australians at Southend in 1948 when they amassed the most runs in any day of first-class cricket (721 in 5 hours 48 minutes), contributing 187 in 125 minutes himself. The first batsman to average over 100 runs during an English season (115.66 in 1938), on each of his four tours of England he exceeded 2000 runs and averaged over 80, surpassing the average of the leading home batsman of that year. In 1930 and 1938 he reached 1000 first-class runs before June. The only batsman to have achieved this feat twice, he also holds the record for the earliest 1000 runs in a season – 27 May (1938). His 452 not out for New South Wales against Queensland at Sydney in January 1930 remained the world's highest first-class innings until Hanif Mohammed overtook it in Pakistan 29 years later. Bradman's 415-minute knock included 49 fours and, astonishingly, was scored in the second innings of the match. He was then only 21. Having scored 205 not out on the Saturday, he resumed on the Monday, adding 90 before lunch and a further 137 by tea when Alan Kippax closed the innings. Had he been allowed to bat through the final session he might well have extended the record beyond the 600 mark. Playing for Bill Woodfull's XI against Jack Ryder's XI in the same season, he completed a first innings century (54 to 124) before scoring a second-innings double century on the same day.

Bradman exceeded 1000 runs in an Australian first-class season on twelve occasions, twice as many as any other batsman, and is alone in scoring 1500 more than twice. His aggregate of 1690 achieved in 1928–29, his first full season and the one in which he began his Test career, remains the Australian record. In 1931–32 he scored 1190 runs against the touring South Africans, the record by one batsman against any visiting team. In 1947–48 his twelve first-class innings included a record eight centuries.

Born in the New South Wales township of Cootamundra, Bradman lived his early life in Bowral and unwittingly taught himself the basis of batting by throwing a golf ball against a large brick water tank and hitting the rebound two-handed with a small stump. His magnificent out fielding owed much to a similar exercise that involved throwing a ball against the upper rail of an open fence and catching the rebounds. His early cricket was played on concrete wickets with a matting cover. On those steeply bouncing surfaces he evolved a technique that enabled him to keep the ball down and stood him in good stead when he began playing grade cricket in Sydney on turf pitches. Such was his mastery of the artificial surfaces that he once added 100 runs off 22 balls in three eight-ball overs. This incredible display occurred in November 1931 at Blackheath, a Blue Mountains town some sixty miles west of Sydney. Playing for Blackheath against Lithgow in a match celebrating the opening of an experimental malthoid pitch, Bradman, having scored 38 off the first over he received, later produced the following sequence: 66424461/64466464/*661*446. The asterisks denote singles scored by his partner, Wendell Bill.

He had watched just two days of first-class cricket – during the fifth Test at Sydney in 1921 – before embarking on his own first-class career. Bradman was completely self-taught as far as technique was concerned. He claims to have never deliberately copied any other player's method. He had an unusual stance, placing the bat between his feet rather than behind his back foot. His pick-up was not text-book vertical but angled towards the slips. Sometimes when he completed a pull shot he would finish up with one foot behind the stumps in the bowling crease. During that first tour of England in 1930, Sir Neville Cardus wrote of him: 'Bradman is not a romantic ever. He is perpetually a realist with the oldest head a boy cricketer has carried on his shoulders since W.G. Grace.'

Being a realist and an arch competitor would have counted for nothing if Bradman had not been blessed with exceptional co-ordination and superb judgement of a ball's potential length and direction from the moment it left the bowler's hand. Contrary to popular opinion, he did not possess above-average eyesight. He often moved into a preliminary position fractionally before the ball was released – forward against a slow bowler or back and across when facing the quicker stuff. Most vital to his method was his footwork. He had little feet and moved lightly and very, very quickly into the correct position.

I first met the Don in 1976 when Richie Benaud introduced us at Yalumba winery on the rest day of an Adelaide Test. He was seated at a long trestle table chatting to an eager group of famous past players. It was like coming face to face with royalty, appropriately enough I suppose as he was undoubtedly a cricketing deity. Adelaide had been his adopted home since 1934. Astonishingly small for a batsman who had extended most batting records beyond the reach of mortal men, I was immediately struck by his alert eyes, incisive mind, sharp wit and easy sense of humour. Justly proud of his achievements, he had dedicated his later life to his family, his business interests and golf, gradually, office by office, relinquishing all his ties with the administration of cricket both nationally and in his state. On later visits to Yalumba I was invited to join that élite assembly. He even agreed to write a generous foreword to my *Wisden Book of Test Cricket* and another for the 1984 edition of the *Daily Telegraph Cricket Year Book* which I compiled with Michael Melford.

By 1988, the Don was very much back in the news in Australia. After shunning the media for many years he emerged in print and on radio to the vast delight of his many fans. First came two sumptuous volumes of *The Bradman Albums*, which were condensed editions of fifty-two leather-bound volumes of the Don's career prepared by the State Library of South Australia from the original scrapbooks kept by his mother, wife, relatives, friends and admirers. Then came the publication of the Bradman tapes, *The Don Declares*, an ABC Radio biography composed of eight hour-long interviews in which he straightened the record on many aspects of his brilliant but often controversial career.

When I went to see him in his eightieth summer, the first overseas player to be knighted for his services to cricket still looked as spry and fit as in his heyday fifty years earlier.

'I play golf every Saturday – A-grade – and can still get round in fewer strokes than my years,' he revealed, eyes sparkling with pride.

To visit his elegant two-storey house in Kensington, a leafy suburb of Adelaide, is to enter a cathedral of cricket. The sitting room with its piano – he once recorded some pieces for the BBC – is a treasure house of cricketana. His portrait surmounts the fireplace. Watched by Lady Jessie, his serene and devoted wife of fifty-five years, he gave wise counsel on a variety of topics. Our discussion soon involved Mike Gatting's recent on-field row with umpire Shakoor Rana.

'An umpire's decision must be accepted, however incompetent he might be. If you don't accept his authority, you have anarchy. The time to complain is off the field afterwards. I don't agree with the idea of selecting umpires for Test matches from a panel of the best officials, regardless of nationality. That would inevitably restrict the field to English and perhaps some Australian umpires because they are the most experienced. How would umpires from other countries ever gain the experience necessary to reach that level? I think that the home country's best umpires should officiate throughout each series.'

Computerised scoreboards now dominate the Test arenas at Sydney and Melbourne. As well as match details, in 1987–88 the giant screens presented the crowd with slow-motion replays of run-outs and stumpings. Bradman was convinced that the umpires should be able to examine these replays before making their decision.

'It is ridiculous that millions of viewers should have the benefit of this aid when umpires do not. But I would not support its use for lbws. There the umpire's unique positioning to exercise judgement should remain dominant.'

His reaction confirmed that, although a renowned traditionalist, he was not totally averse to change, especially if he thought it might be to a batsman's advantage. Many retired players of Bradman's era were scathing in their views on the use of helmets. The Don did not share them. 'If someone had produced a batting helmet during the 1932–33 (bodyline) series, I would certainly have worn it.'

As a statistician, I have long considered that maiden overs should be removed from bowling analyses and records. During the last hundred years the over has varied between 4, 5, 6 and 8 balls. To add such entities together is a mathematical absurdity. Maidens have no significance as far as the result of a match is concerned, nor do they affect personal averages. Since no-balls and wides became universally debited to bowling analyses in 1984–85, any over containing one of these penalties cannot be a maiden even if it includes no runs from the bat. Sir Donald shared my view. 'Any reference to maiden overs has long since become anachronistic and serves no useful purpose,' he said.

John Inverarity, former captain of both Western and South Australia, lived two doors away from Bradman. How close was Invers to becoming captain of Australia instead of Graham Yallop in 1978–79 when England won 5–1?

'I don't know. I wasn't a selector then. But he wasn't a good enough player to get in as a batsman and that prevented him from being captain. By the same token, Mike Brearley would never have skippered Australia,' the Don replied.

Bradman played his 52 Tests over a period of 20 years. Sunil Gavaskar amassed his world record aggregates of 10,122 runs and 34 hundreds during 125 Tests in just 16 years. I asked if he realised that, had he maintained his Test average of 99.94, with a century every 2.75 innings, and enjoyed the same number of completed innings as Gavaskar (198), he would have finished with the useful tallies of 19,788 runs and 77 centuries.

'What makes you think I would only have maintained my average?' he asked. 'If I had had the opportunity of playing in India, Pakistan and Sri Lanka, I think I might have increased it.'

When I suggested that the local umpires might have made sure that he did not hang around too long, he retorted, 'They can't give you out if you hit it for four!' He obviously had not been there.

Soon after my visit, the Bradmans flew to Sydney to attend the Bicentenary celebrations, including the commemorative Test against England. It was fitting that Australia's oldest surviving captain be taken on a lap of honour around the historic SCG turf. His record as a leader was also a tribute to one of the greatest cricketers of all time – 24 Tests, 15 wins, 3 defeats and 6 draws.

I, too, was on my way to Sydney and my first mission on arrival on the eve of the Bicentennial Test was to telephone Sir Donald Bradman's old adversary, Harold Larwood, who had been resident there since 1950. The eyesight may have failed but Larwood's voice with its unblemished Nottinghamshire accent was as strong and cheery as ever and I was soon taxi-bound to see him.

We had first met in 1977 when Nottinghamshire had flown him home to share their celebrations of the Royal Jubilee. He had sat next to me in the *Test Match Special* commentary box chatting about his career to Brian Johnston. It was during an interval of the Centenary Test in Melbourne a few months earlier that I had first set eyes on him. On that occasion, he had taken a mid-pitch bow with his old bowling partner, Bill Voce, and received a tumultuous welcome from the vast crowd.

'Bit different from the last time we were here, Bill,' remarked Harold, referring to the 1932–33 tour. Voce's reply was to hand Larwood his coat and pace out his run at the end from which fellow left-armer John Lever had been bowling. It was a tribute to Bill Voce's strength that his run was barely half the length of Lever's and his contemporaries insist he was a yard or two faster.

When a storm felled the famous Trent Bridge elm known as 'George Parr's Tree' in January 1976, former Nottinghamshire captain and England opening batsman Reg Simpson had arranged for his company, Gunn and Moore, to make a limited edition of miniature bats from the timber. A treasured possession of mine is one of those tiny but noticeably heavy bats bearing the signatures of Larwood and Voce.

When I last saw him in 1988, almost fifty-five years had passed since Harold Larwood ended his controversial Test career at the Sydney Cricket Ground. It was a notable finale, completing England's decisive 4–1 victory in the infamous 'bodyline' rubber. Larwood's five wickets in that match brought his tally for the series to 33 at a cost of 19.51 runs apiece. Furious at being sent to bat at number four as night-watchman after bowling 32.2 overs with a splintered bone in the ball of his left foot, he tried to run himself out before the close. He hit the ball to cover-point and called Hammond for an impossible run. Bradman collected the ball as they crossed in mid-pitch, hurled it at the stumps at the bowler's end and missed. Larwood thus opened his account with a five.

Next morning the mob on the Hill exhorted the Australian bowlers to 'knock the bastard's bloody head off'. In 140 minutes he rattled up 98, hooking and square-cutting nine fours and straight driving a six. Going for his century in the grand manner, he miscued an on-drive and skied the ball to Bert 'Dainty' Ironmonger at mid-on. 'Dainty was a hopeless fielder,' grinned Larwood. 'Couldn't stop a tram. But the beggar clung on to that one.'

The crowd that had vilified him for bowling 'bodyline' treated him to a rapturous reception as he returned to the pavilion. 'They gave me a standing ovation. They were cheering and jumping up in the air. They like a fighter in Australia.'

Since 1950 he had lived just three miles from that famous ground in a cosy house at Kingsford. If the wind was right, he could hear the Hillites in full cry when a major match was in progress. Then 83 and blind, his handshake revealed the immense strength that had made this little former miner from Nuncargate the most feared fast bowler of all time. For two hours I was welcomed into his home, still kept spick and span by Lois, his wife of more than sixty years, and listened enthralled as he returned to that turbulent series. So turbulent was it that an exchange of cables between the Australian Board and MCC, then the governing body of English cricket, threatened to end the tour and sever relations between the two authorities.

Fast leg-theory involved short-pitched bowling aimed at the batsman's torso and head with a menacing ring of close legside catchers to take the ball as it was fended away. It was employed with the solitary objective of curbing Bradman's exceptional appetite for large scores. The Don's genius had created an imbalance between bat and ball that needed to be rectified if England were to regain the Ashes.

According to Larwood, during his innings of 232 in the fifth Test at The Oval in 1930, Bradman had been uncomfortable when facing short-pitched bowling on his leg stump. The Don strenuously denied this and claimed it was merely an excuse to justify the leg-theory plan with its packed onside field. Devised by England's captain, Douglas Jardine, around the accuracy and speed of Larwood and his left-handed Nottinghamshire partner, Bill Voce, it was to prove outstandingly successful. Bradman was confined to 396 runs at 56.57, four times falling victim to Larwood.

The term 'bodyline' was originated virtually by accident on the opening day of the series by Hugh Buggy of the *Melbourne Herald*. Soon after MCC's match against an Australian XI in Melbourne, Buggy had read an article by Jack Worrall. The former Victoria and Australia batsman had used the phrase 'half-pitched slingers on the body line'. Buggy had to send his match reports by telegraph and, needing a concise phrase to catch the lunch-time edition, sent: 'Voce was hit for six, again bodyline bowling'. It was his shorthand telegraphed form of 'bowling on the line of the body'.

Back in the sports office of the *Melbourne Herald*, my friend Ray Robinson, then a sub-editor, latched on to the word 'bodyline' and decided to use it as a headline. His editor, Syd Deamer, forbade it but allowed the word to remain within Buggy's report. So, by an extraordinary sequence of events, the most contentious term in cricket's long history was originated. Ray played down his own role in seizing upon Buggy's phrase but he admitted that as soon as he saw the word 'bodyline' he knew he had found the ideal term for a type of bowling that writers were struggling to describe using a single word.

Back in England after the tour, Larwood was told to apologise to the MCC for his bowling. As he had been obeying Jardine's instructions, he not surprisingly refused. From that moment, he was ignored by England's selectors and, disillusioned, he soon retired from first-class cricket. In 1950 he sold his confectionery shop in Blackpool and, accompanied by his wife and five daughters, sailed for Australia on the *Orontes*, the very ship that had carried the MCC team there in 1932. He found much happiness in Australia and, by 1988, those five daughters had given him thirteen grandchildren and four great-grandchildren. Despite his disability, he could easily find his way around the house the family moved to soon after his arrival. As we looked at his team photographs, his memory of the whereabouts of each player was so uncanny that his blindness was soon forgotten. His impressions of his playing career were so vivid that it was hard to accept that he was describing events that had occurred more than fifty years ago.

Until John Major intervened in 1993 and he was belatedly awarded the MBE, all honours lists passed him by and his lifestyle was in stark contrast to that of the Don in his affluent Adelaide suburb. Larwood's proudest possession was a silver ashtray presented by Douglas Jardine. It is inscribed: 'To Harold for the Ashes. 1932–33. From a grateful skipper.'

We had a beer together and he presented me with a revised edition of his book *The Larwood Story*, sightlessly signing it for me guided by his wife. I photographed them both in front of their house as I waited for my taxi, two delightful people who still cared deeply about each other. Their diamond wedding anniversary in September 1987 had been commemorated by greetings cables from the Queen and Nottinghamshire County Cricket Club. They had also received one from H.S.T.L. 'Stork' Henry, the Australian Test all-rounder then aged 92 and enjoying his sixty-second year of marriage. As I once again felt myself on the receiving end of Larwood's powerful handshake, it was easier to reconcile the personality of this gentle old man with that of cricket's most devastating fast bowler.

FIFTEEN

NEW ZEALAND

My GREAT AUNT Marion, an outstanding nurse who was awarded the Royal Red Cross for her First World War service, was my first contact with New Zealand. She had married an ANZAC soldier whom she had nursed in Plymouth Hospital and had emigrated to the Land of the Long White Cloud in 1932. Twenty years later, spurred on by her niece, my mother, I began writing to her. Apart from wanting to know about New Zealand, I was a keen collector of stamps. She seemed pleased to hear from her great nephew and all went well until 28 March 1955 when Len Hutton's team, having successfully defended the Ashes, laid siege to New Zealand in Auckland and dismissed them for a paltry 26, still the lowest total in all Test cricket. When I foolishly boasted about this feat to my great aunt, a major boost to my burgeoning stamp collection ceased abruptly. Nearly thirty years later and long after her innings had ended, I visited her house in Manurewa, a few miles south of Auckland. The current occupants showed me round and it was fascinating to stand in the rooms where she had lived her later life and written those letters to me. Later, I inherited her collection of photo albums. David McNeill, her younger brother, retrieved them when she died and they were among the McNeill heirlooms that Eadith left me. The photos featured Great Aunt Marion's early life in the Sussex village of Burwash and the servicemen she nursed during the Great War.

After scoring England's 1982–83 tour of Australia, I spent a fort-night driving around the North and South Islands. to set up an expedition for the Maltamaniacs the following year. In 1983 New Zealand was very much like England was in the 1950s, with quiet roads and a sparse population. The proportions of three million people, a third congregated in Auckland, and sixty million sheep was virtually the converse of Britain's and far more acceptable. The population, unstressed by overcrowding, was exceptionally friendly and the scenery breathtaking. One could drive from the southern extreme of South Island to the tip of its northern neighbour in a week, crossing the Cook Strait by means of the Picton-Wellington ferry. Scenery ranged from fiords and glaciers to sub-tropical fruit farms.

Setting up a three-week cricket tour of New Zealand was an absolute doddle. The Auckland Cricket Society insisted that we start our programme with a match on Eden Park's Number 2 Oval, itself a first-class venue. Sir Jack Newman offered to supply coaches and drivers at generous rates, Glenn Turner organised a match at Alexandria and Ian Walter arranged a game on the Basin Reserve Test Ground in Wellington.

Ian Walter (1948–87) was a remarkable and humorous man with an abiding love for sport and for his country. He was a qualified librarian with an MA degree, a regular contributor to the New Zealand *Listener*, a single-figure handicap golfer, an expert on hockey, and the author of a book on soccer. In between, he ran several marathons, survived a shipwreck and revolutionised New Zealand's television coverage of cricket and golf. Cricket was Ian's major passion and, as an off-spin bowler and left-handed batsman, he represented Canterbury and Wellington 'B' teams in addition to captaining New Zealand Universities on a tour of Australia.

I first met Ian when he came to England as New Zealand's official scorer in 1973. He played in a one-day game against Scotland but he was destined never to play first-class cricket, although Wellington once selected him shortly before he fractured a bone in his foot. During a net practice at Lord's before the start of the tour, Jim Laker had his first sight of the visitors and was immediately impressed with a youngster flighting off-breaks to Glenn Turner. It was Ian. 'I should let someone else do the scoring,' Laker suggested laconically.

Ian skippered a tyro called Richard Hadlee at Christchurch Boys' High School, captained Jeremy Coney at the Wellington Club, Onslow, and won the Wellington Cricket Player of the Year award. He had been Graham Dowling's opening partner in Christchurch and the future Kiwi captain's pads accompanied him aboard the *Wahine* when it sailed from Lyttelton harbour, Christchurch, bound for Wellington in 1968. In the early hours of 10 April, the 8948-ton ferry, a steamer express and pride of the Union Steam Ship Company's fleet, battled her way northwards from Cook Strait into Chaffers Passage, the narrow entrance leading to Wellington harbour. Suddenly the ship was struck by a storm of unprecedented ferocity, the gale whipping the sea into steep waves and reducing visibility to zero. The radar system was put out of action and the ship struck Barrett Reef, a chain of jagged rocks in the centre of the passage. By now her engines were out of action. Severely holed, she drifted a few hundred yards before foundering off Fort Dorset.

Ian swam two-thirds of a mile to the eastern shore, his exceptional stamina enabling him to combat those mountainous seas and survive a disaster in which fifty-one people lost their lives. Describing the experience many years later, he said that the incident he recalled most vividly was of a baby being thrown from the ship to rescuers in a lifeboat, only for a large wave to lift the boat out of reach as the child was in mid-air.

He joined NZBC (now TVNZ) in 1974 as a researcher in the sports office. By the 1979–80 season he was in charge of cricket. It was Ian Walter who introduced the pitch microphones much maligned by England's management in 1988. Among the other innovations to earn him worldwide respect were camera cover from both ends and a system of computer scoring that was far in advance of the one used in Australia. Perhaps his only misguided experiment was to invite me to join his commentary team for England's 1983–84 tour. When I photographed commentator Glenn Turner slumbering contentedly in the commentary box, Ian startled the victim by putting the shot on air while he was actually talking – several times. He also encouraged me to suggest to Turner that Jeremy Coney's mother had invented radio (Ma Coney). Surprisingly, I was asked back two years later.

In 1984 Ian married Sally Guinness, who had been his PA during his early years as a producer. They enjoyed one blissful year of marriage before he collapsed with cancer of the sinuses. Three weeks after brain surgery he won the match (top-scoring and taking 3 for 8) in an annual game between the TVNZ staff of Auckland and Wellington, a fixture that he had instituted five years earlier. Later that year, after massive radiotherapy, he covered the Commonwealth Games in Edinburgh, scored an unbeaten century for my Maltamaniacs in Farnham's cricket week, and went hiking around the Swiss Alps with his wife and Glenn Turner's golfing brother, Greg. He returned to Wellington, relapsed, lost his sight and, nursed by Sally, bravely outlived his physician's predictions by six months.

The Ian Walter Memorial Trophy is now awarded by the New Zealand Sporting Journalists' Association to the sports writer of the year. It is a most fitting tribute. Few men have crammed half as many activities into thirty-nine years or contributed more to their nation's enjoyment of sport.

New Zealand's Test match grounds are, with the solitary exception of Wellington's Basin Reserve, primarily rugby amphitheatres with cricket a poor tenant. Auckland's Eden Park, Christchurch's Lancaster Park and Dunedin's Carisbrook are all concrete edifices with scant atmosphere. Eden Park began its sporting life as a cricket ground built over a reclaimed lake that had originally been formed within a volcano. Only its original wooden cricket pavilion initially survived the ground's conversion to a soulless stadium. In 1984 it still housed the clubrooms, library and trophies of the Auckland Cricket Society. A splendidly convivial haven, windows had been added to give its members excellent views of play both on the Test arena and behind to the adjacent ground where Auckland play most of their first-class matches. It was this reserve ground that provided the venue for a Leap Day match between my Maltamaniacs and an ACS side captained by Dave Crowe, father of Jeff and Martin. Dave had been a capable batsman, sufficiently handy to have represented both Wellington and Canterbury (not at the same time). His team that day included former Test stars Bert Sutcliffe and John Sparling, who both scored fifties, richly entertaining us with their strokeplay. It was a tremendous thrill to bowl to Sutcliffe, one of New Zealand's greatest batsmen. Playing his final innings in any grade of cricket, he scored a chanceless 63 off 72 balls. Until Brian Lara amassed his undefeated 501 in 1994, Sutcliffe's 385 for Otago against Canterbury at Lancaster Park, Christchurch, in 1952–53 was the highest first-class score by a left-hander.

The evening in the clubrooms was one of the highlights of a superb tour. The ACS in general and Graham Burgess in particular were most generous hosts. Graham's brother, Gordon, managed New Zealand's 1969 tour of England and his nephew, Mark, captained the Kiwis in ten Tests. Besides being a most active member of the ACS, Graham prepared the pitches at Cornwall Park, a delightful, tree-surrounded ground immediately beneath Auckland's famous One Tree Hill, where I was privileged to play in several friendly matches.

Walter Hammond (he whom Fred Trueman always referred to as 'the great Wally') set records galore at Eden Park in 1933 when he amassed 336 not out, the highest innings in Test matches until Hutton's 364 five and a half years later. He scored 295 on the second day (only Bradman with 309 at Headingley in 1930 has exceeded him), including 111 before lunch. His time of 288 minutes remains the fastest for scoring a triple century in Test cricket, while his 240-minute double century is the England record in terms of time rather than fewest balls received. In Test cricket, Hammond's tally of ten sixes in that innings remained the record for 64 years. He also stroked 34 fours, his total of 196 in boundaries being second only to John Edrich's 238 during his 310 not out against New Zealand at Headingley in 1965. Not surprisingly, Hammond's series average of 563.00 also remains a world record.

Three of Hammond's sixes came off consecutive balls from Jack

Newman's left-arm seamers. Knighted in 1978, Sir Jack was extremely generous when my team toured six years later. Besides arranging a game in his native Nelson, he provided us with his best coaches and driver-guides for our three-week tour. He even invited us to his clothing store and gave each of our touring party a hand-knitted sweater.

For the first time in Auckland's history, club cricket was played on the Saturday of an Eden Park Test in 1984. On big match days the No. 2 ground is used as the main car park. By a stroke of luck, I spent the Friday evening at a barbecue held at the house of Roger Seaton, the Auckland Cricket Board member who controlled the parking arrangements. After much falling-over water, I persuaded that émigré from Leeds, and former captain of the local Birkenhead City Cricket Club, to arrange Saturday's cars in rows of red, white and blue to boost England's effort. The following morning this master plan was brought to fruition. Scores of cars were segregated into the three colours of the Union Jack in swathes across the adjacent ground. With the ball holding sway over the bat and runs being eked out a snail's pace, TV cameramen focused frequently on the bizarre parkathon. Many spectators decided to leave the lacklustre Test early and either go home or follow the club action at The Domain, Davenport, Papatatoetoe and Takapuna. Faced with serried ranks of cars of the same colour, few were able to find their chariots before play ended. It was a scene of splendid confusion and both Roger and I kept a very low profile that evening.

That day will be better remembered for the luckless Martyn Moxon being out for 99. The supreme irony of this frustrating score was revealed later. Early in his innings, a well-timed sweep for three runs off Bracewell had been signalled as leg-byes by umpire Rodger McHarg, standing in only his second Test. The bowler subsequently admitted that the ball came off Moxon's bat. The Yorkshireman earned full marks for diplomacy when he said, 'I don't want to make a fuss about that and I'm not claiming those runs.' He was only the ninth England player (and fourth Yorkshireman) to perish on 99 in the course of 644 Tests to that point. The most recent one had been Graham Gooch whom I saw run himself out attempting a ridiculous single to mid-on to complete his maiden Test century, at Melbourne in 1979–80. I can still recall the horror-stricken expression on the face of his wife Brenda when the TV cameras picked her out as Goochie began his desolate walk back.

One of the other three Yorkshiremen to perish on 99 in a Test was Geoffrey Boycott. I saw him in the ACS committee room after play. 'I were a bloody greyhound compared with this lot,' he growled at the assembled company, referring to England's scoring rate. Realising that he had an audience and referring to an imaginative lbw decision that Rodger McHarg had awarded against Martin Crowe, Boycott tested the piece he had just written for a newspaper: 'Visiting sides have been saying for years how atrocious your umpires are. It's only now they've sawn off your best player that you realise we're right!'

I was covering the 1984 series as cricket correspondent of *The Mail on Sunday*. The announcement of Hadlee's temporary retirement following a leg injury came as a boon that Sunday morning. The time difference of thirteen hours allowed London papers to carry a report of play up to 2.00 p.m. New Zealand time (1.00 a.m. in Britain). My paper could carry a full report of Saturday's play together with a 'runner' describing Sunday's proceedings during the pre-lunch session and for twenty minutes afterwards. This facility demanded that I virtually commentated live by telephone to a copytaker on the sports desk in London. I much preferred sending copy through a Tandy portable computer/word-processor linked to the phone but Bidelia Corrigan, an émigré from Brisbane, eased my ordeal with her extraordinary patience during a late night-shift at the other end of the ether. That Auckland Test's only claim to fame lay in the fact that out of ten Test matches scheduled to include play on 29 February, this was the first to end on a Leap Day! Another 'first' that final day was the news of Jeff Crowe's removal from the captaincy because of his poor batting form. It was sad news for both camps. He was a friendly, popular character who communicated easily and had always handled press conferences with more enthusiasm and common sense than most of his recent England counterparts. He was the first New Zealand captain to be removed from office during a home series. Three others – Harry Cave (1956), Murray Chapple (1966) and Barry Sinclair (1968) – stood down because of ill health or injury.

A bizarre episode from the Auckland Test that sticks in the mind featured a fight on the outfield between two magpies. They stood side by side watching play, apparently secure in the knowledge that they were in absolutely no danger of being hit by the ball, until the TV cameras showed an interest in them. As soon as they were thrust into viewers' living rooms, they started fighting like mad. It was a most dramatic scrap involving beak sparring, jumping, diving, mid-air combat and chasing round in tight circuits, all beautifully filmed in the style of an Attenborough Zoo Quest. When the producer decided he had better get back to the cricket, they immediately stopped fighting and resumed their dignified watch.

Christchurch's Lancaster Park was anything but pretty. Until recently, its spectator amenities were virtually non-existent, unless you happened to be a committee member or were invited to one of a handful of hospitality boxes. There was no watering hole from which you could watch the cricket. I was scoring for TVNZ in 1984 when New Zealand won by an innings and 132 runs, their record margin of victory in this series, after only 11 hours 41 minutes of actual play. For the first time since 1894–95, England had suffered the ignominy of being dismissed for under 100 in both innings. Some spicy accounts circulated of the England dressing-room door being lined with wet towels to confine the aroma coming from within.

In 1988 I was in the Lancaster Park press box on the opening morning of England's Test series when Richard Hadlee needed to take just one wicket to overhaul Ian Botham's world record Test match tally of 373. I could already see the headline to my piece: 'HADLEE BREAKS RECORD ON HIS HOME GROUND'. It would be the bowling equivalent of Boycott scoring his hundredth first-class century in the 1977 Test against Australia at his native Headingley.

Certainly Richard Hadlee richly deserved that record. He had equalled Botham's record aggregate of 373 wickets in 21 fewer matches and with 1774 fewer balls. He also had the superior strike-rate of 51.0 balls per wicket compared with Botham's 55.7, and a lower average of runs per wicket — 22.32 compared with 27.86. Surprisingly, he had taken 196 wickets in 37 Tests overseas compared with 177 in 36 matches in New Zealand. His 32 instances of five or more wickets in an innings and eight of ten or more in a match were then both Test records.

Richard Hadlee was a highly professional cricketer, almost as obsessive about his fitness and pre-match preparation as Geoffrey Boycott. He was probably a decade ahead of his time in adhering to a rigid training discipline. His 1984 'double' for Nottinghamshire was the product of meticulous target-setting. His bowling action was as rhythmic and smoothly honed as any in the history of the game. Designed to produce maximum effect from a minimum of effort, it was a perfect sideways-on example from which his varied hand-actions and subtle changes of pace could propel a bewildering catalogue of deliveries. Richard Hadlee was the Mean Machine of bowlers and by far the most dangerous New Zealand had produced.

The thought that Hadlee might fail to capture a single wicket in that three-match series never entered anyone's head. When the press box ran a sweep on the number of balls Hadlee would bowl before putting everyone out of their misery, the highest was 67 by Peter Roebuck (*Sunday Times* and then captain of Somerset). John Thicknesse, a master bookie thinly disguised as the cricket correspondent of the London *Evening Standard*, was involved in the identity of victim No. 374 and predictably Martyn Moxon was easily the favourite. Just in case all that activity was insufficient to tempt fate, I had been rash enough to set as the opening question in a quiz in the imminent new edition of the *Playfair Cricket Annual*: 'Whom did Richard Hadlee dismiss to become the leading wicket-taker in Test cricket?'

Walter Hadlee, captain of the 1949 New Zealanders and Richard's father, sowed the first seeds of doubt when I had asked him if the champagne was on ice. Sitting just below our press area, Wally solemnly rebuked me. 'Remember Leeds in 1983, our first win in England? Richard bowled 47 overs in that match and didn't take a wicket.'

Conditions were perfect for swing bowling when Hadlee took the new ball, a 'Kookaburra', at 11.00 on a battleship grey morning. It was humid and the heavy cloud obliterating most of the Cashmere Hills would have done Old Trafford proud. His first ball, from the Southern End to the left-handed Chris Broad, was allowed through to wicket-keeper Ian Smith. His second pitched on off stump before snaking past the bat's groping edge. The third swung in late to strike the pad. Hadlee leapt in the air, forefingers aloft as he roared his appeal, and landed astride the pitch. 'Not out,' was Steve Woodward's verdict. Hadlee's Nottinghamshire colleague played at and missed the next one before safely middling the last two balls.

Those with numbers 7 to 12 in the sweep grinned smugly as Hadlee began his second dramatic over, to Moxon. The first ball was pushed nervously to mid-on, the second was edged into the pad, and the next, a swinging yorker, was stabbed out at the last second. Hadlee polished the ball harder and, straining for extra pace and bounce on the slow surface, committed the rare mistake of over-stepping. Two deliveries later he beat the Yorkshire right-hander all ends up, shaving bat and off stump by the narrowest of margins. So the saga dragged on. Soon Hadlee looked under more pressure than the batsman. The crowd, much smaller than anticipated, tried to boost his efforts with chants of 'Had-lee! Had-lee!' as he ran in, arms parallel to thighs like a sprinter. It was all to no avail and he reluctantly ended his first spell after 56 minutes, 7-2-16-0.

Wally Hadlee sat at the end of a small VIP enclosure, chatting animatedly with two other former Test players, Jack Kerr and Sir Jack Newman. Throughout those seven overs his reactions to his son's frustrations were recorded by a TV camera crew. He handled it with great aplomb.

England had reached 50 for 1 when Hadlee returned for the last three pre-lunch overs from our end. Broad was in touch by then and steered two offside boundaries. Five more overs immediately after lunch were equally unsuccessful and Wally Hadlee's grim reminder about Leeds in 1983 began to bear more significance. At 3.21 p.m.

Hadlee came back for the last three overs before tea from our City End. Tim Robinson safely blocked a yorker and off-drove the second ball imperiously for four. A thundering straight-drive was brilliantly fielded by the bowler, diving forward. Soon afterwards, with two balls remaining before the interval, Hadlee gingerly felt the back of his lower leg and completed his over off a four-pace mini-run. He had bowled 18 overs and been no-balled eight times, probably more than in an entire season of first-class cricket in England. The camera crew left Walter Hadlee to have his tea. If his son did manage to snare his elusive wicket, Peter Roebuck would carry off the sweep, his 67 balls being the outsider in a closely packed field.

But Richard Hadlee did not return. The irony of his injury was enhanced when he said, 'I had never broken down in a Test before or left the field for more than fifteen minutes.' The damage was diagnosed as a sprained calf muscle and it was packed in ice – probably the ice that had been ordered for the champagne. His father's wry look from across the gangway said, 'I told you so.'

Next morning I anticipated a severe reprimand when Wally beckoned me to join him in his enclosure and was a tad mystified when he showed me his copy of the *Wisden Book of Obituaries*. 'You work for these publishers, Bill. What can I do about this section?' he asked, showing me some totally blank pages. I said that he should write to them and I would make a call to ensure he received a replacement copy. Looking up at our press area, Wally said he wanted to meet Peter Roebuck, which I was happy to arrange. Wally showed him the faulty section of the book. Totally oblivious to the significance of the book's title and trying to be sympathetic, Peter said, 'That's bad luck, Wally. Were you on that page?'

Fourteen years passed before I returned to Christchurch in the role of *TMS* scorer at the start of England's 2002 tour. I soon discovered that something nasty had happened to my printer during the flight. It was responding to my laptop's bidding but would only produce the most alarming whirring and metallic crunching sounds. After much trade directory searching and a $20 taxi journey, I delivered it to a suitable repairer. Later in the day I received a call to tell me that the cause of the problem was £1.15 – the total of the coins that had slipped from a plastic packet into the machine's innards while it was in my briefcase. The cost of the repair was $78 (£25).

Played on a drop-in Lancaster Park pitch that started damp, the opening Test of that 2002 three-match series was full of drama and inspired performances. Nasser Hussain lost a vital toss and, inevitably put in to bat, England lost two wickets without a run scored. A tenacious 244-ball innings of 106 by their captain took the tourists to 228, but that modest total assumed almost gargantuan proportions when Matthew Hoggard's late outswing snared 7 for 63 and gained a lead of 81. A low-scoring match and at least a day's wine-tasting were in prospect when England collapsed to 106 for 5 at their second attempt. Then, as the pitch dried into a featherbed, Graham Thorpe and Andrew Flintoff turned the match on its head with a record England sixth-wicket stand of 281, Thorpe's undefeated 200 being his highest score in Test cricket while Freddie notched his maiden hundred (137) at that level. The hosts were set to score 550 off a minimum of 201 overs, a seemingly impossible target considering the record winning fourth-innings score was then 406.

Nathan Astle almost achieved the impossible with the innings of his life. Without doubt it was the most exhilarating and prolonged exhibition of audacious strokeplay that I have ever seen. His first hundred took him 114 balls in 148 minutes and included two sixes and 17 fours. His second took a mere 39 balls in just 69 minutes, his 153-ball double-century being the fastest in Test cricket history. He had scored 134 when the ninth wicket fell and he was joined by an injured – and reluctant – Chris Cairns accompanied by a runner. Cairns blocked two balls from Andrew Caddick, whose analysis was then 6 for 77. The pair savaged 23 runs, including a six apiece, from Hoggard's next over. Astle drove 38 off Caddick's next seven balls (4664666). The final straight hit lost the ball and compelled an early drinks break. Caddick was expelled to pasture with his plundered analysis reading 6 for 122. The fifty partnership came from 24 balls in 21 minutes. Ashley Giles stemmed their flow by bowling slow left-arm over the wicket into the legside rough and conceded only three singles in as many overs but the carnage continued against the pace of Flintoff and Hoggard. The hundred partnership came from 55 balls in 46 minutes and the target dropped into double figures as the scoreboard clicked past 450.

With defeat in prospect, England's fielders grew alarmed. Up to then they had weathered the storm by assuming that eventually Astle would make an error and be caught in the deep or bowled, but it wasn't until 5.07 on the fourth evening that Hoggard ended one of the most astonishing innings of all time. A slower short-pitched ball, well outside Astle's off stump, lured him into a square-cut and a top edge to the keeper. England had won by 98 runs but Astle, with 222 off 168 balls, won all the plaudits. His tally of 11 sixes in a Test innings was second only to Wasim Akram's 12.

A few days before that Test, Lancaster Park had staged a major rugby match, necessitating a drop-in pitch for the cricket. Tickets for the rugby had been at a premium and Christopher Martin-Jenkins had been overjoyed to purchase the last one available. He soon realised why nobody had wanted his seat. Set in a far corner among a sea of scaffolding, its entire view of the action was restricted to the goalpost area immediately to his right.

I had spent the week's interval between the limited-overs frolics and the Test series at Karaka Point, a headland in the hills overlooking Marlborough Sound. My temporary haven was a sumptuous bed and breakfast chalet with panoramic views stretching around three sides of the headland. The extensive wooden bungalow had a decking verandah on two sides giving views of the water and hills from Picton on the distant left to a mile or so up the Sound towards North Island. There was a constant flow of boats – yachts, cruisers, ferries and barges. This was March and the early autumn weather was perfect, similar to June in England without the rain.

No breakfast has bettered those I enjoyed on the verandah, watching the Wellington ferries sail towards nearby Picton, preceded by a brace of playful dolphins. It required monumental discipline to retreat to my laptop and complete the final copy sending and proof-checking for the 2002 edition of *Playfair*. For once, the technology was without hazard and using a modem and phone line I was able to send, receive, check and amend all 304 pages and meet my deadline. With the exception of excellent dinners featuring the local smoked salmon provided by my generous hosts, I withstood all temptations apart from the irresistible lure of the Marlborough vineyards barely half an hour's drive distant. Most had free tastings and excellent restaurants. It didn't help that I had rented a rogue car that automatically detected and navigated itself to wineries throughout the two major islands.

Despite the attractions of Karaka Point, if I were to make my home in New Zealand, I would probably choose to live in Wellington. Tucked neatly away in a vast bay, confusingly named Port Nicholson, it is situated in the very south of the North Island. That central location has made it an obvious choice as New Zealand's capital city since 1865. Built on a fault line and subject to numerous minuscule earth tremors each year, Wellington is excitingly hilly and often alarmingly windy. Many of its third of a million-strong population live like troglodytes in houses burrowed into the hillside or perched precariously on vicious slopes. Most domestic buildings are wooden, because of the risk of earthquakes, timber being more pliable than bricks and mortar. Hillside residences with access roads are in great demand and highly priced, the alternative being extremely steep footpaths up which all shopping and deliveries have to be carried. The city itself is a thriving commercial centre with a wide necklace of high-rise office blocks. Unlike the haphazard monstrosities in Auckland, most of Wellington's new architecture is pleasing and many buildings share similar features, an arch motif being especially popular.

The aptly named Beehive is the most striking of Wellington's parliament buildings, while the Government Building (1876) is thought to be the largest wooden structure in the world. The best vantage point is the summit of Mount Victoria, from where the breathtaking view takes in the whole city, the harbour, the airport, which is situated dramatically between Mounts Victoria and Cook, and the Basin Reserve itself. Originally a lake, the Basin was elevated into a swamp by the 1855 earthquake before being drained by prison labour. It was the only New Zealand Test ground where cricket did not have to play second fiddle to rugby. Completely surrounded by a one-way road system, it could claim to be the only venue where Test cricket is played on a traffic island within a city. Protected by Act of Parliament, the Basin Reserve, which staged its first match in 1868, is New Zealand's only sports ground to gain a place on the National Heritage List.

Although many of its capacity 11,600 spectators watch from a grassy bank on the eastern side of the ground, the press, radio and TV facilities are sited along a vast gondola in the roof of the members' R.A. Vance stand. Although this giant gantry provides a panoramic view of the ground, Mount Victoria and the approaches to the airport, it is seldom warm. When a southerly is blowing, it is positively freezing. The wind blows into your face before rebounding off the wall behind you to attack on a second flank.

In addition to scoring five Test matches at the Basin, I had the honour of skippering the Maltamaniacs to victory on the main square in 1984 when we won a most enjoyable contest against the Midlands-St Pats Cricket Club. The fixture was confirmed only after protracted negotiations with groundsman Wes Armstrong, who tried to prevent the game being played despite our hosts having booked the ground months in advance.

Our scorer for that match and throughout my tour of New Zealand was Cheryl Styles. Based in Johnsonville, she scored for that club and also for Wellington in first-class and limited-overs games. One of the first to use the linear method, she soon progressed to scoring Test matches at the Basin Reserve, usually for the visiting countries. She operated from within one of the most shambolic scoreboards on the international circuit. Players' names were assembled, letter-by-letter, on sticky back plastic and pressed to its green background. Sometimes the odd letter fell off. Sometimes they ran out of a letter and had to put up another one sideways or back to front. Mike Selvey memorably described the overall effect as looking like a ransom note.

Cheryl, the only international scorer to keep our linear sheets, was one of those whose help was indispensable in keeping the Frindall XI books over three decades, joining Jacky Frindall, Wendy Wimbush, Michael Fordham, Roger Dean, Sarah Cannon, Debbie (Brown) Frindall, Sue Bullen, Carole Sangar, Jane Widmer and Andrew Roberts.

Wellington now stages its limited-overs internationals at a far less attractive, but much bigger, venue with a vastly superior capacity of 33,500. Officially named the Westpac Trust Stadium, the locals call it 'The Cake Tin'. I have scored one game there and don't plan to repeat the experience. Visibility of the playing area was poor, that of any scoreboard non-existent and a door opened into my left elbow every few minutes. The only memorable feature of the day occurred in the interval and was totally unrelated to cricket. New Zealander Peter Jackson was filming the *Lord of the Rings* trilogy. In fact, there are precious few denizens of 'Welliwood', as Wellington is now known in the film industry, who did not appear as extras in the films or were related to someone who did. During the break between innings he stood, bare-footed and with microphone in hand, directing the vast crowd as he recorded sound effects for the third film, *The Return of the Ring*. He had them shouting, murmuring, beating their chests and leaping up and down. The noise was absolutely deafening. Every time the outside door attacked my elbow, the roar invaded our commentary box where Peter Baxter was broadcasting a special feature. Heaven knows what our listeners made of it.

Carisbrook in Dunedin is the world's most southerly Test ground. Another rugby venue, until recently its facilities were minimal with just concrete terracing down its longer sides. Spectators would bring their own seats and cushions. Before a limited-overs international against Australia in 1986, I watched a group of students carry in a dilapidated sofa and set it down in the middle of the terrace on our left. The terrace soon filled and by mid-afternoon the sofa had become a focal point of noise and activity. Fights broke out and the police moved in. I later discovered that the sofa was a Trojan horse of grog, its springs and upholstery replaced by bottles.

Dunedin was settled by Scots — its name derives from Edinburgh — and some of its many fine buildings are constructed from stone imported from Scotland. The town is surrounded by much exquisite scenery and it has an albatross colony. It is also home to one of New Zealand's most famous sports broadcasters, Peter Sellers. We met during my first visit in 1983 and have kept in touch ever since. His first broadcast was almost his last. Asked to do a live interview with members of the Carisbrook catering staff on the eve of a rugby international, he asked how many pies they had in stock. Told a tally in the tens of thousands, he responded with, 'Jeez, that's a load of bloody pies!'

I had met Glenn Turner during his early days at Worcester and we enjoyed each other's company during my summers with TVNZ. I was privileged to be his house guest both in Dunedin and at his 'batch' in the lakeside resort of Wanaka. He has long enjoyed iconic status in Otago and his Indian-born wife is now the city's mayor. He introduced me to one of his most successful, if belated, protégés, Peter James Petherick. Peter was the first New Zealander to take a hat-trick in Test cricket and the second bowler after Maurice Allom to achieve that feat on his debut.

An off-spinner from Ranfurly in Central Otago, Petherick learnt his cricket on matting pitches based on concrete before moving to grass pitches at Alexandra. The presence of the Alabaster brothers, both spinners, delayed his debut for Otago until 1975–76 when Greg Alabaster, a fellow off-spinner, was unavailable before Christmas. Selector/captain Glenn Turner invited Peter for a trial and he duly made his debut at the advanced age of 33. He relied on rhythm, line and length rather than pace variations. A big turner of the ball on spin-friendly pitches such as Otago's at Carisbrook in Dunedin, his armoury was the basic one of away drift followed by off spin. He spent a fortnight practising with Turner before making his debut. His skipper shifted his line from outside off stump to middle and off and set stronger legside fields. In his initial nine first-class matches, Petherick took 42 wickets at 20.16 apiece and he was chosen for the tour of Pakistan before the start of the following season. He celebrated his 34th birthday on the flight out, 'a very expensive exercise', he remembered.

'I didn't expect to play in that opening Test in Lahore. On the eve of the match the pitch was a green top, but Glenn didn't trust them and named thirteen with me included. He didn't think they would leave all that grass on with Richard Hadlee in the side. Sure enough, the grass had all gone the next day. The pitch was white and they had called up three extra spinners during the night. There were eighteen in their dressing room when Glenn tossed and lost. So I played. We had them 55 for 4 before Javed Miandad and Asif Iqbal put on 281. I had none for 96 off about 17 eight-ball overs on a low, slow pitch and wished I could go home!'

Then, on his very first day of Test cricket, 9 October 1976, he dismissed Javed Miandad (163 on debut), Wasim Raja and Intikhab Alam with successive balls. 'Miandad was batting magnificently,' Peter recalled. 'I bowled a ball that was slightly short, he went for the big hit over square-leg and got a top edge. Raja had been waiting about four hours with his pads on. A left-hander, he came down the wicket and I anticipated the turn would take his hit towards cover. He hit it in the air and I moved across and held it shoulder high to my right. Inti, who was about my age or even older at this stage, came in on the hat-trick. We had fielders all round the bat. I thought he'd probably play forward so I dropped it a bit shorter and flatter. I just hoped it would bounce. It did bounce and it hit him on the glove. Geoffrey Howarth, fielding at silly point, had moved in as I bowled and he caught it with his right hand, fully stretched. I turned and appealed. I was convinced it had hit him on the glove but the umpire was unmoved. I thought, "Oh, no!" Then he slowly put his hand up. Inti had actually walked but I didn't realise that as I had my back to him. I was getting bashed on the back by players I had known for only a few weeks. Then Danny O'Sullivan came running over and said, "Jim Laker's got nothing on you!" and I thought, "Who the hell's Jim Laker?" '

Having been 336 for 4, Pakistan were eventually dismissed for 417. New Zealand batted poorly, made 157 and 360 and lost by six wickets. Petherick added the scalps of Zaheer Abbas and Mushtaq Mohammed in the second innings to finish with 5 for 229 from 22.7 eight-ball overs. Turner lost all six tosses on that tour of Pakistan and India so Petherick never had the luxury of bowling on a worn fourth-innings pitch. He missed the third Pakistan Test and ended the tour with 16 wickets from five Tests. The following season he was overlooked for the first Test against Australia in spite of taking 7 for 65 against the tourists for Otago. Picked for the second Test on a green pitch at Eden Park, he bowled only four overs and his international career ended there. He was unlucky not to be picked for the 1978 tour to England.

During England's 1988 tour I drove their scorer, Warwickshire's Peter Austin, from Dunedin to Christchurch. We made a little three-hour detour to see Mount Cook. Sadly, we saw very little because the mountain was shrouded in mist but we lunched extremely well at an adjacent hotel. As we returned to the car, a party of Japanese school-girls asked if I would take their photo. I spotted that there were 11 of them and, to their confusion and Peter's amusement, I arranged them in two rows like a cricket photograph. Cricket seems to have taken off in Japan from that date.

My favourite ground in New Zealand is Pukekura Park in New Plymouth on the south-eastern flank of North Island. It has to rank high on my list of the world's most delightful cricket grounds and it was a joy to report a match there on England's 1987–88 tour. A small-ish playing area is surrounded on three sides by steeply banked grass terracing surmounted by a framework of exotic trees. Perched precariously atop the middle summit in the press tent, I had a perfect view down the pitch and beyond to a colourful medley of roofs with the shimmering Tasman as its backcloth. Seated around this terraced amphitheatre were a thousand sparingly clad spectators on slatted benches, their sun brollies adding more colour to a kaleidoscope of green. The cricket ground is just a small part of a stunning park and botanical gardens, featuring a huge variety of native trees, king ferns and rhododendrons. In the park's centre is a long, thin lake spanned by The Poet's Bridge, named after the horse whose winnings paid for its construction.

SIXTEEN

INDIA AND SRI LANKA

WHEN, IN 1968, I first met Clive Lloyd at the start of his illustrious career with Lancashire, I asked him about the tour of India where he made his Test debut. He pulled a face indicating abject horror and said with feeling, 'India – where a fart's a luxury! One of our players called his diary *Loose in India*.' Happily, things have changed a great deal in the last thirty years and I would recommend everyone to visit India. My daily 'medicine', consisting of a small dish of raw chillies with dinner, has proved infallible on four visits. Not being a consumer of four-legged beasts, I have usually kept to a fish and seafood diet and enjoyed some fabulous meals. I adore curry and most of the local dishes. Outside the large hotels, which have their own water purification systems, it is wise to avoid salads, because they will have been washed in unpurified water, and don't add ice to drinks. Another precaution is to clean your teeth in bottled water. Some use gin.

Back in 1967, I had my first view of those four wonderful Indian spinners, Bishan Bedi, Bhagwat Chandrasekhar, Erapally Prasanna and Srinivas 'Venkat' Venkataraghavan. My first sight of them was at Worcester when I stood with John Arlott watching them practising in the nets. John surveyed the entire touring team, turned to me with his Tony Hancock hangdog expression and said, 'What a terrible waste. We shall never be able to identify them. The only one with a beard is also the only one with a turban!'

In those early days of my broadcasting career I usually carried my cricket case in the boot in case England were one short. When rain delayed the start of the tour match against Warwickshire, the Indians' captain, 'Tiger' Pataudi, sent a message to our box asking me to meet him in the indoor nets. We had met seven years earlier when he was at Oxford and I was stationed at RAF Abingdon. He had a cunning plan, the victim of which was to be the visiting Indian commentator, Pearson Surita. I changed and, under Tiger's instructions, spent the morning practising bowling with my left-arm. With Bedi's help I was soon reasonably proficient. I was also shown how to put on a patka and given an Indian sweater. When the weather cleared in the afternoon, Tiger, Farokh Engineer and Dilip Sardesai went on to the field in front of the pavilion to bat against three slow bowlers. It was a manoeuvre timed to coincide with Surita's daily radio report to India. Afterwards, our producer, Dick Maddock, told me that the report went something like this: 'It has stopped raining but there is more to come. Some of the team are having a bit of batting practice down there in front of me. Bedi is bowling to Pataudi, Prasanna is bowling to Sardesai, and Bedi is bowling to Engineer. Oh my God! I can see two Bedis! Back to the studio!' Surita had lunched well but not that well. As he left the box to see the Bedi twins at first hand, Dick gave the signal that led to my speedy replacement by Venkat. The rain returned and play didn't start until the following afternoon.

When a ball from the Sikh spinner lifted, turned sharply, beat both the batsman and wicket-keeper and went to the boundary, Brian Johnston seized the moment. 'Ah, it's gone for four byes,' he said. 'Have you scored those as Beddibyes, Bearders?'

John Arlott referred to that ghastly pun in his next stint – 'I suppose if this bowler beats bat and keeper, you will record them as Abid Ali-byes, Frindalius!'

I had long wanted to view the delights of India at first hand, especially after meeting Reita Faria, Miss World, at Edgbaston. She was the first Indian to win that title and she subsequently qualified as a doctor and brought up a family. Visits to what John Arlott referred to as the

'Incontinent' were barred for a long time by my history of allergic reactions to various inoculations and remedies. However, by 1991 medical progress had overcome those problems and my GP gave me the go-ahead to join the three-week joint Sutton CC and *Cricket World* tour to Delhi, Agra, Jaipur, Bombay and Goa. So, in my 53rd year, I was introduced to the most exciting and dramatically different country of all those I had visited and I was utterly bewitched by it. India is divided into 28 states and seven union territories. All are different. To say that you have visited India is as vague as saying you have been to Europe.

Flights on India's domestic airline were terrifying experiences. There appeared to be no limit on the amount of hand luggage one could take into the cabin. Rolls of carpet were commonplace. So were large framed pictures wrapped in brown paper, which were often leant against the cabin walls, blocking emergency exits. One aged passenger squatted on the floor in front of an exit, piled his luggage behind him to cushion his back and calmly lit a small primus stove. Cabin staff seldom bothered to check that the overhead lockers were properly closed and I was nearly knocked unconscious when the one above me opened and a case fell on my head.

The cricket was entertaining and competitive. We won three of the five matches in which I played. We had the honour of playing against the Bombay Gymkhana and the Cricket Club of India on Bombay's first two Test match grounds. I should have had a wicket with the very first ball I bowled in our opening fixture in Delhi. The fielder was Baroda's left-handed all-rounder, Tilak Raj, whom we had borrowed, and he dropped an absolute sitter at short-leg. I suspect he may have dropped it deliberately. When we were introduced before the match, I made the great mistake of asking him about his over of orthodox spin that had been struck for a world record-equalling six sixes by Ravi Shastri. 'I was very unlucky,' claimed Tilak. 'Shastri was actually caught at deep midwicket.' I showed surprise. 'Unfortunately, the catcher was at the top of a stand.'

That tour provided my first visit to some of the world's greatest buildings. The awesome Taj Mahal, the classical parliamentary buildings of Edwin Lutyens in New Delhi, the Amber Fort in Jaipur and Calcutta's Victoria Memorial were the highlights of some astonishing architecture. Jaipur, dubbed the Pink City because most of its main buildings are coated in a pink wash, was a great delight. Not so my journey by elephant up a steep and narrow path to the Amber Fort. Four of us were seated atop Jumbo on a howdah, in back-to-back pairs. I was on the left side so my legs dangled desperately close to the edge of an unfenced drop of several hundred feet. The sheer terror of this ordeal was increased by our elephant being slightly lame and having a heavily strapped knee. It just had to be his left one! Every few steps he would buckle slightly and we would lurch a few degrees closer to our doom. That was the longest ten minutes of my life. Two pieces of advice if you visit the Amber Fort and decide to take an elephant ride – don't get on one with a damaged undercarriage and remember to sit on the right-hand side. Incidentally, Jaipur's pink wash was introduced in 1876 to honour Prince Albert's state visit. Bearing in mind that Queen Victoria's husband was German, I have often wondered if their tally of nine children may have accidentally resulted from his confused sovereign wife's plea of, 'Nein!'

In January 1993 I returned for a memorable month to score England's three Tests at Calcutta, Madras and Bombay for *TMS*. Although India is such a vast, teeming shambles that the most glorious cock-ups are bound to occur, I soon discovered that no country makes its visitors more welcome. Those involved with national touring teams are treated like gods. It may have helped that I asked an Indian Test cricketer to organise my flights and accommodation. My choice of left-arm spinner Dilip Doshi (33 Tests plus eight county seasons with Nottinghamshire and Warwickshire) proved to be inspired as his contacts at Air India led to the warmest greeting ever received at a check-in counter, followed by instant upgrading. There was a slight hiccup in the form of a ninety-minute delay when one of the crew went missing, but the unscheduled interval spent in terrible comfort in the airline's VIP lounge proved a useful rehearsal for eight hours of wine tasting and food sampling cunningly disguised as a long-haul flight to Delhi. I was even presented with a beautiful minakari tray, the prelude to a month-long succession of gifts, which eventually threatened the world excess baggage record.

My crumpled 1 a.m. arrival was considerably eased, first by an Air India official who sped me through the immigration formalities, and second by two local cricket writer/statisticians. They epitomised their country's hospitality, sacrificing their night's sleep to welcome me, transport me to the domestic airport, persuade its manager to open up the VIP suite, and guard me while I dozed until my breakfast flight to Calcutta. One of that splendid duo, Rajesh Kumar, has become my main statistical contact in India,

Again the gods were with me and the month-long pilots' strike, which had already condemned Graham Gooch's team to several marathon surveys of India's erratic rail system, had been lifted the previous day. 'Doshi Tours' came up trumps again when Dilip's father, Rasiklal, met me and chauffeured me to my haven for the next nine days. Despite being fully booked when, just a fortnight earlier, my contract with the BBC had finally been confirmed, thanks to Sam Bhadha, general manager of the Taj group's London showpiece, St James's Court, the Taj Bengal Hotel miraculously produced an excellent room and VIP service. I had never spent so long in one hotel nor found one where there was absolutely nothing to complain about. Completed less than two years earlier, this vibrant, friendly haven owed its happy atmosphere to an unusually youthful staff, the oldest member of which had reached the ripe old age of 40.

My first jetlagged day continued until 3 a.m. After a poolside lunch, Professor Doshi's car braved the maelstrom of livestock and ageing vehicles that constitutes normal traffic anywhere in India. His guided tour included a suspension bridge that had taken seventeen years to build, the cleanest underground railway in the world, a visit to his tailor that doubled the volume of my luggage, and ended in a garlanded welcome at the college he had helped to found.

The hotel management's invitation to cocktails awaited my return. There I met two hazards. The first was the discovery that, contrary to many reports, the available falling-over water included dry white wine and the second was the hotel's assistant sales manager, Partha Chatterjee. A few glasses of the first led to my accepting from the second an invitation to attend a pre-Test match bash at the Calcutta Cricket Club. Next morning I awoke at 11 a.m. in far better order than I deserved, having obviously found the perfect remedy for jetlag.

An advance party of the Gullivers Travels tour group adopted me as their mascot, ensuring that I never ate alone or had to worry about transport to and from the cricket grounds. All I could offer in return were invitations to the commentary box and the autographs of its occupants. At Eden Gardens, one of the world's largest sports arenas, commentator, summariser and scorer were cramped into a minute area in which our bucket bench seat enjoyed a combined width of barely five feet. I was on the extreme left, touching a wall with a nail that protruded at elbow level. Small scars are testament to my forgetting to pack a pair of pliers. Summarisers Vic Marks and Tony Lewis alternately occupied the seat next to me. They could only gain access if commentators Jon Agnew or Christopher Martin-Jenkins vacated their seat and continued describing the action while bent double under the shelf housing the TV monitor.

Excluding the Bengali engineers, who understood little English, certainly not the vivid Anglo-Saxon with which our producer berated their unsuccessful efforts to connect the lines to London, I was privileged to be the sole listener to the first forty minutes of commentary during that dramatic series. It began at 9.15 a.m. local time (lunch was at 11.15, tea at 2.00 and stumps at 4.20) with Marks suddenly thrusting his left wrist between his knees. I thought he had been sharing Mike Gatting's prawns but he was merely trying to muffle the alarm on his watch. Vic's duty-free purchase in Dubai had not included instructions for manipulating the alarm and he was condemned to its daily 9.15 morning call, and the goading of Aggers, for the rest of his tour.

Although India won an important toss, England had already committed the gross blunder of picking four seamers on a spinner's pitch. This not only allowed India, thanks to an innings of astonishing brilliance by Mohammad Azharuddin, to amass a large total and remove much pressure from their inexperienced spin trio, but it also confirmed total lack of confidence in John Emburey and Phil Tufnell when they chose Ian Salisbury ahead of the experienced Middlesex pair.

England's intensive preparation at Lilleshall did not seem to have prepared them for the ear-shattering background at Eden Gardens. At times 80,000 strong, the crowd maintained an almost incessant din, their chanting, clapping and whistling interspersed with Mexican waves that circumnavigated the vast arena in ten seconds. Every English wicket was celebrated with thunder-flashes. The din on the final morning was so great that I could not hear the broadcaster barely a foot away. An unbroken sequence of 125.2 overs of spin bowling in England's second innings produced a scoring exercise straight from a time warp. By 12.44 p.m. on the fifth day, India had achieved only their second win in 26 Tests and the presentations were being made on a ground covered in oranges, paper darts and jubilant Bengalis.

England's scorer, Clem Driver of Essex, was taken ill with heart problems on the first morning. Luckily, Dermot Reeve's mother, Monica, was in the crowd. An experienced scorer at Middlesex county youth matches, she was roped in for the rest of the tour. I had a chance to chat with her beside the pool at the team's hotel and asked her if she had any offspring in addition to Dermot. She told me that there were three other sons. I asked if, like Dermot, they had all been born in Hong Kong. 'Oh, no. And Dermot wasn't conceived in Hong Kong.' I took a deep breath and asked where he was conceived. 'In Southport, on Independence Day.' I never found a way of including that gem in his entry in the *Playfair Cricket Annual*.

England's demise allowed some extra sightseeing, including a visit to the Victoria Memorial with its unique collection of paintings of India by British artists dating back two centuries to the era when Calcutta was the source of the East India Company's fortunes. A mile away was the Mission of Charity founded by that remarkably alert octogenarian Mother Teresa, who made time in a crowded schedule to meet the Gullivers group and one hanger-on. It was undoubtedly the most moving moment of this memorable tour.

Just six MCC members remained domiciled in Calcutta and they generously invited visiting MCC members, including Ted Dexter, Tony Lewis, Henry Blofeld and me, to cocktails at the historic Bengal Club. It was good to see Pearson Surita, aged 79, for the first time since 1967. I decided not to mention the incident of Bedi's double.

When England moved on to Vishakhapatnam for the final non-international match of the expedition, I flew to Bangalore, India's garden city and birthplace of Sir Colin Cowdrey. Its abundance of colourful trees and shrubs set in spacious parkland was an abrupt contrast to the smog, decay and bustle of Calcutta. From the Taj West End Hotel, a series of colonial houses surrounded by tropical gardens, I walked to St Mark's Cathedral and found Sir Colin's entry in the Baptismal Register. The cathedral organ had been presented in his grandparents' memory by his aunt.

Bhagwat Chandrasekhar, tragically confined to a wheelchair after being run over eighteen months earlier by a truck while on a scooter waiting at traffic lights, spent a happy poolside hour or two chatting about a career that snared 242 wickets in 58 Tests and caused Tony Greig to invent the ungainly lofty bat guard, copied by many opening batsmen.

Deciding to visit the hill stations, I hired a car and its driver. For the first mile I sat in the front passenger seat, mostly with my eyes closed as we overtook in the paths of oncoming livestock and thundering trucks. I soon switched seats and spent the next few hours cowering in the rear of this hired death chariot, hurtling along the pitted track that doubles as the main road to Mysore and the hill stations of Ootacamund ('Ooty'), Wellington and Coonoor. I frequently asked Ben Hur to stop, more to recover my shattered nerves than to photograph the breathtaking scenery featuring mountains and terraced tea plantations. In 'Ooty', C.T. Studd (five caps for England in 1882–83) had started his Union Church mission as a quiet net before tackling the Belgian Congo. Returning to Mysore's Lalitha Palace, I shared my room with seven lively companions. Sadly, they were all cockroaches.

Taking the train from Bangalore to Madras, scene of the second Test, I enjoyed my first experience of India's railways. I had expected total chaos with no reserved seats and hordes of passengers clinging to the carriage roof and footplate. The computer has changed all that. Tickets list carriage and seat numbers and passenger lists are displayed outside every compartment. Six hours of first-class air-conditioned comfort with a constant stream of peddlers bearing tea, coffee, soup, ice cream and snacks cost me about £4.

Our box at Chepauk's Chidambaram Stadium was mercifully larger than its Calcutta counterpart but it lacked ventilation, a distinct downside in the steamy heat of Madras – or at least my allotted corner did. Our producer had decided to remove the air-conditioning unit from the rear of the box and take out the middle of three windows at the front. The tepid breeze enjoyed by commentator and summariser did not reach the scorer's position. After a day of sweltering discomfort, a large electric fan appeared. My relief was swiftly dispelled when the engineer interrupted my attempt to aim it more in my direction. 'Not for scorer, sahib. Fan to keep equipment cool.' In India, Bearded Wonders were obviously deemed to be expendable.

Joy at escaping from the heat, humidity and sewers of Madras easily dispelled any disappointment at England's innings defeat. My premature escape allowed a swift tour of the city before I joined the Gullivers party for a three-day break at Fisherman's Cove, an idyllic holiday complex some thirty miles south. Former England fast bowler Chris 'Chilly' Old was guiding the latest influx of tourists. Forgetting his nickname, I startled him at breakfast by ordering a chilli omelette. At Fisherman's Cove, he dragooned me into joining a sophisticated game of beach cricket against the staff of the hotel, giving me a fearful rocket for misfielding in the loose sand. It was all great fun and mercifully injury free. An inspired piece of umpiring produced a tied finish to the delight of everyone.

Thankfully, the box in Bombay's third Test arena, the challengingly named Wankhede Stadium, was roomy and air-conditioned.

A thrilling double-century by Vinod Kambli enabled India to complete their spinwash with another innings defeat. Occasionally, commentators get their words in a twist or produce juicy *double entendres*. Not often do they compete with the following three that occurred during a post-lunch half-hour at Bombay: 'It's been a good partnership by the two little bumboys' (Agnew, meaning to say Bombay boys); 'Kapil's not a natural bonker' (Marks, meaning slogger); 'DeFreitas really has lost his zip' (CMJ).

The prestigious Cricket Club of India (CCI) invited visiting MCC members to dinner on the outfield of their Brabourne Stadium, India's main Test arena until the feuding Bombay Cricket Association built its rival two blocks away. There I met B.B. Nimbalkar, the only batsman to score 400 in a first-class innings and not become a Test player. I introduced him to Brian Johnston, revealing that Nimbalkar's innings of 443 not out was made in only 8 hours 14 minutes and was terminated when a dispirited opposition conceded the match with him just nine runs short of Bradman's (then) world record. Johnners startled the great man by asking him why he had not played a few strokes and scored more quickly! My last meal on that tour was a magnificent seafood curry shared at a table on the floodlit outfield in the company of such cricketing legends as Lala Amarnath, 'Polly' Umrigar, Dilip Sardesai, Hanumant Singh, the Apte brothers and Ramesh Divecha.

Sponsored by British Gas, I returned a year later to set up a short tour for the Lord's Taverners in Delhi, Calcutta and Bombay. I was able to invite Bapoo Mama to lunch. For more than twenty years he had been a highly industrious source of Indian cricket data and a most tremendous help. His task in those days before the advent of the internet was monumental. India is a vast country with a host of first-class teams and players. All his data had to be gathered from an erratic press or via an even more eccentric postal system. Bapoo and I had met just once previously. When I first flew to Australia in 1976, he had arrived at Bombay airport the previous day, bribed a security man and got into the VIP lounge to wait for me. When I left the plane for the transit lounge, a stewardess clutching my photo nabbed me and took me through a maze of corridors. I thought I was being arrested. Suddenly we entered the lounge and there, at 3 a.m., was a beaming Bapoo.

Thoughts of transit lounges remind me of a lovely story Brian Johnston told against himself. He was stretching his legs in Dubai when he spotted a fellow staring at him. Eventually, the man began to approach him. Thinking he wanted his signature, Johnners started to get his pen out. 'I never forget a face,' boasted the fan. 'I'd know yours anywhere.' Johnners preened himself. 'Oh, yes, I know you. You used to drive my bus in Watford.'

During that short visit to Bombay I met the Royal Yacht's cricket team. Although their ship was docked nearby, they assured me that they tended to play mostly away matches. I had the honour of entertaining them at a lunch in the Brabourne Stadium hosted by the Cricket Club of India president, Raj Singh Dungarpur. They presented me with one of my proudest possessions – a navy tie bearing the inscription 'HMY BRITANNIA CC' beneath a set of white stumps and a gold and red crown, the motifs sandwiched between two narrow gold and orange stripes.

Sadly, I have been able to make only the briefest of visits to India since then. With Chris Cowdrey as co-speaker and accompanied by Debbie, we were flown to Bombay at the expense of various sponsors and under the banner of the Lord's Taverners, just to attend one dinner. A limited-edition print of Jack Russell's painting of the old Tavern at Lord's was auctioned for £14,500 when two rival tycoons, one female, tried to outbid each other. Instead of being proud that his picture had raised such a vast sum, Jack was very cross when I told him some weeks later. 'Why didn't you phone me?' he demanded. 'I'd have flown out with another one!' Our appearance was part of the Indo-British Partnership Initiative and also to promote a British Trade Fair. The Royal Yacht, bereft of its regal residents, was again moored close by and helped earn a host of valuable orders during its week there. We were privileged to be invited to parties on board on successive evenings as the Band of the Royal Marines played on the quayside below. When we were invited to tour the engine room, Debbie, wearing a long white gown, asked if it was clean enough for her to visit. 'Oh, yes, madam,' the sailor assured her with a grin, 'your dress won't dirty any of the brass work.' The engine room was as clean as an operating theatre. Every piece of metal gleamed, probably the result of hundreds of hours of elbow grease.

*

Sri Lanka, which I still think of as Ceylon, as do many of its older inhabitants, is totally different from India. Hilly, with lush vegetation and an abundance of tropical flowers and shrubs, it is an island paradise when its people are not killing each other. I have been there twice. In 1981 I toured with the *Guardian* cricket team and played in some of the hottest and most humid conditions I had encountered. They were useful practice for my visit to Malaysia a year later. Having had my glasses smashed while batting in 1970, I wore hard contact lenses for the next twenty years. Twice on that tour sweat washed one out of my eye as I bowled the ball. Each time there was a ten-minute delay while everyone crawled around the pitch searching for this tiny circle of plastic. Each time it was found and each time the batsman, probably having lost the will to live, was out to my next ball. A cunning ploy!

Our arrival in Colombo was memorable. The traffic halted in a very poor area on the outskirts of that teeming city. A small boy ran out of the door of a small hut on our left and darted on to the road in front of our stationary coach. Suddenly he turned, ran up the path and bowled a tennis ball through his front door. At that moment the coach moved on so I couldn't tell if someone was batting at the far side of the hut. We continued down the Galle Road. Spotting a partially constructed two-storey building festooned with bamboo scaffolding, I said, 'Here we are folks. That's our hotel for the next week.' The weak laughter turned to moans of horror when the coach turned into its entrance and we were directed to the rear of the building. I was grateful that my companion on that trip was the assistant matron of the Royal Masonic Hospital. We weren't the only occupants of that room. A colony of bandicoots were in permanent residence. A breed of destructive Asian rat, they had free access to the entire hotel via an open drainage system. When I mentioned this problem to our tour operator, we were swiftly moved into luxury accommodation in the city.

I was soon in need of a nurse. Batting on matting in the nets at the Nondescripts Cricket Club, I was struck on the jaw by a ball that flew from a length. Fearing a fracture, I was taxied to the main hospital. Flies were everywhere and hardly any of the medical staff wore uniforms that had escaped blood. My trepidation at the thought of having my jaw wired under those conditions was dispelled by an X-ray, but bruising limited my diet to pineapple and bananas for a few days. After that, I was persuaded to bat in a helmet. As well as impairing my vision and feeling so weighty that it affected my balance, it was also a gleaming white target for the Sri Lankan quick bowlers. I soon exchanged it for my cap and have never donned a helmet since.

Our most spectacular venue was the Dimbula Cricket Ground, located in a valley within the terraced tea estates at Radella. We batted first and, as I was well down the order, I set off up the hillside with my camera. It was quite a climb and, near the vantage point I was searching for, my shin collided with what I thought was a twig bearing tea leaves. At that moment of agony I discovered that tea bushes have extremely substantial hardwood branches and are more than a match for an aging shin. A glance at the blood seeping through my cricket trousers confirmed that I had a problem. I bound it up with a hand towel that I carried as a sweat mopper. Determined to get my photo, I continued my climb but with extreme care. I found the perfect place and took several shots. Far below the receding rows of bushes lay the cricket ground, the players tiny white dots, and beyond that a fertile valley, a few houses and a low mountain range. It proved to be the most acclaimed photograph I have taken. Besides appearing on a magazine cover and in several cricket books, Patrick Eagar included it in his MCC exhibition at Lord's.

I took another photograph when we played on what was to become the Test ground, the Asgiriya Stadium, in Kandy. To take a distant view, I had to gain access to a cinema and climb to the top of the projection room where there was a small window. Our opening partnerships had been fairly dismal, and I volunteered to go in first, so I opened both the batting and the bowling on a future Test ground. We put on nearly 50, of which my share was 10 plus half a dozen bruises, and I was invited to tea by a family living beside the boundary. When I wasn't selected for the final match, the opposing president's XI requested my services and I took an early wicket thanks to an amazing reflex slip catch, high above his head, by a sixty year old. Afterwards, we lined up in the pavilion to receive commemorative butter dishes. Mine still survives. Then we all had to go up again, one by one, and solemnly accept a green string bag to carry it in.

My other trip was in 1987 when the *Mail on Sunday* sent me to report the England Young Cricketers' Tour. It was my baptism as their newly appointed cricket correspondent. I also reported it for *Wisden Cricketers' Almanack* and *Cricket World* magazine, in addition to doing some commentary for Sri Lankan radio's ball-by-ball coverage. The England side, all under 19 on 1 September 1986, included six future Test cricketers, two of them destined to become captains. That inspired selection provided an uncanny glimpse of the future. In alphabetical order the touring team read: Mark Alleyne, Michael Atherton (captain), Martin Bicknell, Simon Brown, Mark Crawley, Alastair Fraser, Warren Hegg, Nasser Hussain, Mark Newton, Mark Ramprakash, Oliver Smith, Martin Speight, Lloyd Tennant, Harvey Trump and Trevor Ward.

Curiously, their solitary win was a limited-overs game. They dominated all six of their longer matches, drawing the three 'Tests'. Ramprakash and Hussain looked prospective international cricketers of great flair, while the extremely determined Atherton looked as though he might become an opener in the Boycott mould.

Three memories stand out – play being stopped by an iguana being allowed to cross the ground when the England fielders feared it was a mini-crocodile; the tortured expressions of the players lunching at Kandy after I had complained that the previous day's curry was too mild; and the sight of a crowd of 47,000, mostly children admitted free, watching the first international at the new Khetterama Stadium, a match that was televised ball by ball.

SEVENTEEN

THE MALTAMANIACS

L IKE MOST wandering cricket teams that parade under strange banners, the Maltamaniacs evolved by accident. The label was first used in 1979 but it camouflaged a habit that had its origins twenty-eight years earlier when Bill Frindall's XI first took the field.

My inaugural eleven was two short and not very tall. The playing area was a balding recreation ground at Tattenham Way, near Banstead in Surrey, and the average age was 10½. The collective will to win fell not far short of that instilled by Duncan Fletcher and Michael Vaughan in England's victorious Ashes team and doomed this initial contest against Tommy Slaughter's XI to a tearful abandonment. When their leader fell victim to an imaginative lbw decision that would not have required consultation with a replay umpire, my opposing captain's reaction was to storm off the ground with our only bat – his! Unlike most of our subsequent fixtures, that one was never renewed.

A decade passed before I rounded up another eleven. During that interlude I was introduced to the rudiments of captaincy by leading my House XI at Reigate Grammar School and skippering Banstead Cricket Club's Colts team. Only half a dozen games were involved in that span of experience, but my teams were never defeated and I won the toss every time. During those games, I returned my personal bests at that time – 42 and 7 for 20. My RAF sojourn with NATO at Fontainebleau provided my next chance to emulate those prodigious tour masters H.D.G. Leveson Gower, E.W. Swanton and D.H. Robins. The first serious contest took place at Camp Guynemer on 4 September 1963, just up the road from the scene of Napoleon's famous final farewell before he began an enforced holiday in St Helena. My unbeaten run was preserved when we beat Afcent's Joint Communications Agency by 41 runs. My communion with NATO developed a latent ability for bludgeoning reluctant, and frequently retired, cricketers into turning out and travelling vast distances. Tours were arranged throughout Europe, the great attraction being that they were financed totally from public funds.

My next opportunity for team recruiting did not present itself for another eight years when, following a visit to the delightful Kent village of Benenden to be guest speaker at their annual dinner, I was invited to bring an eleven to play on the green. Benenden first featured in *Scores and Biographies* as early as 1798 and by 1830 had become an exceptionally strong club. In or around 1835, the parish challenged any other parish in England for £100. The challenge was accepted by William Clarke, founder of Trent Bridge Cricket Ground, on behalf of Nottingham, but the contest never took place because Clarke refused to play at Benenden. Their club's stature had declined somewhat by 26 September 1971 when my first adult civilian team defeated them by 18 runs. The village school, the wall of which formed a boundary, doubled as the pavilion. Two handsome sightscreens had been lost when their winter storage in the garden of the neighbouring vicarage coincided with the arrival of a new incumbent who used them to support his runner beans.

My team for that initial match included Pakistan batsman Alimuddin, sports writers Steve Whiting, Norman Harris and Claude Duval, BBC commentator Norman Cuddeford, Surrey's scorer Jack Hill, and Robin Bligh, my maths master from Reigate Grammar School. It typified the curious blend that was to be preserved throughout the next thirty years.

Invitations from cricket clubs swiftly mushroomed. During the 1980s we played up to a dozen matches each season, mainly in cricket weeks or on the rest days of Test matches. Recruiting players for such games can be a nightmare, especially when several drop out at the last minute. Fortunately, I never managed to emulate the despair of Denis Compton, who ended up with a team comprising himself just forty-eight hours before an event featuring his annual invitation XI. On one ghastly occasion we did appear as the A.A. Milne eleven (*Now We Are Six*). Debbie Brown (Mrs Bearders since Leap Day 1992) played a key part in bullying players to abandon a cosy domestic day at home to join our expeditions. In the mid-eighties we used the games to raise money for Guide Dogs for the Blind in the hope that they would lend us one to help boost our eccentric fielding by providing us with four short legs and some collecting boxes. One season we raised £2500, enough to train two and a half novice dogs. Any blind person given a half-trained dog now knows who to blame.

My couple of seasons on European matting when I played in France, Holland, Switzerland and Germany during my time at Fontainebleau in 1962–63 had given me an appetite for touring. I must confess that I am a tad envious of the school teams that nowadays enjoy winter tours to the Caribbean or Africa on a regular basis. In the 1950s my school team's only venture out of Reigate involved a ramshackle coach ride to Guildford or Tunbridge Wells. Cricket tours are the perfect solution for those who have a low beach-boredom threshold but who love trespassing abroad and playing cricket. There is now a vast list of fabulous venues that guarantee an abundance of sun, falling-over water, seafood and beautiful ladies. Touring does present a major challenge. If you manage to survive your hosts' over-whelming hospitality and actually get on to the field, you will then have to revise your batting and bowling skills to cope with pitches and weather very different from those at home. The match-winning formula is to savour every moment, make lots of friends and always try to play with a smile.

I had to wait until 1974 (when I was 35) before I visited Malta on my first overseas tour as a player. That trip led to the formation of my own touring XI, which eventually became The Maltamaniacs. For three decades I managed to sandwich expeditions overseas between compiling tally sheets for *Test Match Special* and doorstops for cricket reference libraries. If you throw in a dozen working trips to Australia, five to New Zealand and sundry trips to Asia and Africa, it could be said that I have just about compensated for the slow start. In 1975 the organisers of the Malta Cricket Festival invited me to take a team to join two other sides from the UK. That first expedition included Khan Mohammad, Fazal Mahmood's new-ball partner in Pakistan's early Tests, who, twenty-one years earlier, clean-bowled Hutton, May, Bill Edrich, Evans and Bailey in a Lord's Test that, due to rain, began in mid-afternoon on the fourth day. Also in our touring team were Stewart Storey of Surrey and Sussex, Frank Keating of the *Guardian, Punch* and, subsequently, *Oldie* magazine, and Phil Gould, star of a revue entitled *Irreversible Brain Damage*. This stage successor to *Monty Python* had found its way from the Edinburgh Festival to London's West End. Phil was also the co-scriptwriter of the successful TV medical comedy series *Rude Health*.

Keating arrived at Heathrow late and in considerable disarray. His entire luggage for a two-week tour was contained in a supermarket plastic bag. The previous evening he had discovered that his passport had expired and only phone calls to friends in high places and a frantic journey by a courier had saved the day. He said that he would like to play in the first match but then would have to concentrate on writing 100,000 words for a book on George Best. He vanished and no one saw him again until the final day of the tour. His skin was untanned, his legs still milky white, but he looked content.

'How's the book going, Francis?' I asked.

'Wonderfully well, my dear. I couldn't have managed without this break. Thank you so much for asking me to Malta.'

'Great!' I said. 'How far have you got?'

He hesitated, then sheepishly replied with a grin, 'I'm already to start.'

The Kent connection had been maintained by Micky Back (West Farleigh and The Mote), George Baker (Gravesend and The Mote) and three stalwarts from Linton Park – Nigel Thirkell, Trevor Back and

Brian Piper. Kent 2nd XI failed to make the most of Nigel's all-round talents. Perhaps Canterbury's lack of interest inspired him to play several outstanding innings in Malta and the Cape, and, when his back allowed, to swing the new ball at a lively fast-medium pace. Probably his proudest honour was the Man of the Match award he received when Linton Park won the 1978 National Village Cup final at Lord's.

The forces entertained us superbly, hosting visits to the fortress at St Angelo and various ships, including the magnificent aircraft carrier HMS *Ark Royal*. The crew challenged us to a match but, sadly, insisted that we couldn't make it a 'home' fixture on their ample flight deck.

When the RAF team was diverted on to a NATO mission, I organised a single wicket contest for our touring party. Khan Mohammad and Phil Gould were the finalists, a pair of outstanding bowlers, late swing and left-arm chinamen being their respective specialities. Gould emerged the winner and I had to find a suitable 'trophy'. That night's end of tour dinner at the Marsa Sports Club was a lounge suit affair. Unfortunately, Phil had not brought one with him, so there is a bizarre photograph of him receiving the award, his own brandy, while wearing my spare suit.

Alan Lee, future cricket correspondent of the *Mail on Sunday* and *The Times*, and the latter's award-winning racing correspondent, was one of several newcomers who joined the second tour to Valetta. Alan overcame an alarming series of injuries and refusals by writing a therapeutic diary of the tour. Typed in red ink, symbolic of his manifold injuries, physical and mental, but necessitated because he had exhausted the black half of the ribbon, the diary ran to eleven sides of quarto flimsy paper and was entitled *MALTAMANIA or the Full and Unabridged Diary of the Bill Frindall XI's Tour of Malta and Gozo, October 1976*. It began 'The laughter never stopped' and that was just my fielding.

We enjoyed four tours to Malta (1975–78), all under the Bill Frindall's XI label. The Maltamaniacs tag was not assumed until 1979. Unbeaten on our last two expeditions, we defeated All-Malta in both year's 'Tests' and won all ten matches on our final visit. The highlight of that final tour was the match against a Combined Civilians XI, our rigorous preparation for which had been an all-night engagement party for Carmen and Peter Baker, younger brother of Surrey all-rounder Ray. We played a 50-overs match and the opposing captain beseeched me to declare after 48.3 overs when Baker reached an inspired century and the primitive scoreboard showed a score of 373 for 3. Baker's partner in an unbroken stand of 281 was former Warwickshire, Army and Combined Services batsman, Richard Davies. The latter's score of 212 not out is the highest on a Tuesday in Malta by a batsman a stone underweight with his jaws wired together. Three weeks earlier, while playing for me at Benenden, he had fractured his jaw trying to hook one of the local hairdresser's bouncers. A liquid diet based mainly on gin and tonic had reduced his weight by a stone but obviously not affected his energy levels. From that tour on, he has thrived on the appellation of 'Jaws' and become a much respected coach and groundsman at Lancing College. A decade later, Jaws was to survive the Zeebrugge ferry disaster.

Possibly our victory by 240 runs accelerated the British withdrawal from Malta on 1 April 1979. The back-up of civilian staff and teachers, which had swelled the island's cricket strength to two leagues and a dozen teams, left with all the servicemen. No attempt appeared to have been made to attract the indigenous youth of Malta on to the cricket field and, apart from a Canadian chicken farmer, an aged English carpenter, a few Asian doctors and a handful of middle-aged Maltese, the island was left almost bereft of cricketers. It was unlikely that a multitude of immigrants from Libya and China would provide too many replacements. The time had come for a change of touring venue.

A visit to Guernsey with the Lord's Taverners led to the first of our annual mini-tours there in 1979. John Arlott's transfer to Alderney the following year demanded an annual match on The Butes and gave us an excuse to visit The Vines, raid his cellar and assault his unbounded hospitality. It also attracted the recruitment of Roy Marshall of Barbados, Hampshire and West Indies, actor Jeremy Kemp and author Leslie Thomas, who had brought *Virgin Soldiers* into thousands of bedrooms. The unattached ladies of Alderney were an added attraction. On the day of one annual match, accompanied by Roy and Leslie, I was fortunate to be invited to lunch at Arlott Towers. To our barely concealed glee it was pouring with rain and we settled down to one of John's traditional three-hour feasts. Leslie Thomas achieved an unprecedented feat by out-talking John. The anecdotes flowed and so did the wine in copious amounts. Around 3 p.m. some clot noticed that the rain had stopped and the sun was blazing. A phone call confirmed that play could begin at 4 p.m. Alderney is a tiny island, with a pub for every ten houses. Tracking down the remainder of my team and extracting them from the clutches of the local handmaidens was exceptionally difficult. Certainly, it was the most reluctant and ill-prepared team I have ever commanded. I remember our youngest player, Stuart Chambers, diving around on the rough outfield and making some incredible stops. At the party afterwards, John Arlott, president of Alderney CC, told Stuart that it was the bravest fielding performance he had witnessed on The Butes.

'Young man, did you notice all those white flecks on the outfield?'

'No, sir,' replied a puzzled Stuart.

'Fielder's teeth!' grinned John wickedly.

Guernsey now has one of the stronger and better organised teams in Europe and has attracted some exceptional cricketers, none more so than Mike White. Notwithstanding his exalted rank, Brigadier W.M.E. White, CBE, wanted to be remembered as a soldiering cricketer rather than the reverse, a wish confirmed by his wife and daughters when they announced his death after a long illness by stating that he had 'finally declared at 89'.

He had been enticed by cricket at the age of nine after watching Frank Woolley and James Seymour stroking hundreds against Lancashire at Dover, where he was to be educated at the County School. Tall and powerfully built, he honed his medium-fast bowling and aggressive batting in Kent with the Dover and Hythe clubs before going up to Trinity Hall and playing eight first-class matches for Cambridge University in 1937. To his eternal disappointment, a future captain of England, Norman Yardley, won the all-rounder's berth and a blue. Commissioned in the RASC later that year, his war service embraced France, North Africa and Italy, gaining him a Mention in Despatches and the OBE in 1944. He still managed to play for the British Empire XI in 1941 and subsequently appeared in matches on such unlikely venues as a Tunisian hillside and a Roman sports stadium. After the hostilities, his performances for Army and Combined Services teams prompted Northamptonshire to register him and in 1947 he celebrated his debut with spells of three wickets in six balls in each of Somerset's innings.

The feat that gave him most pleasure, and earned him a place in the *Guinness Book of Records*, was achieved on 23 July 1949 when he scored two separate hundreds in a day for Aldershot Services against the MCC. In 21 first-class matches he scored 398 runs at 13.72 and took 42 wickets at 36.28. Promoted to Brigadier in 1959, his post-war roles included Commandant of the RASC Training Centre and Director of Supplies and Transport, Far East Land Forces. After six years (1963–69) as aide-de-camp to the Queen, during which period he was promoted to CBE, he retired to Guernsey to indulge in cricket, golf and sailing. In addition to serving as president of the island's golf and cricket clubs, as well as of the illustrious Incogniti CC, he also became commodore of the island's royal yachting club.

It was a delight to visit him at home, talk cricket and be shown his cricket net in his terraced hillside garden with spectacular views across the Channel to several of the neighbouring islands. At 72 he finally hung up his cricket boots after heading the Guernsey Island CC bowling averages but finding 'that fielding had become a bit of a bore'. His final public appearance was to watch his daughter, Julia, make her cricketing debut for the Guernsey Sirens, whom she now skippers.

I decided that a major tour to escape some of the nastiest midwinter months was needed and, in 1980, we inflicted three weeks of Maltamania on Cape Province. Given South Africa's abundance of wine, barbecues and friendly handmaidens, it is hardly surprising that this was the most popular destination for England's touring cricketers

in the immediate post-war years. Our preparations would possibly not
have met with the approval of modern regimes. At a pre-tour dinner,
26 Maniacs enjoyed a fair net by consuming 30 bottles of falling-over
water. Moreover the combined ages of our 22 players registered a formidable 824 years, giving the frightening average of 37½, a tally that was
unlikely to permit hectic chasing on the field or off it. As my carefully planned itinerary included several wineries and a brewery, the hospitality was limitless. We managed to withstand it sufficiently to win
more matches than we lost, gaining notable victories against Green
Point CC, who included England players Graham Barlow and Allan
Lamb, and also against the Western Province CC on the famous Test
arena at Newlands, where A.W.H. 'Tony' Mallett of Kent came to
watch the great moment of victory. At Beckenham in 1947 he had
been E.W. 'Jim' Swanton's opening partner in the first game of cricket
I ever saw. Tony joined us for a post-match party in the pavilion and
delighted a fascinated audience with his wartime experiences in the
Royal Marines and tales of university and county cricket immediately
after the war.

I joined the tour after scoring Australia's first season of Tests following the Kerry Packer schism. Three matches against England, without
the Ashes being at stake, were intermingled with another trio against
West Indies. Writing in our tour brochure, Michael Melford, then senior cricket correspondent of the *Daily Telegraph*, revealed that he had
decided that the best way he could further the team's success was 'by
undertaking to get the manager-captain on to his flight in Melbourne
on February 5th clear-eyed, bristling with health and bursting with
potential efficiency. Rest assured, therefore, that in the previous week
those hours which he has not spent in spiritual meditation or in turning his final plans over in that voluminous brain will have been spent
in the gymnasium. Prepare for the arrival in Cape Town on February
6th of one combining the most successful qualities of Dr W.G. Grace,
Thomas Cook, the Archangel Gabriel and Sir James Goldsmith.' He
failed miserably.

On an earlier tour with a wandering London club, I had fallen victim to a cunning ploy by the Stellenbosch Farmers' Winery team. We attended a magnificent thrash in their pavilion the evening before the match. Small barrels of wine were in abundance and were replaced from the adjacent winery as soon as they were emptied. The host team was smartly dressed in green blazers and club ties and we all wore our tour uniform. By 2 a.m. the jackets and ties had been discarded as we began to make serious inroads into the Cape's wine stock. Reassured by the presence of the entire opposition team, our leader confidently led our excesses. After a couple of hours of fitful sleep we returned to the scene of our crimes to discover a totally different team of players pitted against us. We had been socialising with the SFW Drinking XI. Inevitably, we lost the toss and spent the next three hours leather-chasing in blazing heat. Batting at first drop for the hosts was Peter Kirsten, a future Test player. I did have him caught, on the long-on boundary, off the third ball I bowled to him but he had scored 87 at the time. Wary of a repeat performance, my team enjoyed its social evening at Stellenbosch a week before the match.

Two years later I organised a second major tour. The destination was decided on a whim when I saw a photograph of the cricket ground at Kuala Lumpur on the cover of a travel brochure. Thanks to the enthusiastic assistance of a cricket-devoted travel agency, Singapore Airlines and the secretaries of the Malaysia and Singapore Cricket Associations, my dream was swiftly converted into reality. Within a couple of months six fixtures were arranged, flights and accommodation booked and eleven other players recruited. We left Heathrow on 2 April 1982 and returned undefeated three weeks later, in spite of appalling heat and humidity and injuries to three of our players, including me.

Bearing in mind the extreme heat, I had arranged for a Singapore hotel tailor to make each member of our touring team a lightweight beige suit. We all filled in forms containing a series of cartoon bodies. The tailor and his wife joined our flight at Singapore for the final leg to Kuala Lumpur. To avoid Malaysian import duty, they simply added two large holdalls containing our suits to our group luggage. I still have one of the holdalls. When we reached our hotel and tried on the suits, we found that remarkably few alterations were needed. A demi-lifespan has reshaped all of us except Phil Gould, who can still squeeze into his suit.

It was in Malaysia that I first reduced my run-up from twenty paces to eight. The end product appeared at much the same rat-power and I managed to snare a brace of victims in each of the six games. The first was against the Selangor Club at Kuala Lumpur's famous 'Spotted Dog' ground, named after a Dalmatian that originally held sway there. Outside the pavilion I interviewed the Selangor Club's unique head groundsman, Lall Singh.

An aggressive right-handed batsman and outstanding fielder, Lall Singh (1909–1985) was born near Kuala Lumpur and played his early cricket there. Lala Amarnath heard of his prowess in the field and nudged the selectors. He was invited to play in the Indian trial matches of 1931–32, when he made his first-class debut. Subsequently, he appeared for Southern Punjab (1933–34 to 1935–36) and the Hindus (1934–35 and 1935–36). His spectacular fielding was a feature of India's first tour of England in 1932. Jim Swanton remembered 'his slight figure with a light blue turban gliding swiftly over the ground like a snake'.

He played in India's inaugural Test, at Lord's, scored 15 and 29, the latter in a stand of 74 in 40 minutes with Amar Singh. He also held a catch and ran out Frank Woolley with an exceptional display of antic-ipation, picking up and throwing.

Lall Singh remains the only Malay to have played Test cricket. When I reminded him of this in our interview, he chortled and added proudly, 'I am also the only Test cricketer to have owned a nightclub in Paris.' Before I could follow up that claim, he trumped it with, 'I think I am also the only Test cricketer to have run off with his cap-tain's wife.' That could explain why he appeared in just that one Test.

His first-class career lasted just 32 matches (1931–32 to 1935–36). Returning home to Kuala Lumpur he spent the rest of his life coach-ing and looking after that historic ground.

After Kuala Lumpur, we travelled by coach to Ipoh and were

billeted with various English and Australian families. Several were housed in a mansion belonging to the chief of a local bank, who ruled the community like a potentate. Having shown his 'hostages' around the vast residence, revealing the price of every item of furniture and showing off vast quantities of booze and cigars that he had extracted from his customers, he invited our entire party to a Chinese restaurant. We sat around one vast table with a revolving centre that allowed dishes to be circulated easily. Perhaps to get us in festive mood, he arranged for a chicken's head to be placed in a dish, and spun the table. Whoever was the poor unfortunate it settled in front of had to eat it. We all stared in horror as it slowed and finally landed in front of Debbie Brown, our scorer and my wife to be in a decade's time. She was not amused and I stood up and told our host exactly what I thought of him. He looked as though he had been shot between the eyes, quickly apologised and had the offending dish removed. I doubt if anyone had ever stood up to him before. Certainly his customers had not. One had been invited to join us and was promised a loan if he could equal the pace of our drinking. He went very quiet after a couple of hours. Then there was a crash as his chair fell backwards. The staff, accustomed to this ritual, pulled him across the floor by his shoulders and I turned round just in time to see his feet leave the room.

All this time a small group of musicians had been playing quietly in the background. They were squatting in the dark, unable to read their music until I demanded that, if they were to continue to play for us, they should have some light. Again the banking god acquiesced but, unwittingly, he exacted his revenge on me. To avoid him earlier that day I had spent several hours in his swimming pool. With dense cloud overhead I had no fear of getting sunburnt. How wrong I was. By the time we drove up to Penang and took the ferry across to the Australian Air Force (RAAF) base at Butterworth, the top of my back was a mass of large blisters.

We lost the toss and I had to bowl my eight overs. As soon as their innings ended, I arranged the batting order with myself at number 10 and went to the Station Sick Quarters. The gorgeous Malaysian nurse who carefully swabbed and dressed my back was wearing an identity tag that read '001'. When I reckoned that she could inflict no further pain, I asked if she wished she had joined six nurses later. She looked extremely puzzled, then smiled and said, 'My name Daisy Ooi.' This event was reported in the *Daily Telegraph*'s Peterborough column but not with great accuracy, unless you want to believe that the incident occurred in a massage parlour.

I returned to find us seven wickets down and 20 runs short of victory. I just had time to pad up before another wicket fell and I was in. Angry that the batsmen had made such a hash of things and determined that I was not going to bat for long, I quickly ended the game by slogging a few straight boundaries. I have never sunbathed since.

By the end of the next match, also at RAAF Butterworth, we had lost two players to injury and could raise only ten for our final game in Malaysia. Breakfasting in the hotel after a heavy night, I was told that Angelo Porcaro, an Australian staying in the hotel, had played grade cricket in Perth and was eager to play for us. He was in room 344. I put a note with the details of the match inside one of our brochures and slipped it under the door of 344. By dinner on the eve of the match, Porcaro had not contacted me. I checked his room number with reception. He was in 433. I put another brochure and invitation under that door. Next morning I had two phone calls. One from Porcaro saying he had brought his gear with him and would be delighted to play that day. The other was from an Australian with a much older voice. 'I'm really thrilled to be asked to play. No one has invited me to play anything for thirty years. I'm eighty-four.'

I lost the toss, took the field, stationed Porcaro at mid-off, and ran in to bowl. An enormous bellow of 'Come on the Maltamaniacs!' from my left stopped me in mid run. Everyone else on the field froze and we all stared at Porcaro like in a Bateman cartoon. Until the more excessive Australian habits hit our culture in the early nineties, fielders remained silent unless something exceptional merited a subdued comment or polite clap, or we were making an appeal. The game continued peacefully for the remainder of my over. Porcaro claimed to be a swing bowler so I gave him the next over with just one slip. His first ball swung away late and beat the bat. I summoned a second slip. The next outswinger took the edge and was caught by second slip. Porcaro leapt and screamed. I moved in a third slip and he held a beauty off the last ball of the over, causing more leaping and screaming. For his next over I introduced a fourth slip and the inevitable happened. Porcaro could not believe it. 'Best bloody fielding side I've ever played for. No one catches those buggers at home,' he bellowed, beaming from ear to ear. I gave up on silence after that.

We had won all our five games in Malaysia. Could we maintain our success against the Singapore Cricket Club? Back in Penang we celebrated long into the night with Porcaro setting a fierce pace. He told me that he worked for Toyota in Perth and that if I was ever there, he would make sure that I had a free car for the duration of my stay. Although he looked astounded when I told him I would be arriving on 7 November at the start of England's 1982–83 tour, he kept his word. I was contributing my scoresheets of the Tests to a *Daily Telegraph* book of the tour and I persuaded them to include a credit for Toyota. In return, I was given a free car in every city that I stayed in. In Sydney, the manager supplied me with a brand new exotic sports car and apologised for it having 10km on its clock. At the end of England's tour, I flew to Auckland to set up a Maltamaniacs tour of New Zealand for 1984. Porcaro had contacted Toyota there and I was given a free car and permission to drive around both islands as far as Dunedin and back.

Porcaro asked if he could have some more copies of the Malaysia and Singapore tour brochure. Next morning I took them to his room and knocked on the door. A very ancient beaming lady in a vast nightdress greeted me. Behind her was an elderly man. 'You've got the wrong bloody room again!'

Three years later, the Maltamaniacs joined me in New Zealand for a four-week tour at the end of my second season of scoring duties with TVNZ. We were shown unrivalled hospitality and were allowed to play on the Test grounds at Auckland's Eden Park and at Wellington's Basin Reserve, as well as at several other first-class venues on both islands. We even broke our homeward journey to play matches in New South Wales and Western Australia.

That was our last major venture overseas. My involvement with numerous publications made organising such ventures impossible and most winters have been taken up with scoring official England tours for *Test Match Special* or undertaking minor MCC tours to California and British Columbia as an aged player.

In March 1985 the Maltamaniacs became formally constituted as a club. Our aims were to celebrate cricket on and off the field and to raise money for various charitable causes. Membership was by invitation and subject to the approval of the club committee. Candidates for membership could either be sponsored by two committee members or play in two Maltamaniacs matches. Although no annual subscriptions were levied, members were asked to make an annual donation of at least £5. This, match fees, fines (a bountiful source of revenue and a tribute to the much-neglected kangaroo court system) and donations were given to a charity chosen at each AGM. Club expenses involving administration, equipment or presentation shields were met by other donations and sponsorship.

In 1975 I had chosen for our inaugural tour a Maltese Cross surmounted by crossed cricket bats and the international broadcasting signal as the Maltamaniacs' motif. It had already featured on a variety of touring ties and ladies' head squares. The club's colours were confirmed as (Surrey) chocolate and gold. Roger Dean, a tireless veteran from my very first tour and handy off-spinning all-rounder for the Northampton Exiles, organised a wide range of Maltamaniacs clothing, including cricket and leisure sweaters, and caps in the baggy Australian style. All profits from those sales went to the charity.

Two personal anniversaries came round in 1996 – thirty years since my debut for *Test Match Special* and twenty-one years since our inaugural tour to Malta. In celebration, the Maltamaniacs embarked on a minor overseas expedition – to France, where we played at the beautiful Chateau de Thoiry ground near Versailles. As usual, new friendships were forged, marriages wrecked and manifold injuries sustained to pride and limb.

One failed ambition was to take a team to play in Italy. I reckoned we had an excellent chance of winning there because they would probably declare before the start, just in case! As our players have aged, our tottering distance has been limited to the Channel Islands. The annual visits to Guernsey have coincided with my duties as public-address announcer at an annual match involving two county teams that raises funds for the Lord's Taverners and the beneficiary of one of the invited counties. It was there in 2003 that I skippered the Maltamaniacs to defeat for the final time. I thought I ought to retire before I started drawing my pension and I managed to win that race by five months. My last foray with the bat, at number 11, shared in the highest stand of the innings, just reaching double figures, and spanned a lengthy interval for lunch. Celebrations continued at a splendid hillside tavern almost into October.

Research of the scoresheets has revealed an extensive Maltamaniacs cast list of notable cricketers, writers and actors, recalling a host of matches and incidents worthy of their own tome. David Morgan (not the ECB supremo) is worthy of special mention. Our friendship dated from the 1960s when he played for Cheam against Banstead, and he was my vice-captain on all the major tours and in most of our home matches. Cheam Cricket Club's outstanding slow bowler, he was one of the greatest exponents of flight and drift never to have played first-class cricket. He meticulously recorded in a prized ledger details of nearly 4000 wickets taken in 60 seasons, from the age of 10 until two years before his death in 2004 at the age of 71. Maintaining a precise control of line and length, allied to subtle changes of pace and gravelly voiced appeals, he was for three decades one of the most effective bowlers in club cricket, taking a record 1325 wickets in Surrey Championship matches, including more than 100 five-wicket hauls.

Born in Elstree and educated at Dulwich College, it was as a fast-medium bowler that David took the first of his hat-tricks while on national service in Malaya with the 17th Ghurka Regiment during the Emergency. He also represented his host country at rugby. David had been compelled to re-invent himself, from a bowler of fast inswingers to a master of slow away drifters, on medical advice after daily six-hour coaching stints on concrete-based pitches in Denmark had wrecked his knees. Retaining his opening bowler's action, he found that his attempted off-spin would drift away before pitching and become a bouncing leg-cutter. At 57 he became the oldest player to appear in the Club Cricket final at Lord's. Even after major surgery for cancer he represented Surrey in Over Fifties matches. Touring South Africa, Malaysia, Singapore, New Zealand and Australia with my Maltamaniacs in the 1980s, he was inevitably last to bed and the first at breakfast. His booklet, *How to Think Batsmen Out!*, remains essential reading for all aspiring bowlers.

Although he never played cricket at the highest levels, the Reverend Canon Hugh John Pickles, who died at Blewbury Vicarage on 24 September 1987 in his 71st year, was a singular man. Overcoming fierce opposition he was probably the most eccentric cricketer to wear Maltamaniacs colours. Few clerics can have made as strong an impact on such a wide variety of people. Father Hugh had three main loves – his religion, cricket (his second religion) and the ladies. No man has pursued such a trilogy with greater relish.

We met at Worcester in 1971 when I was broadcasting a county match with Brian Johnston. We were off air when Johnners leant out of the window, waved to a passing cleric, as one does, and shouted, 'Hello, you old ram, how are you?' He then explained that Father Hugh had almost been defrocked for associating with a neighbouring parishioner. 'The Bishops don't like you straying outside your own parish,' explained Brian. When we were introduced, Hugh asked if I played cricket. That meeting produced an enduring friendship and resulted in many enjoyable guest appearances for the Oxford Clergy, and I achieved my career bests of 91 not out and 9 for 21 (all bowled) for his team. We played many matches together and he bravely toured Malta with my XI. Hugh was an automatic choice as the first president of the Maltamaniacs.

A defensive opening batsman with an impeccable technique modelled upon that of Tom Graveney, he was an able coach. As chaplain to Worksop College (1953–63) his influence extended to the young Philip Sharpe. Originally a fast-medium bowler, he later became a temptingly slow off-spinner, who, at the age of 69, took a hat-trick for the Oxford Diocese against Cuddesdon College.

As vicar of Blewbury from 1963 until his death – duties that he combined from 1974 with those of rector of neighbouring Upton – he was a familiar figure, inevitably emerging from a battered car with his faithful dogs, Pax and Jessica. Their predecessor, Justice, had often 'sung' in the choir and when the dog died, he was given prime billing by Hugh in a toast to 'absent friends' – 'Let us drink to Justice and the late Bishop of Oxford.'

After the war, Hugh had revived and captained Wantage CC, an association rekindled annually by his XI's September visit. In 1977 he was compelled to delegate the captaincy to me when he was summoned from the field by an irate parent – an unfortunate case of a forgotten christening. In 1951 Hugh had helped to found the *Church Times* Cup competition and guided first London and later Southwell to victory in those early finals, twice carrying his bat through an innings. For his final twenty-five years his burning ambition had been to lead Oxford to victory in the final. Although terminally ill with stomach cancer, he bravely travelled to Southgate and watched his charges complete an emphatic win against Rochester. At his team's insistence he accepted the trophy and, to quote the Bishop of Oxford when he gave the eulogy at Hugh's funeral, 'It was at that moment he entered paradise.'

Hugh was accorded a requiem mass and his coffin was adorned with his bat and a cricket ball. Catherine, the last of his great loves, was responsible for arranging those artefacts. When I congratulated her on that feat, she looked crestfallen. 'No, Bill. I didn't get the bat quite straight – and Hugh loved a straight bat.'

Among those overflowing St Michael's Church at Blewbury were the victorious *Church Times* Cup team, England women cricketers Avril Starling and Megan Lear, cricket biographer Dr Gerald Howat (who gave an address) and Hugh's great mentor, Tom Graveney.

MALTAMANIACS LIST OF NOTABLES

Test cricketers: David Allen, Jan Brittin, Godfrey Evans, Richard Hutton, John Price, Harold Rhodes, John Snow, 'Butch' White (England); Dilip Doshi (India); Alimuddin, 'Billy' Ibadulla, Khan Mohammad, Mushtaq Mohammed, Younis Ahmed (Pakistan); Roy Marshall (West Indies).

Other first-class cricketers: Andy Babington, Ray Baker, Alan Burridge, Byron Byrne, Tony Clarkson, Richard Davies, Ian Davison, Nick Faulkner, Anthony Fincham, Vince Hogg, Richard Hoskin, Arnold Long, Majid Usman, 'Laddie' Outschoorn, Bob Parks, John Pretlove, Qamar Ahmed, Neil Smith, Stewart Storey, Stuart Surridge jr, Ken Suttle, Brian Taylor, Roy Virgin, Dennis Yagmich.

International footballer: Gary Lineker.

Actors/artistes: Tony Ainley, Robin Asquith, Colin Baker, Christopher Blake, Larry Dann, Johnny Dennis, Phil Gould, Jeremy Kemp, Ian Liston, Malcolm McFee, Bill Pertwee, Duncan Preston, John Rawnsley, Struan Rodger, Bill Simpson, Richard Stilgoe.

Broadcasters/writers/publishers: Jeffrey Archer, Michael Blumberg, Trevor Bond, Tony Cozier, Norman Cuddeford, Bill Day, Ralph Dellor, John Dunn, Claude Duval, Barrie Fairall, David Frith, Andrew Green, Norman Harris, Tim Jollands, Frank Keating, Chris Lander, Alan Lee, Ian Marshall, Frank Nicklin, Keiran Prendiville, Brian Scovell, Robin Simon, Leslie Thomas, Steve Whiting, Graeme Wright.

EIGHTEEN

PLAYING AND CHARITY HIGHLIGHTS

HAVING PLAYED hundreds of innings since 1949 without seriously threatening three figures, I still feel desperately envious of any player achieving the magic hundred. I used to think I had played a major innings if I reached 10. The nearest I have got so far – yes, I am still creaking around cricket grounds despite being exactly six months old when Neville Chamberlain called Hitler's bluff – is 91 not out in an hour during a 40-over game for the Oxford Clergy. I appeared in disguise as 'Father William' against an Abingdon School XI on an artificial pitch at Blewbury and hit three sixes and 11 fours (they forgot to set a long-on). I must confess it was not their strongest eleven, nor their oldest. On another occasion I was allowed to score 80 in a benefit match for Robin Jackman before a large crowd at Roehampton. Sadly, I am almost certainly the only member of that impressive congregation who recalls my innings despite some of it curiously being featured in a televised documentary.

My approach to batting has always been that of an incurable romantic and optimist, not unlike Robert Browning's 'high man' in *A Grammarian's Funeral*:

> That low man goes on adding one to one,
> His hundred's soon hit;
> This high man, aiming at a million,
> Misses an unit.

As Courtney Walsh and Danny Morrison discovered, it is all too easy to register that round unit.

While I was playing for Northallerton during my time at RAF Leeming, the club celebrated its centenary by staging a benefit match for Ray Illingworth. As twelfth man for the Northallerton Invitation XI, I had bribed a student pilot to take over my stint as Duty Officer and, still in uniform, escaped to the ground in the hope that one of the host side had not woken up in the best of health. They were all fit but the Yorkshire team were mostly late. John Hampshire arrived demanding breakfast. A yellow Ford parked just behind me. The driver, wearing spectacles and thinning hair, came over to me and, pointing to a large cricket case, said, 'You can call me Geoffrey and that's my bag.' I touched the peak of my RAF cap and said, 'Good morning, Geoffrey. You can call me Bill and your dressing room is up there.' He scowled and lugged his bag up the steps of a new pavilion about to be opened by the Yorkshire President, Sir William Worsley, a former Yorkshire captain (1928–29) and father of the Duchess of Kent. When Illingworth found that he was three short, Close, Ryan and Trueman having found better things to do, I was invited to play for Yorkshire. So were the groundsman's young son and our 2nd XI captain, who had sustained a black eye batting the previous day. Using the term loosely, *we* declared at 250-5. Boycott scored 77 out of 189. At one end there was a Test match, at the other total carnage. When we took the field, Illy handed me the ball. 'They tell me you take the new ball for this lot. Good luck. You can come up the hill. I want 'Wills' (Don Wilson, slow left-arm) to bowl down it.' I had never been down that end of the ground before. Facing me was Alimuddin of Pakistan and Peter Kippax of Yorkshire, who had amassed most runs in the league the previous season. Thanks to some superb fielding by four outstanding cover fielders, I escaped with figures of 5-2-12-0. None of them shook hands for a week. Banished to deep square-leg, I easily converted a brutal, flat, head-high pull for six. The Northallerton XI was bowled out for 83, Wilson taking 7 for 35 to prove that Illy could read a pitch better than most. Years later, Brian Johnston received a letter from a Northallerton listener revealing that I had once played for Yorkshire and he confronted Illy about it.

'Did the Bearded Wonder really play for Yorkshire, Illy?'

'Aye,' responded Illy with a pained smile, 'but beggars can't be choosers.'

I can also claim to have captained England once and it happened in the most unusual match I have ever played in. Billed as the 'Battle for the Bush Ashes', it took place in deepest New South Wales at a tiny outpost called Tilpa on 8 January 1983, the day after Bob Willis's team had surrendered the real urn at the SCG. Tilpa's official population was eight, but hundreds came to watch this 40-overs game played on a matting-on-concrete pitch in a desert of red sand. We had flown from Sydney in a private jet. Tilpa's airfield was a strip of tarmac in a flat wasteland with the scrub removed. The only airport buildings housed a telephone and a kharsi. Neither worked. We lunched well in an enormous air-conditioned hall and I suggested we played the match inside it. Outside the temperature was 40°C and walking out into it was like walking into an oven. They had linked an old freezer to a truck's battery so we could have a drinks break every four overs. Encouraged by the concrete under-surface, I foolishly opened the bowling off my usual 20-yard run. Although I took an early wicket, I was soon exhausted. After an hour's break, I had another spell but, with the ball in shreds, I decided to re-enact my Bishan Bedi impressions and bowl slow left-arm. To everyone's astonishment I took a wicket in my first over. We celebrated coming second long into the night before being driven through the bush to a homestead. Next morning our pilot was absent. He had set off to find the home of a girlfriend and was eventually found fast asleep in the cab of a truck with his feet sticking out of the window. Restored by a cold shower and a vat of coffee, he led us reluctantly to the plane. We had to clear a dozen sheep off the strip before we could take off.

Back in Sydney, I went straight to a lunch party at Gamini Goonesena's house. A leg-spinning all-rounder, Gamini would have played many Tests if his native Ceylon had gained full status thirty years sooner. During a first-class career that extended from 1947–48 until 1968, he played for Nottinghamshire and New South Wales and gained four blues at Cambridge, skippering them in 1957. He twice achieved the double of 1000 runs and 100 wickets, scored 211 in the varsity match and returned match figures of 10 for 57 in his final first-class game. His small garden ended in a sheer rock face and when I arrived he was talking enthusiastically to Trevor Bailey. The Boil was showing off a new film camera. When his efforts were developed he discovered that the only segment of sound that he had managed to record as a back-up to the pictures had Gamini saying, 'Those bloody birds perched up there have been shitting all over my vegetables!'

Thanks to John Arlott I played in one match for Hampshire 2nd XI, in August 1972. When asked how this came about, he would tell the enquirer, 'They were desperate – and they never asked him again.' I had been scoring a Sunday League match with John and Jim Laker at Portsmouth and the Hampshire coach came to chat. The first team had several injuries, which had depleted the second team to ten men. With a two-day match against Gloucestershire beginning next day at the Dowty-Rotol Sports Club Ground outside Gloucester, a replacement was urgently needed. John mentioned that I opened the bowling for the MCC and I was immediately selected.

The weather was perfect and so was the pitch. I was given one six-over spell as second change after John Holder, S.J. Taylor and Jon Rice. The bowlers' run-up was similar to the Kirkstall Lane End at Headingley, with a slope leading to a high ridge, the square being elevated to a plateau by years of top dressing. I couldn't find any rhythm but my figures of 6-1-22-0 were quite acceptable. On the debit side was a sharp slip catch, which I stopped with my shin and a comical slow-motion fall when I trod on a loose lace while trying to move forward to field. I scored a single to midwicket before bringing joy to a left-arm spinner by donating a low return catch. The game ended with Hampshire just one wicket short of victory and Gloucestershire 53 adrift of their target. As John said, they never asked me again.

That game also turned out to be the final county appearance for two Gloucestershire stalwarts, Barrie Meyer and Mike Bissex. I shared a room with Daintes Abbia 'Danny' Livingstone, an extremely useful left-handed middle-order batsman from Antigua, who scored two fifties in this match. He ordered breakfast in our room and warmed up for it with a series of prolonged headstands. Suddenly there was a knock on the door and a young maid entered with a breakfast tray. Seeing a very black man clad only in white underpants standing on his head she shrieked, dropped everything and fled.

Ten years later, on the final day of the Maltamaniacs' tour of the Far East, Singapore Cricket Club phoned before breakfast asking if I could provide them with a bowler, a batsman and a wicket-keeper. The latter two roles were easily filled but my bowlers opted for a day's poolside laze before our night flight home, so Muggins played. Our opponents were the Western Australian Veterans and only later did I discover that they included two former Test cricketers and several ex-Sheffield Shield players. In blinding heat and excessive humidity we worked up a sweat just walking out to field on this famous ground set in front of parliament buildings on one of the most valuable pieces of real estate in the world.

Singapore's regular opening attack comprised two large, fit, fast-medium bowlers. When they conceded 50 runs in eight overs, I was summoned to the bowling crease. It seemed churlish to refuse and I reluctantly marked out my new eight-pace run. The second ball must have hit a stone because it pitched leg and removed the off pole. Jon Harris was an outstanding keeper who had played for the MCC at Lord's. In the next over, I bowled a legside ball and Jon brought off a brilliant stumping. After four overs I could hardly breathe and had to stop bowling. Lunch couldn't come quickly enough. Refreshed by a cold shower and a few beers, I was brought back to bowl at the other end. Facing me on 49 was Paul Barton. Now settled in Perth, he had gained seven caps for his native New Zealand, scoring a century against South Africa at Port Elizabeth in 1961–62. By now, I had just about become acclimatised to the heat and bowled one of my best overs of the tour, a maiden. Barton watched his partner receive the next over and looked restless as he faced my first ball. It was a yorker and he kept it out. The next one was a slower yorker. He missed and, as he was bowled, lost his grip on the bat, which sailed out of his hands and above the keeper. There was flying wood everywhere but no one to capture it on film. The next over I took my fourth wicket when John Borrell, the third guest Maltamaniac, ran 20 yards and held an unbelievable diving catch in front of the sightscreen to give me career figures of 8-1-18-4 for Singapore. A few hours later I flew home and battled to stay awake while spending the next two days doing PA commentary at the Wadham Stringer County Indoor Tournament at Brighton Arena.

I wonder how many cricketers have played in two matches at different venues on the same day. On Sunday, 5 July 1984 I played in two games of cricket for Roger Knight's benefit. The main one was at Sanderstead where, batting number three on a flat track with a lightning outfield, I scored 31 off 30 balls with six fours before getting greedy and caught in that order. Roger then despatched me to Kenley to guest for his Mixtures XI. Batting number four on a very different surface, I nudged my way to 26 off 47 balls, completing an interesting half-century for the day. Opening the bowling, it took me six overs to take a wicket and free up a member of the Kenley Club to return me to Sanderstead. There I took the field and watched Sunil Gavaskar keep wicket.

In 1989, in response to an SOS sent to the *TMS* commentary box by a touring team called the Old Gordonians, I seized the chance to play in two matches against Somerset village sides, took eight wickets and won their bowling cup.

Between 1971 and 1994 I played in 56 matches for the MCC, including tours to California and British Columbia. The California expedition in 1992 was the inaugural members' tour, the club's first to be funded by the participants themselves, and was led (astray) by R.M.O. 'Bob' Cooke (Essex and Cheshire). United Airlines won the tour's first major award when they solved their overbooking problems by separating our leader from his motley crew. The rest of us, led by me, won the Gower Award with consummate ease after a stewardess had unwisely wagered against our consuming the flight's considerable stock of champagne. Although the cricket clubs of Marin and Hollywood first played each other in 1932, the game failed to develop in California until the early 1980s heralded a large influx of immigrants from the Indian sub-continent and the Caribbean. With a climate permitting an eight-month season, extending from the end of March into early November, the Marin Club alone stages nearly 100 matches each year and has played a central role in expanding the game in Northern California, where there are now sixteen clubs fielding twenty teams in two divisions.

The MCC took part in Marin's annual festival, which also featured British Columbia CC (a mix of the Vancouver and Victoria clubs) and Lucaya CC (a Bahamas team augmented by several members of London's Mill Hill CC). Few grounds can match the superb wooded scenery of Piper Park. Set within the U-bend of a small river and surrounded by mountains, hills and houseboats, it commands vistas on every side. With the river restricting the square boundaries to 50 yards, ball-retrieving forays frequently advanced into alligator country. While most of the grass outfield was well manicured, Captain Cooke managed to despatch me to a sector that had been reduced to a dusty minefield by its double duty as a soccer pitch. During the Festival, the lack of a pavilion was overcome by the use of two tents – a changing den and a 'Tavern' housing inexhaustible supplies of varied falling-over water and an impressive display of trophies and shields presented by visiting teams.

The matches produced a succession of last-over finishes. A brace of outright wins plus a draw gained the MCC a handsome carved-wooden trophy, which was presented at the closing dinner/dance by Sir Garfield Sobers. The game's greatest all-rounder, now employed by the Barbados Tourism Board, captivated a large, youthful audience with his coaching class the following day. The Cooke school of fitness training demanded tasting raids on the wine-growing valleys of Sonoma and Napa, plus journeys to Fisherman's Wharf and Alcatraz, the latter happily not one-way. One splendid expedition just happened to coincide with the annual Sonoma Wine Festival.

After that, our four minibuses journeyed south via Yosemite National Park to Los Angeles, where we were defeated by two different teams representing the three-division Southern California Cricket Association. Woodley Park had three grounds with grass squares and was busily constructing a fourth. Owned and maintained by the Department of Recreation and Parks, it would be the envy of every city and town council in Britain. It is also home to the Hollywood Cricket Club, their famous but rented Sir Aubrey Smith Field in Griffith Park now being part of an equestrian complex. Happily, their original pavilion survives as an historic monument to some memorable cricketing actors, whose ranks included, in addition to the man who uniquely captained England in his only Test, David Niven and Bill Pratt (aka Boris Karloff).

The MCC's tour to British Columbia in Canada two years later enabled me to return to Vancouver after an interval of forty-six years. Journeys down memory lane included a visit to my former home at 4789 Dumfries Street where the present owners, a very welcoming Chinese couple, revealed a very different interior from the one I had lived in. The greatest thrill was to open the bowling at Prospect Point in Stanley Park, the venue where the scenic beauty had so impressed Sir Donald Bradman. My first visit to Vancouver Island included an exhilarating whaling trip and a walk around the famous Butchart Gardens, where Debbie shamefully wrote in the visitors' book, 'Found a weed.' Linked by microphone to the local radio station, and with Don Oslear umpiring, I commentated as I bowled my last spell for the MCC. Not many bowlers have had a chance to describe their final wicket for the most famous cricket club of all. I probably deafened hundreds. Fred would have been very envious.

Most cricketers who have visited the late Sir Paul Getty's cricket ground on his estate on the Buckinghamshire/Oxfordshire border would happily never play cricket anywhere else. Set in a wooded valley within the Chilterns, it has every amenity money can buy and upstages the Arundel Castle ground, its closest rival for natural scenic beauty, by having an exceptional view on all four sides. An imposing thatched pavilion stands alongside a bank with a large marquee housing massive hospitality. Champagne and Pimms are served by waitresses to invited guests and the lunch interval, officially an hour, once stretched to 89 minutes when Dickie Bird was umpiring. Across the immaculate playing area, with its stripes perfectly mown by groundsman Simon Tremlin and his staff of one, is the neat thatched scorebox. Behind that is a hillside once devastated by a massive gale but now flourishing with 90,000 trees planted by Sir Paul. It must have been a shock to the nursery orders department when they took the phone call. Nesting down the valley are Portuguese red kites, reintroduced to England from Wales by the RSPB. Thriving in their dream environment, the little devils have bred their way down to the New Forest. Sir Paul's magnificent library, a cathedral of books housed in a small Gothic castle, is open on match days to players and guests.

It was through Brian Johnston that I met John Paul Getty II. During the 1980s Johnners frequently began his first session of commentary each day by greeting 'my friend who overlooks Green Park'. At first he was rather evasive about the identity of this mysterious friend. If we hadn't known him better, we might have suspected an intriguing liaison with one of the ladies who baked cakes for *TMS*. No such fun, sadly. We were all taken aback when his mystery friend was revealed as Paul Getty and even more astonished to discover that this reclusive American millionaire was hooked on cricket. We had read over the years that he'd been hooked on just about everything else. Anyone who named a son Tara Gabriel Galaxy Gramophone must have been severely trolleyed at the time. That was in the 1960s when he was at the height of his hippy, velvet kaftan period. Married to the sublimely beautiful Talitha Pol, daughter of Dutch painter William Pol and stepgranddaughter of Augustus John, he had held open house in his Moorish palace in Marrakesh. There he bravely hosted the Rolling Stones and met Mick Jagger. After the tragic death of his wife in Rome in 1971, Paul came to England and lived close to Jagger in Chelsea's

Cheyne Walk. It was Jagger who introduced him to cricket, took him to Lord's and inspired him to buy his first *Wisden*. In 1993 he bought John Wisden & Co Ltd.

Besides much of Britain's threatened heritage, his boundless philanthropy embraced many cricket clubs and grounds, including a £1.6 million donation towards the new Mound Stand at Lord's. There, at all major matches, he could be seen hosting a variety of celebrities and former international players in his private box. By 2002 he was confined to a wheelchair, as was the legendary Australian all-rounder, Keith Miller. Paul adored Keith and arranged for a private car to bring him to Lord's for all the major matches as well as to his private ground at Wormsley, where he always sat at the host's exclusive table in the pavilion corner of the 200-seater marquee.

Paul met Johnners after one of the latter's three sons installed a satellite dish at Getty Towers and Paul revealed his ambition to recreate cricket at Wormsley. They toured the estate looking for a suitable pasture, a task that would have been eased considerably if he had not constructed a lake where the original cricket ground had been. They chose a sloping undulating field close to the Hall, and Harry Brind, Surrey's head groundsman and the ECB's inspector of pitches, was called in for advice. Work began on constructing the ground in 1991 and the Paul Getty XI played its opening match the following June.

Brian Johnston extended his career prospects at the age of 80 by being appointed Paul's cricket co-ordinator, a role that gave him a huge say in selecting the team. Thus Aggers, CMJ and I played in that inaugural game, and Bob Wyatt rang the bell donated by Johnners and inscribed 'To MFWOGP From Johnners' after his daily *TMS* greeting – to my friend who overlooks Green Park. Fred Trueman raised the Wormsley flag and those in attendance included the Queen Mother and Prime Minister John Major. Faith Hawkins, an energetic South African émigré cricket devotee, was the real power behind the Getty cricket throne. Originally nanny to Lady Getty's children, she became Wormsley's Miss Fixit and quickly established good relationships with the counties so that current professionals were queuing to play at Wormsley.

Although Paul had seen neither my birth certificate nor my fielding, invitations to play ceased after we failed to win a match in our first two seasons. To keep me off the field, I was installed as his cricket archivist. Besides reporting the matches and keeping the team's records, I introduced signature albums to display the players' autographs opposite team photographs for each match. These albums feature all the major cricketers of the last decade, including several touring teams. When the 1997 Australians played there, Martin Crowe overcame a major knee injury to score one of the finest hundreds of his life. Players scoring centuries or taking five wickets in an innings for the Getty XI have those feats celebrated by plaques in the pavilion. Paul granted a plaque to just one opposition achievement, Brian Lara's unbeaten 103 for the West Indians in 2000. It is a special burgundy one. Sadly, Sir Paul Getty passed away on 17 April 2003 but his widow, Lady Victoria, has ensured that this unique oasis of country-house cricket continues.

Charity matches can be a great boost to the career averages. Batsmen have no need for helmets, umpires seldom give lbws and fielders are not expected to dive or even chase too frantically. On the other hand, bowlers know that even ace players feel compelled to give their wicket away once they have reached 50. Apart from the chance to mingle with celebs and Test cricketers, the best feature of charity matches is often the catering. I was lucky enough to be selected for an event staged in aid of raising funds to combat famine, a contest played either side of a three-hour seafood feast washed down by copious amounts of falling-over water.

The game was staged at Finchley with Viv Richards as captain. I had strained a calf muscle a few weeks earlier and was supposed to be doing the PA. Viv would have none of it, insisted I played and gave me the new ball. I thought I would go flat out and, if it went again, I could have a relaxing day behind the mike. In my second over I bowled M.J. Smith of Middlesex in his back-lift and Mike Brearley came in. 'I've never put too much of a strain on your scoring, Bill,' he pleaded before miscuing my second ball to short midwicket. A member of England's women's team had taken two wickets from the other end and the opposition were 15 for 4 after four overs. After the match organiser came on to the field and spoke earnestly to Viv, Richard Stilgoe and a boxer recently released from Her Majesty's care were put on to bowl and the score quickly rose to 200.

After the feast, I had just taken my place at the PA table when Viv told me I was opening the batting. Off I went with Terry Blake of the ECB and we put on 50 before he was out. Viv came in, blasted his first ball, the last of an over, and it teetered all the way to silly mid-on. He frowned at his bat. I decided I wasn't going to hang around and slogged a couple of boundaries to my favourite long-on. At the end of the over he grabbed my bat. 'Where did you get that, man?' he demanded. I told him it had been Bob Woolmer's and he had given it to me for playing in some of his benefit games. Viv handed me the piece of firewood. The bowler tried to bounce him, Viv was early into the hook and the ball sailed over the marquee off the back shoulder of the bat. He signed the dent afterwards. Viv hid the bat from me so I had to face the next ball of Mike Smith's left-arm spin with the piece of firewood. I swiped it mightily. From the 'sweet' part of the blade it teetered gently into the bowler's hands. Beside the pavilion was an oil drum adapted as a rubbish bin and I threw the bat into it as I passed.

I first played for the Lord's Taverners in 1972. My skipper in that match was Jack Martin, the first England cricketer I ever met. Since then I have had the delight of playing alongside many famous cricketers and stars of other sports, as well as a host of celebrities including actors, comedians and singers. We have a great time and raise a lot of money for handicapped and sick children. Never did I expect to open the batting with Jack Robertson, take guard against John Snow and Dennis Lillee, or bowl to Reg Simpson with Godfrey Evans behind the stumps. Willie Rushton was one of the wittiest characters I shared a cricket ground with. As I ran in to bowl in one game, my boot split and the heel fell off. 'Your foot's just exploded, Bearders,' he chortled. 'Is that another of your wicket-taking gimmicks?' I once took four wickets in an over and wasn't allowed to bowl for two matches. Allowed to open at Arundel, I scored my only 50 for the Taverners. 'Butch' White was probably under orders when he deliberately ran me out in the next game.

Taverners' tours are rather special. The first one I went on was to Guernsey where Debbie and I were billeted, along with John Cleese and his wife, at the house of former Hertfordshire captain John Appleyard, the linchpin of Malta's cricket when I took my teams there. One morning John's young son insisted that I bowled to him on the main lawn before breakfast. The sound of my appeals woke Cleese. He opened his window and I expected a Basil Fawlty stream of sarcasm. Instead, he shouted, 'I'm in next!' Wearing a silk dressing gown over his pyjamas and sporting a beard he had grown for the part of Petruccio in *The Taming of the Shrew*, he gave us a cameo of the elegant strokes that had earned him a place in the Clifton XI.

Next day, I was asked to do a stint of commentary. I had never done this before and was rather nervous. Cleese was batting and putting the bowler off by lifting his front leg in a goose step. He cover drove a half-volley. Two fielders dived and missed it, another chased and gave up. The ball scuttled over the boundary into some trees and a spectator got out of his deckchair, retrieved it and threw it back. Heavens knows why but I picked up the mike and said, 'That was a wonderful cover drive by John Cleese. Any batsman would be proud of that stroke. We'll just look at that again in slow motion!' Bless 'em, the bowler ran slowly in and pretended to deliver the ball, Cleese did a slow-motion cover drive, the fielders repeated their failures and the spectator slowly rose and retrieved the imaginary ball. Commentary was dead simple after that. I soon became sufficiently confident to do impressions, especially of the *TMS* team. Once at Blenheim (we rarely played where there wasn't a palace or a brewery) I imitated Harry Secombe's famous *Goon* laugh. I put the mike down just before my bottom was pinched and a huge raspberry blown behind me. It was Harry. 'Hello, folks,' came the familiar falsetto.

Visits to Gibraltar, Portugal and Ireland have followed. Neil

Durden-Smith led the Portugal expedition. We all went to a beachside
bar on the first night. Neil ordered all the food and commanded proceedings with great flair. The bill arrived and he read out 21,988 escu-
dos. We all paid our share and the waitress took away the loot. Five
minutes later she returned and handed most of it back. It was the 21
September 1988 and he had paid the date.

In Ireland there was a bomb scare when we were in the middle of
the main fund-raising dinner. It was the era of the Troubles and our
hotel must have been in the thick of it, as scarcely a window had not
been replaced by wooden boards. Compere Richard Stilgoe had just
completed the preliminary part of his main act. This involves the audience contributing a dozen or so totally unrelated subjects, all of which
he has to compose into a song. He had just disappeared into a back
room with his list when we were told to leave the building immediately. We filed out into the cold, drizzly night. Debbie and I, together with
a few others, were invited into a house nearby, before being evacuated
from there to a distant rugby club. More than an hour later we
returned to our seats. Stilgoe, wondering where we had all got to, continued with his act as though nothing had happened. It was a brilliant
piece of showmanship, as is Richard's double act with singer/song-
writer/pianist Peter Skellern. Their cabaret at a dinner in a large illuminated cave was the highlight of our Gibraltar mission.

With one notable exception, my other contributions to charity
have been limited to speaking at dinners and donating books and scoring charts. The exception was the inaugural Botham walk from John
O'Groats to Land's End, a 986-mile trek that Ian undertook in aid of
Leukaemia Research in the autumn of 1985. I volunteered to do a day's
walking with his followers in Scotland and arrived at Pitlochry a day
early to visit a few National Trust buildings. Someone dropped out (the
story of my life) and I ended up doing two days and a total of 57 miles
from Blair Atholl to Kinross. Afterwards, with my feet, shins and knees
in some disarray, I vowed never to repeat the exercise.

A few weeks later I had a phone call from Cornwall. Could I please
drive to Redruth immediately. A slight altercation with a policeman

had occurred on Bodmin Moor and Ian was keeping a low profile that evening. Could I come down, receive some money on his behalf, make a couple of speeches and do the final leg to Land's End the following day. I agreed the first part but said that my undercarriage had only just recovered from the Scottish jaunt. No problem, I was assured, I would be sitting behind a microphone in the cab of a truck, persuading the public to put donations into a bucket. I drove to Cornwall and did what was required.

Next morning it was raining heavily when we assembled in the dark. The truck was a notable absentee. Conveniently, it 'had broken down'. I feared I might well follow it into oblivion, especially when I was asked to lead the walk. They wanted me to set the pace because they had to reach Land's End at a certain time scheduled for live TV camera shots from a helicopter. I was not happy as I steamed off from Camborne. The long strides that had caused such problems in my marching days took me along at a rapid pace. In less than two hours I was on the threshold of Penzance. Ahead of me were crowds of people, banners welcoming 'Beefy' and a brass band. I looked behind me – no one, not a soul for at least a mile. Should I slip past as though I was an anonymous traveller totally unconnected with the walk, march purposefully under the banners and wave, or stand and wait for them. My predicament was solved by a shout from a pub – 'Bill! What are you doing here? Come and have a drink.' Two pints later the main procession arrived. My legs having stiffened up, I had a battle keeping up with them.

Early in the afternoon we reached the First and Last Inn. The four who had walked the entire journey – Ian, Alan Border's brother, sports writer Chris ('Crash') Lander and a Manchester hairdresser whose father had died of leukaemia – went into the inn to change. Half an hour later they emerged wearing top hats and morning suits and carrying silver canes. Bearders had decided not to stand in the rain while this metamorphosis was taking place. He was the first to complete the final stage of the walk and be driven to a warm bath in a Penzance hotel. After Botham had thrown all his friends into the sea, we enjoyed a celebration dinner. The hero of this amazing feat of endurance initiated the traditional throwing of bread rolls. Some thought he should have taken it off his side plate first.

The fund-raising walk did not end there, though. Unhappy at the meagre contribution made by the striped suits of London, Ian organised a final mini-walk of the City a few days later, starting at Lime Grove Studios. Again I was summoned and could not think of an excuse in time. It was a brilliant sunny morning. This time I was rewarded with the testing task of shepherding a wheelbarrow full of champagne. Luckily, Ted Moult volunteered to help and our load soon lightened. It was even more fun when Linda Lusardi joined us. A vivacious brunette, she had a great sense of humour in addition to those more publicised attributes that had prevented most male readers of the *Sun* venturing beyond its third page.

Late in the walk an elderly gentlemen sidled up to me and, in a stage whisper, asked, 'Excuse me. Didn't you used to be Bill Frindall?'

NINETEEN

BLIND CRICKET

F RANK MCFARLANE, a teacher from Liverpool, introduced me to blind cricket. Frank had been totally blind since birth. We met at Old Trafford when he was interviewing members of *Test Match Special* for a series of tapes that he circulated to members of an association of blind sportsmen. When he invited me to watch a blind cricket match at Ealing, I had no idea what to expect and wondered how on earth you could play cricket if you could not see the ball. Of course, the answer was to use a ball that makes a noise.

Blind cricket was invented by the nursing staff of St Dunstan's in the 1920s to provide exercise and entertainment for servicemen who had been blinded in the First World War. St Dunstan's itself had been established in 1915 by Arthur Pearson, a newspaper proprietor who owned the *Evening Standard*, founded the *Daily Express*, and who had lost his own sight. Two years earlier he had been made president of what was to become the Royal National Institute for the Blind. Pearson's objective was to provide a training centre and workshops for hundreds of blinded servicemen. His mission proved astonishingly successful and within three years, over 1500 people had been taught a variety of new skills, regained their confidence and begun to take up independent lives.

The original ball for blind cricket was made of thick cane and contained the type of bell used as a baby's toy. This extraordinary cane 'cage' was the size of a soccer ball and caused painful injuries if it struck a fielder or batsman in the face. After the Second World War it was eventually replaced by a size three white plastic soccer ball containing ball bearings that rattled loudly when it moved. This ball was not too large to be gripped by one hand and bowled overarm. The wicket was a larger version of the standard one and built as a single section gate, making it easier for partially sighted players to see and for batsmen and bowlers to touch to orientate themselves. The pitch was reduced to 18 yards. Teams were a mix of totally and partially blind players but all were 'registered blind'. Batsmen were guided by the bowler calling play before every ball and by the ball's sounds. Bowlers were guided by shouts from the wicket-keeper.

The Laws of Cricket were adapted to allow totally blind and partially sighted players to compete on equal terms. Bowlers had to pitch the ball at least once to a partially sighted batsman and at least twice (without rolling) to a totally blind one. A 'total' could not be stumped and was given one 'life' before being given out lbw. A 'total' fielder could dismiss a batsman by catching him after the ball had bounced once.

Once I had accepted the vastly increased size of the ball, my first impression was that it was a game of cricket rather than a game for the blind. It was played on grass within a cricket ground but it did not have to be played on the square itself. Usually a pitch was cut beside the square. Sightscreens had to blacked over or moved out of the line of the white ball. Some of the fielding was quite outstanding and the game produced an even balance of batting and bowling skills. Although Frank had never seen anyone bat, he executed several immaculate cover drives and timed the ball easily. Most blinded people have exceptional hearing and the rattling ball bearings allowed him to pinpoint the ball with precision. My second impression was that the players contributed a great deal more enthusiasm and effort than I had seen in a recent sighted club game.

In 1984, Frank invited me to meet some of the committee of his association, a registered charity, which then had the convoluted title of BASRAB (The British Association for Sporting and Recreational

Activities of the Blind). We discussed many blind sporting topics and the possibility of expanding their cricket on an international basis. At the end of the meeting I was invited to become the association's first president – probably as a tribute to my fielding. I immediately accepted and was delighted and proud to hold office for twenty years. We soon decided that the charity needed a snappier title and eventually settled for British Blind Sport. Possibly a major reason for my surviving in office for two decades was my refusal to attend any blind archery event.

The charity had been formed in 1975 by blind people who wanted to manage their own sporting affairs. It soon gained worldwide recognition and became responsible for sports' organisation, training and selection at all levels from grassroots to international events. Much of the charity's effort has been concentrated on helping blind children attending mainstream schools, who are disadvantaged where sport is concerned. All too often they are excluded from sporting activities because there is no member of staff qualified to coach visually impaired children. BBS became the voice of the blind sporting community for a range of activities that included archery, athletics, bowls, cricket, football, goalball (a sport devised especially for the blind), judo, martial arts, sailing, skiing, shooting, swimming and tenpin bowling. In the past two decades, blind cricketers have frequently paraded their skills during lunch intervals at Test matches. During the final Test of the 1997 Ashes series at The Oval, their demonstration included two players who had flown over especially from Brisbane. Their presence was especially remarkable because it would have been the first time that they had played the British form of the game.

Although blind cricket was played in many parts of the world by the mid-eighties, at least three totally different sets of rules and equipment were in use. The Australians and New Zealanders played on 22-yard concrete pitches and bowled underarm with a baseball-sized sphere made from plastic-coated wire and containing bottle tops. It looked like a cross between a small lobster pot and a hand grenade. Curiously, catches did not count as a dismissal. The Indians and Pakistanis also bowled underarm on 22-yard pitches but they played on grass using a white plastic ball containing beads. Until all the countries involved could agree to adopt one of these vastly different formats, or find a workable compromise, blind cricket at international level would remain a pipe dream.

During one of several visits to Adelaide to speak to their Cricket Society, I discussed the problem with representatives of Australian blind cricket. Their aims had already moved beyond mere international tournaments to a blind world cup competition. The BBS cricket committee took over these initial discussions with the Aussies but it took the enthusiasm, energy and organising skills of George Abrahams of India to break the stalemate. Astonishingly, in September 1996, after a conference in India lasting just two days, delegates from seven countries (the Test-playing nations of that time, without West Indies and Zimbabwe) settled for the Asian format – a white plastic ball containing beads, underarm bowling, catching, and 22-yard grass pitches. Each nation was allowed two years in which to train a squad of players in the new format.

The inaugural Blind World Cup tournament was held in New Delhi in November 1998 and was won by South Africa, who comfortably beat Pakistan in the final. Two years later I flew to Brisbane to witness a week of tri-nation cricket involving Australia, New Zealand and England. The tournament marked the first visit to Australia by blind cricketers representing England. Managed by John Barclay, a former Sussex captain and England manager, they did extremely well to reach the final. There was no disgrace in losing to a very talented Australian team. In Christopher Backstrom, a 36-year-old right-handed former grade cricketer from Brisbane, now partially blind (B2), they had an outstanding batsman. The lightweight plastic ball did little for the game, offering negligible bounce when bowled underarm and proving difficult to hit with perpendicular bat strokes. Most batsmen relied almost totally on the sweep but Backstrom employed the straight and on drives that had served him well in his fully sighted days. The New Zealanders employed an extremely irritating tactic, which has subsequently been outlawed for being against the spirit of the game. To block the favoured sweep shot, they placed three totally blind fielders in the short-leg area. This formation, introduced but abandoned by the Australians, was known as 'The Wall'. It not only blocked the sweep but ricochets were frequently caught off the bodies of the crouching trio.

In 2004 a stump was burned to inaugurate the first ECB/Sport England Blind Ashes series. The burnt remains of the stump were sealed in the Blind Ashes Trophy. It had to be a stump because bails are not used in blind cricket. Venues for the five matches included Lord's and the Rose Bowl. The series had largely been initiated, promoted and organised by Tim Gutteridge of BBS and it was appropriate that he should play a decisive part in clinching the three-wicket win that gave England a 3–2 victory. His 138 in his final international innings deservedly earned Gutteridge the match award.

Johnners had been an enthusiastically active president of the Metro Club for the Blind and his regular plugs for the Primary Club on *Test Match Special* had greatly boosted that famous charity's membership. Since his death, the Brian Johnston Memorial Trust has sponsored many blind cricket events and contributed considerable sums to the Primary Club's coffers. One of Brian's favourite stories involved his interview with a blind parachutist.

'I'm full of admiration for what you do,' said Johnners. 'Incredibly courageous. But how on earth do you know when you're about to land?'

'Oh, that's no problem,' replied the blind man. 'The lead on the guide dog goes slack.'

Under its new president, Sally Gunnell, the former Olympic 400 metres hurdles champion and world record holder, BBS is going from strength to strength. Development officers and 'Have a Go' days have encouraged many young blind and partially sighted people to join BBS. In 2002 Chris Cowdrey and I were guest speakers at a London dinner celebrating BBS being chosen as charity of the year by the Industrial Agents Society. Combined events, including a raffle and auction, raised a staggering £16,800 for the charity. Long may it continue. Blind sport has changed many young lives.

TWENTY

GUEST SPEAKING

I T TAKES A fair amount of courage to stand up in front of an audience and make a speech, but confidence soon builds after one or two successful attempts. Fortunately, my amateur dramatics exploits in the RAF and the experience of teaching art in the latter stages of that career had given me that confidence. It is important to speak to an audience and not at them. Most cricket functions are held in rectangular rooms, like a tennis court, with the speaker level with the net. It is vital that you keep both sides of the room involved by constantly switching your attention from side to side – rather like watching tennis. Growing up in the golden age of radio comedy had developed my skill at impersonations, as it had for most of my schoolboy contemporaries. If you can do Cyril Fletcher, Max Wall, Tony Hancock and the entire cast of the *Goon Show*, then imitating Messrs Arlott, Johnston and Trueman is a piece of cake – sorry Johnners!

Not until the end of my third season with *TMS* was I invited to speak at a dinner. Then I received a letter from Eric Blott, a journalist and keen cricketer who had opened the batting for Wallingford when I played there for RAF Benson during my early national service days. We met again when I was stationed in Yorkshire and he had become editor of York's local paper and a leading light in the NUJ. Recklessly, he invited me to be guest speaker at the annual dinner of Clifton Cricket Club in York and I made my debut in that role on Friday,

1 November 1968. Luckily, my tales from the commentary box and impressions of its occupants were well received. I thoroughly enjoyed the evening once I heard the first laughter. Other invitations soon followed as word got round and there were very few Friday evenings during the winter months when I wasn't driving to some of the remoter parts of Britain to address cricket clubs and societies.

One of the smallest audiences awaited me at the Wombwell Cricket Lovers' Society when I drove through a blizzard and fog from London to Barnsley. It was an horrendous journey. Visibility was so poor that we had to complete the final few miles with my wife Jacky peering out of the open side window. We arrived about twenty minutes late to find the organiser, Jack Sockell, standing in the porch looking pointedly at his watch. I apologised for being slightly late and hinted that it had not been the easiest five-hour journey I had undertaken. He led us into the hall where ten members of the society were seated in a room set for 100.

'Oh, I'm not the last to arrive then,' I said with some relief.

'Oh, yes you are,' replied Jack. 'You don't expect folk to drive all the way from Leeds on a night like this, do you?'

I did return about a year later when, on a fine evening, a grand total of twenty-three turned up. That wasn't my smallest audience. When I addressed the Western Australian Cricket Society at the WACA ground in Perth, I brought the total attendance up to eight.

One of the worst aspects of cricket functions is frequently the catering. Some has been outstandingly good. At Outwood, a tiny village club in Surrey, players' wives, partners and daughters prepared a fantastic meal for their annual dinners. There are many small local catering firms that produce excellent food, but mass catering is seldom mouth watering and I soon discovered that the standard inevitably decreases with large attendances. It is impossible to forget, and I have tried, a dinner at a major club in Southampton thirty years ago. I knew it was going to be bad when a coven of elderly waitresses served the minestrone soup from kettles. This was followed by something reminiscent of the worst in-flight meals. Dominating a sparse main course was some form of meat sliced so thinly that it was transparent and could have been beast, bird or plastic. I read that Clement Freud so despaired of mass catering when he attended functions that he asked his hosts to leave his table empty. He would arrive with a hamper of food, wine, cutlery and condiments and lay out his own feast. I may well emulate him.

It is usually wise to inspect the 'office' at speaking engagements and check that the microphone works. It's also a good idea to find out where the sound engineer is sitting – or hiding. One of my favourite tasks for more than a decade has been to MC and provide the PA commentary at the finals of the Under-15 Club Cricket Championships. For many years they were sponsored by Sun Life of Canada and held at Basingstoke. One year, when Leslie Crowther was the guest speaker, rain enforced an extended lunch and I was called upon to do twenty minutes after Leslie. I did query whether it would be better for me to precede such a great and experienced entertainer but I was overruled. Leslie began and, to his horror, the battery operated microphone broadcast in three word bursts with silent gaps in between. Norman Collier, a veteran music-hall artiste from Hull, built an entire act around a malfunctioning mike. Leslie struggled on and the audience, thinking he was doing it deliberately, roared with laughter. Realising that I had to use the same piece of equipment gave me no pleasure and, for the only time I can recall, I was dreading having to get up and speak. Eventually, the moment arrived and Leslie handed me the mike with a 'good luck' mumbled through gritted teeth.

I decided to move as little as possible and held the fiendish instrument rigidly still in front of me. The audience thought I was doing it as a gimmick. For twenty minutes I remained immobile, speaking around the mike like a ventriloquist. They were soon laughing so much it didn't matter what I said. Miraculously, I got through my stint without mishap. The rain had stopped. I dumped the wretched mike on my table and fled outside to watch some cricket. Leslie joined me and asked how I had managed to make that mike work. I told him I had frozen in a position where it didn't cut out. At that moment, Sandy Pearcey, the lady in charge of the microphone, hurried over to us.

'Excuse me, Mr Frindall, have you got a microphone in your pocket?' I couldn't resist the obvious retort. 'No, I'm just pleased to see you, Sandy.' The poor girl turned beetroot and Leslie's latent fury erupted. 'No one's ever given me that line,' he fumed.

A few months later Alice Katharine was born. Among some wonderful cards of congratulation was one from Sandy inscribed, 'I'm glad you don't always keep it in your pocket!'

Most functions lose valuable time in getting the diners seated. Very rarely does 7.00 for 7.30 p.m. come to pass and you are lucky if you start by 8 p.m. It gets worse when the guest speaker follows three club members eager to make an impression. We have all suffered the club captain with twenty-three pages of script. Years ago at the Bromsgrove Cricket Club I followed the chairman, then Worcestershire opening bowler John Inchmore and finally a barrister. The chairman did twenty minutes, Inchmore, who never forgave me for discovering that his middle name was Darling and couldn't utter a sentence without the f-word, did twenty-five. Incredibly, the barrister did forty minutes without mentioning cricket and simply strung together a series of sex stories that apparently demanded that the female had a French accent, at which he was quite outstanding. I stood up at 11.50 p.m. After congratulating the club on organising a function that would go into a second day, I assured them that it would not venture very far into it. I also revealed that I now knew why most court cases lasted considerably longer than Test matches. I've not had to go back.

Probably my worst engagement was the Sandy Cricket Club centenary dinner. The ubiquitous Eric Blott, who had shifted south to Hertfordshire, invited me to be the principal speaker. The fellow who preceded me had researched the entire hundred years of history, 73 of which he knew from personal experience. He droned on and on. After thirty minutes he had reached 1925. During the next twenty minutes the audience started to drift out to the bar. Later, the bar staff said that members were escaping the dining room looking as desperate as the cast of *Ice Cold In Alex* when they had just crossed the Sahara. It was now 11.40 p.m. I printed 'YOUR FLIES ARE UNDONE' on a card and slipped it in front of him. He ignored it. At last he reached the hundredth year. Then he said, 'I just want to look ahead to the future,' to which I responded, perhaps too loudly, 'There won't be one unless you sit down!' In the face of sustained applause and cheering from the few remaining listeners, he capitulated.

Alec Guinness could forecast the reception a play was going to receive by peering through a backstage spyhole at the theatre audience before the curtain went up. You can usually assess the potential of a cricket function audience by the pre-dinner drinks atmosphere. If the noise level is high and they are enjoying each other's company, they will be receptive and eager to enjoy the entertainment. But even if the audience is on your side, there are many other hazards to be overcome. It is no fun being the last speaker when you have followed three amateur windbags, a 'heads and tails' session, a raffle, the presentation of scores of cups, shields and plastic miniatures, and the inevitable auction of twenty-four items, many of which involve illegible signatures of kickballers on their shirts and balls.

One of the best-organised events in recent winters was a sportsman's dinner held in the pavilion of Marple Cricket Club in Cheshire in November 2005. Keith McGuffie had masterminded several of these highly successful annual fund-raising events and he cleverly restricted the auction to a dozen items. He also had the brilliant idea of splitting that auction into two sections of six items apiece, one before the speeches and one after. The evening, attended by 150 guests, raised an impressive £5000 and was hugely enjoyed by everyone.

Keith, a senior banking official, came to my rescue the following week when I had to speak at two dinners on the same night. A confusion of dates involving two different agents resulted in my being booked to speak at league dinners in Stoke-on-Trent and in Stockport on Friday, 25 November. Probably the obvious solution would have been to cancel whichever one had been booked second, but I have always preferred to take the positive route. Using the AA website, I discovered that the venues were only thirty-seven miles apart and that the journey should take sixty-one minutes by road. A helicopter solution was discussed with the organisers, both of whom were splendidly co-operative. Finding a landing spot in congested Stockport, allied to that town's close proximity to Manchester Airport, killed that option. When I mentioned the problem to Keith, he volunteered to accept the commission and be my chauffeur. I drove to the Stockport venue where I was to spend the night. Keith arrived from Marple, just three miles east, at 5.30 p.m. and, in spite of the Friday evening traffic, we arrived at Trentham Gardens exactly on time, ninety minutes later. It had been agreed that I would speak from soon after 9 p.m. and be out of the door forty-five minutes later. Stockport agreed to put their comedian on first and I would speak there at 11 p.m. Again, Keith avoided the motorways, took some rat runs around Congleton and Macclesfield, and delivered me to the second function with two minutes to spare without ever breaking a speed limit.

The two functions could not have been more contrasting. Trentham Gardens, where I received my honorary doctorate from Staffordshire University in 1998, had demolished its magnificent main hall. While a successor was being built, functions were held in a vast marquee capable of seating 600. Temperatures that night had already dropped below freezing. I had left Wiltshire under an inch of snow and ice that morning and blizzards farther west had trapped hundreds of motorists on Bodmin Moor. The interior of the mega tent was not a lot warmer, especially as the attendance of 300 rendered it half empty. Access to the Portakabin kitchen was via a large hole in the side filled with hanging plastic strips. Those seated near this passage were rewarded with a fair impression of Siberia. Many diners retrieved overcoats and scarves from their cars. Two very pretty girls, whose scanty choice of dress could have been excused in wartime days of clothes rationing, scurried around the tables borrowing any available garments. Never have two sirens so swiftly been transformed into bag ladies.

My view of these remarkable proceedings was from a darkened dug-out masquerading as the top table. It consisted of a line of a dozen small square tables set on uneven ground beneath an unlit sloping side of the marquee. Seated on the central summit, I commanded an extraordinary view of my table companions as they drifted downhill on either side. Our red plastic chairs were so unstable that any attempt to lean back in one would have catapulted its occupant into the tent's flaps. They were so low that the table surface was at nipple height. In front of me, a twenty-foot section of white clothed trestle tables bore the League's prizes. In addition to some impressive silverware, there were several platoons of bronze plastic batsmen posed with bats over their left shoulders after completing a classic cover drive. As the evening wore on they assumed a more threatening role. They appeared to be advancing up the sloping trestles on either side and, without my glasses, they looked like soldiery bearing rifles. The sixtieth anniversary of the start of the Nuremburg Trials had been marked just five days earlier. Sitting in this darkened bunker, I realised how those twenty-two Nazi leaders must have felt.

The meal was surprisingly good, the audience splendidly receptive – they probably clapped to keep warm – and the auction highly successful. On these occasions, I usually donate one or two limited-edition copies of my radial charts of famous recent innings and these raised £795. Seated on my left in that cramped dug-out was the North Staffordshire and South Cheshire League's president, Russell Flower. A tall, rangy, slow left-arm spinner, he had enjoyed a remarkably long career with Staffordshire (1964–88), continuing to weave his spells well into his 46th year. Ten years earlier he had been recruited by Warwickshire to play in nine championship matches. His tales of the Warwickshire dressing room during that summer centred on his great friend, Dennis Amiss. The Packer Revolution of 1977 terminated the Warwickshire opener's Test career and only legal action enabled the English players who had joined that circus to continue playing county cricket. Many Warwickshire members were openly hostile to Amiss and even his own dressing room was divided in its support. It was an unhappy time for Flower to be introduced to major county cricket at the age of 35.

The Stockport dinner was completely different in both temperature and organisation. Escaping the Stoke igloo, I was whisked into the sauna of the hotel's overheated ballroom. The scene in front of me was the closest to bedlam I had ever witnessed at any function. Jackets and ties had been discarded over mainly empty chairs as their occupants had fled being individually victimised by the high-volume exhortations of a very blue comedian. Their haven was the elevated long bar situated along the back wall of the hall. Their ranks numbered at least 100 and were growing rapidly. I was advised to do no more than twenty minutes and I soon discovered why. Totally oblivious to the entertainment below them, the bar crowd had swiftly doubled and was increasing by the minute. Even savage impersonations of Fred Trueman failed to grab their attention and I was relieved to hand back the mike after fifteen minutes. Never should a speaker follow a comedian but the organiser had suggested it and it did solve a conundrum that I hope will never be repeated. They never got round to the auction so my charts, still unframed, had to await another day – or eBay.

TWENTY-ONE

THE ASHES REGAINED

T HE ASHES SERIES of 2005 has already been hailed as the great-est ever and, having had a box seat from which to record every single nerve-racking ball, I certainly would not argue with that assessment. Only the 1981 Ashes series dominated by Ian Botham ranks anywhere near it among those I have been lucky enough to score. Ludicrously crammed into virtually the last eight weeks of the longest-ever English first-class season, it was certainly the most tense, exhilarating, emo-tional and dramatic of any I have chronicled over the last forty years.

Even though the early season hype gave prominence to England's having won their last five series, few expected the Ashes to change hands. Even ace coach Duncan Fletcher thought that they would have to wait until the 2006–07 tour Down Under. The wily Zimbabwean had only a premonition of the glory to come when England routed a very undercooked Australian side in the 20-over bun fight at the Rose Bowl. Victory by 100 runs in that mini-frolic represented a monumental hid-ing. Then there was the saga of Andrew Symonds being fined and dropped for a late-night binge on the threshold of a shock defeat by Bangladesh. Next day came Kevin Pietersen's first major assault on the Australian bowling to snatch an England victory at Bristol. Ricky Ponting tried to laugh off these defeats as being totally irrelevant as far as the Tests were concerned but Fletcher had spotted three major chinks in their armoury. Their batsmen were struggling against swing, reverse or orthodox, their bowling relied too heavily on Glenn McGrath and Brett Lee, Shane Warne having retired from the limited-overs game, and, like all bullies, they did not like it up them. Matthew Hayden's reaction when a return to the keeper from Simon Jones hit him on the chest, and the fielders immediate support when Hayden gave Jones the benefit of his thoughts, were indicative of the Australians' alarm at discovering that the Poms had grown teeth.

English hopes were severely deflated after Australia's 239-run victory in the First Test. McGrath rashly predicted a 5–0 drubbing and few would have bet against it except the weather lords. Fletcher emphasised the one key positive that could be taken from Lord's – England's bowlers had unexpectedly taken 20 wickets. The team had dropped a sackful of catches, batted poorly and Andrew Flintoff had looked totally out of sorts in his maiden Ashes Test, but England had bowled them out twice. Flintoff went on a short break to think things over and returned in a very positive frame of mind. He was going to take the fight to the enemy and enjoy himself. He can never have dreamt what a formidable all-round impact he was to have on the remainder of the series. The summer was to earn him icon status and a fist full of awards.

After prolonged and agonised discussion, the selectors had replaced Graham Thorpe with Kevin Pietersen. Apart from allowing Thorpe to take his tally of Test caps to three figures, they should surely have brought Pietersen in to the side against a pathetically weak Bangladesh team. KP's outstanding performances in the NatWest limited-overs matches made it embarrassingly difficult not to pick him and he immediately justified their decision by scoring fifties in each of his first three Test innings. After that initial run he did little of note, apart from shelling six catches, until his match-saving 158 on the final day. At the time I thought that Thorpe was very unlucky and that England needed his vast experience, grittiness and left-handedness in the middle order. Crucially, he played Warne well. Although Ian Bell had scored a stack of easy runs against Bangladesh, he is, to quote Rod Marsh, 'a nicker'. In other words, he will edge balls that most other players will miss completely. Apart from twin fifties at Old Trafford, Bell had a dire series with only one other score over eight and a pair at The Oval. Thorpe immediately announced his retirement from Test cricket. I was very sorry to see him leave the stage, having been a great admirer of his batting since he scored a pre-lunch hundred against my Maltamaniacs in Farnham's cricket week when still at school. Although he had made himself unavailable for England's winter tours by accepting a coaching engagement in Australia, Thorpe's inclusion would have shored up our brittle middle-order.

To everyone's amazement, the England team had not been cowed by the Lord's experience. They rallied and charged into the Australians at Edgbaston with all guns blazing. Two bizarre events changed the course of the series on that first morning at Edgbaston and they occurred within 75 minutes of each other. The pendulum of fortune began its swing at 9.15 a.m., as soon as I rolled that errant ball under McGrath's foot as he was warming up with a rugby ball! Before he was carted off in a buggy with a torn ankle ligament, Australia's key new-ball bowler knew that he was out of that Test. From that moment it seemed that the force was firmly behind England and it remained there. At 10.30 a.m., with conditions overcast and the pitch impossible to predict, Ricky Ponting decided to bowl first. We later heard that his choice had not been emphatically supported by his team. At lunch, when England had rattled up 132 for 1, any support must have thinned considerably. All remnants would have totally vanished by tea when the scoreboard showed 289 for 4. At stumps, rebellion must have been threatening after England had rampaged to 407 all out at 5.13 runs per over, becoming the first team to score 400 in a day against Australia for 493 Tests since 1938.

Pietersen and Flintoff (five sixes) provided the centrepiece of this magnificent display with a stand of 103 off 105 balls in 74 minutes. Even allowing for the reduced playing area at Edgbaston, a tally of ten sixes and 54 fours confirmed the power of England's strokeplay. Australia's batsmen struggled after Hayden had miscued his first ball to short extra-cover to register his first golden duck in 120 Test innings. Flintoff left a rampant Gilchrist marooned on 49 when he reverse swung a brace of yorkers to put himself on a hat-trick for the second innings.

Warne (6) and Lee (4) shared the spoils as England were dismissed for 182, Flintoff adding four more sixes in his 73. Australia had two and a half days to score 282 and set a record for the highest winning fourth-innings total at Edgbaston. When the eight-hour playing day ended with Michael Clarke being completely bamboozled and bowled by a brilliant slower ball from Steve Harmison, Australia were 175 for 8 and seemingly defeated.

The owners of the secluded cottage in Worcestershire's Clent Hills where I base myself for Birmingham Tests had tickets for Sunday's fourth day. Realising that they might see only two balls, David was reluctant to forfeit a day's golf but Sheila, who had never attended a Test match, won the verdict. What an incredible 99 minutes of drama they saw. In a seemingly hopeless position and therefore with nothing to lose, Warne and Lee attacked from the start. They added 45 in 38 minutes before Warne, moving across to leg glance Flintoff, kicked his wicket. Last man Michael Kasprowicz joined Lee with 62 still needed. In exactly an hour the pair added 59. Tension mounted in the cramped *TMS* box and we all began to fear the worst as Harmison ran in to bowl the third ball of his 18th over. Short-pitched and lifting viciously at his upper body, it had Kasprowicz evading inside its line and gloving it down the legside. Geraint Jones dived forward, low to his left, and held a fine catch. At the non-striker's end Lee sank to a crouch, head over his bat, a picture of utter dejection and disappointment. Flintoff inter-rupted his victory leaps and hugs, walked over to him, put a hand on his shoulder and said a few comforting words, unwittingly creating the most emotional picture of the year. England had scraped home by two runs, the narrowest margin of any Ashes Test. Had they lost from such a strong overnight position and gone 2–0 down in the series, their spirit must surely have been broken and the series gone.

Edgbaston's was the key result. After that, England were able to take advantage of a bowling attack that was unable to call upon a fit McGrath until the final Test. Jason Gillespie and Kasprowicz appeared spent forces at international level and Lee, although spasmodically successful, was frequently expensive. Only an incredible performance by Warne with an Australian record 40 wickets in a five-match Ashes series, kept the tourists in the hunt. As Fletcher had spotted early on, Australia's technique against the swinging ball was poor. They continued to commit themselves too early. Special fields were set for each batsman. Gilchrist, cramped by the ball angled in at his off stump from around the wicket, kept edging to slip and gully. Lack of success with the blade badly affected his keeping. England would have won at Old Trafford but for the weather and their miserable over rate. They almost faltered at Trent Bridge, losing seven wickets in squeezing 129 to win and relying on a brave rally by Ashley Giles and Matthew Hoggard. Had Warne not dropped Kevin Pietersen on 36 on the final morning at The Oval, the Ashes would almost certainly not have been regained after a wait of 16 years and 42 days, and we would not have witnessed those exultant scenes in central London when man of the series Freddie Flintoff proved that there is life on other planets.

The over-excited scenes in the *Test Match Special* box during the closing stages of those last four Tests reminded me of the rocket-launching control at Cape Kennedy, and my own experiences when charting hits and missiles on WW3 rehearsals with NATO. Somehow I managed to switch my emotions to neutral and concentrate on the accountancy. I found it especially hard to do this if Aggers or Blowers were commentating. Their descriptions became louder, more frenzied and distracting. Behind us the noise level rose abruptly, led by the squeals and shrieks of Shilpa. For the many spectators who keep the score for their own pleasure, maintaining their scoresheets must have become impossible as those around them bellowed and leapt around.

Australian guest commentator Jim Maxwell did exceptionally well in the enemy's lair. Surrounded by pommie broadcasters eager for revenge after nearly two decades of coming a poor second in Ashes contests, he was surprisingly fair and calm. So were the three Aussie summarisers we used. Merv Hughes had the easiest ride because he just did the Lord's Test, which Australia won comfortably. Geoff

'Henry' Lawson handled the Edgbaston and Old Trafford epics with aplomb and obviously enjoyed the time he spent with us. Highly intelligent and witty, he made copious notes in pencil. At least once a session the Lawson hand, like the pincers in a fun-fair scoop, would silently grab my pencil sharpener from the box in front of me. Rod Marsh, who joined us for the last two Tests, had the most difficult mission. Quite apart from commenting on the finale of this extraordinary series, he had a foot in both camps. Amazingly, he managed to tread the tightrope between his Australian nationality and his post as Director of the English Cricket Academy. I doubt if he could have maintained this neutral façade if he had not resigned as an England selector before the season began. He seemed genuinely pleased when England won the series but was not happy that it was he and not Mike Gatting who had to remove his whiskers as a result of a Ladbroke's charity 'Tashes' bet, which swelled the Lord's Taverners' coffers by £8000.

As someone with an interest bypass where soccer is concerned, it was highly satisfying to see cricket dominating the front and back pages of all the national newspapers for more than a month. When I collected my daughter from her primary school the day after the series ended, I was dragooned into joining an impromptu cricket match on the playing field. Cricket had usurped the kickball kingdom and for the remainder of September this was a common scene throughout the country. Now we must build on this great enthusiasm and do everything to ensure that these millions of youngsters remain hooked on our wonderful game. The timing of the loss of televised international cricket to all but the affluent could not be more devastating.

Ashes contests are very special. Just as it is every England and Australian cricketer's ambition to play in them, it is the pinnacle of a scorer's career to record them. It was an immense privilege to have been part of a commentary team that, through the wonders of modern technology, was listened to in some of the remotest parts of the world. No matter how many Ashes series I score for *TMS*, the next one always rekindles the old excitement – and nervousness.

TWENTY-TWO

WILTSHIRE HAVEN

W HEN DEBBIE gained the headship of Steeple Ashton's Primary School in September 1989, she was advised not to live too close to her work. So she opted for a twenty-minute drive, preferably to the east to avoid having to drive into the sun. Urchfont, five miles south of Devizes, a Georgian town in the centre of Wiltshire, ticked both boxes. The village, with just over 1000 inhabitants, lies on the northern perimeter of Salisbury Plain, 100 miles west of London. It contains many thatched cottages, a recently re-opened shop and post office, a pub, two greens, a church and a duck pond. Two years earlier I had escaped from London to Hereford but kept the flat in Fortis Green as my main office. Hereford is a delightful city but it's a three-hour drive from London and the arrangement was not working. I had known Debbie since 1978 when we met on a rainy day outside the pavilion at Kent's St Lawrence Ground in Canterbury. We decided that I should move to Urchfont but retain my office in London.

Opposite Debbie's house, a 1950s bungalow, with extensions, was set in nearly an acre of woodland and water gardens. The woodland included over seventy trees, many of them subject to preservation orders, including two giant beeches that gave the property its name. It had been on the market for more than a year when the owner was advised by a building society chief, who just happened to be on the Devizes Town Council, that she should apply for planning permission to demolish it and some of the woodland, build three four-bedroomed houses with double garages, and run a second drive through the water garden to another entrance. Curiously, this permission was speedily granted much to the dismay of the villagers. It inspired me to enquire about the price and measure the space available to erect a two-storey building to house my study and collection of books, records and score-sheets. By incorporating the garage with part of the ground floor extension and rearranging the rooms in the bungalow, it was just possible. The sale was completed in April 1990 and immediately work began on further extending and refurbishing the bungalow. My mother, then aged 81, moved into the completed new wing that June. She survived two fractured hips and lived for another eight years, spending her final days in residential care close by.

That August, work began on the new building and I moved nine tons of books, files, photographs and pictures from London, temporarily setting up my office in the main room of the bungalow. I completed the season's broadcasting, enjoyed my first cricket tour of India and moved into my new quarters a few days before Christmas. My study overlooks the grounds of Urchfont Manor, now a residential education centre owned by the Council. Beyond that lies the ground of Urchfont Cricket Club where, for several seasons, I opened the bowling uphill on a pitch of little bounce. Interestingly, it gained pace and bounce after I stopped playing there. It was for Urchfont that I scored my final fifty (51 not out at the age of 51), and bagged my last five-wicket haul (6 for 35 in 13 overs unchanged to dismiss Ramsbury for 74 and win by 11 runs) in 1991. I was also instrumental in persuading Urchfont to enter the Village Knock-Out Competition and we reached the third round at our first attempt. After 1994 my few creaking appearances on a cricket field were limited to the Rector's XI in village fete week, the Salisbury Clergy (as 'Father William, the hired assassin'), the Wiltshire Queries, who couldn't think of a proper title when they were formed in 1934 and consequently have a question mark as their badge, the Maltamaniacs and charity games.

On Christmas morning 1991, I 'popped the question' to Deborah

Brown who, considering we had first met thirteen years earlier, cannot have felt rushed into making a decision. We were married in Devizes on Leap Day, with a Service of Blessing immediately afterwards in Urchfont parish church. The date was not chosen to reduce anniversary presents by 75 per cent, as was mischievously suggested in the *Daily Telegraph*'s Peterborough column, but to coincide with Debbie's half-term. After the ceremony, Rector Ivor Hughes, a sage and witty former teacher, clad majestically in his gold and white robes, insisted on leading the wedding procession out of the church. Outside, an HTV camera crew was poised. Ivor halted in the porch and posed. Turning his head slightly, he remarked in a stage whisper, 'They've come to see me, not you two!' Beyond the porch were six members of Urchfont Cricket Club in two ranks with bats raised to form an arch. Debbie and I posed between them for the TV crew and photographers. After a few minutes, one of the bat holders, Tim Ducker, a perpetual last man, rebuked me wearily, 'For Christ's sake, hurry up, Bill. This is the longest I've ever held a bat.' Brian Johnston (who was presented with his own cake by a devoted listener), Trevor and Greta Bailey, and a host of Maltamaniacs were among the wedding guests.

Early in 1996 we were blessed with a delightful daughter, Alice Katharine. One of the bonuses of working from home, apart from my broadcasting and speaking engagements, has been that I have spent more time with her than most fathers are able to spend with their daughters. She is now one of just twenty-nine children attending Chirton Primary School some three miles away. There Debbie teaches the youngest three years and we have both been conscripted as governors. When Urchfont's primary school gained Beacon status, its numbers grew rapidly. It soon passed the hundred mark and Alice became totally lost in a class of more than thirty. She has blossomed since her move two years ago.

After more than sixteen years here, I have grown to love Wiltshire. It seems ridiculous to recall that I used to regard the county merely as somewhere rather quaint that you passed through on the way to Taunton and the west. My only childhood memory of this region involved a visit to Salisbury with my parents and my first view of its spectacular cathedral spire. That launched a fascination with architecture which developed into my first career. It also produced a furious outburst from my fiery mother when my father forgot where he had parked the car and we spent an hour searching for it. One of my earliest broadcasts was from Wiltshire, when a *Sporting Chance* programme was recorded at Dauntsey's School in West Lavington, now a mere ten minutes from home. When I spent that night at The Bear I could never have predicted that Devizes would eventually become my nearest town.

The garden had received scant attention during the seven years before I took it over. The previous owners were a married couple of teachers and, after he left her for a younger model and a smaller garden in 1984, she hardly ventured outside. Until volume of work compelled the occasional assistance of a proper gardener, Malcolm Smith (who just happens to be an Urchfont cricketer), my role was that of destroyer. I cut down brambles and small diseased trees, mowed lawns, moved shrubs, trimmed hedges – including a ten-foot beech one – and borders. Only under strict supervision from Mrs Bearders was I permitted to undertake elementary basic weeding. Debbie does constructive gardening, such as planting and dreaming up new projects. Until she resumed full-time teaching, she was able to combine her supply work with motherhood, gardening, running my office and chairing the village school's PTA.

Life here is delightfully relaxed when deadlines are not threatening. First David Court and, more recently, Harry Hampson have performed technical miracles as computer gurus and saviours of deadlines. As well as cricket in the first half dozen seasons here, my contributions to village life have been restricted to amateur dramatics, consisting mainly of cameo roles in the village panto, but they are still talking about my Abanazar! More embarrassingly, few have forgotten my unfortunate spoonerism involving Widow Twankey.

Reliable medical care is essential as advancing years take their toll and it is fair to say that my body has been well lived in. After all, there is no point in leaving behind one in perfect working order. In Paul Wylie I have the best dentist who has ever attacked me. He was also an outstanding captain and all-rounder for Urchfont. Richard Sandford-Hill is an excellent GP with a hunger for wine and cheese bordering on John Arlott's levels. Husband to a GP shopping companion of Mrs Bearders and father to Alice's closest friends, he is a fervent Welsh rugby enthusiast with debenture seats in Cardiff's Millennium Stadium. Dick also loves cricket and has been known to watch England's overseas Test matches from this room when I am scoring them for Sky and *TMS* and for my 'Billboards' in *The Times*. Gazing around the pictures, books and files during an advert break, he once shocked me by asking, 'What are you going to do with all this when you go, Bill?' I stared at him in feigned horror. 'Have you been studying my case notes, Dick? Is there something I should know?' On another occasion, after I returned from an overseas tour with a spot of tummy trouble, he was conducting an impromptu surgery over a glass of wine in the conservatory. Glancing up from his notes, he asked, 'What about sex?' Flabbergasted, I replied, 'Do you mind if I finish my wine first?'

TWENTY-THREE

FOUR DECADES OF CHANGE

W HENEVER ANYONE asks me what has been the biggest change in cricket during my four decades on the broadcasting circuit, I reply with three words – the Packer Revolution. World Series Cricket, created by Kerry Packer when the Australian Cricket Board refused to grant him exclusive television rights for a Test series, transformed cricket when it was introduced in 1977. He recruited thirty-five of the world's best cricketers into three teams – Australia, West Indies and a World XI – running WSC for two Australian seasons, including matches in New Zealand and the Caribbean.

Helmets became accepted as essential headgear for batsmen and close fielders because of WSC. Advertising around major cricket grounds and on players' equipment increased dramatically, as did players' incomes. Television coverage of cricket changed considerably, with an increase in camera angles created by the use of more cameras. No longer was all the coverage from the same end of the ground. In the last two decades, technology involving slow-motion replays has advanced rapidly, slowing and magnifying the action to show the faintest edged catch. Other innovations such as 'Hawkeye', the 'snick-ometer' and wicket-to-wicket guidelines have put umpires in a no-win situation regarding leg before and caught behind decisions. Stump cameras and microphones have added considerably to the entertainment of viewers.

Apart from ground and individual advertising, now involving even the umpires, Test cricket has changed little as a spectacle. Mercifully, it is still played in white clothing with a red ball and white sightscreens. Sunglasses, wristwatches, sun block and bizarre hairstyles such as Kevin Pietersen's, all now accepted as essential, were hardly ever seen when I began scoring Tests. Overs now universally consist of six deliveries, whereas Australia, New Zealand and Pakistan all employed eight-ball overs until the late 1970s. Commercial television compelled their demise because a six-ball over allowed more advertising breaks. Deliberate time wasting has necessitated a mandatory 90 overs per day but that has not alleviated a dire average over rate. The admission of Sri Lanka (1981), Zimbabwe (1992) and Bangladesh (2000), plus the reinstatement of South Africa (1991), have increased the number of Test playing countries to ten.

The amount of international cricket now staged to comply with the requirements of the ICC's Test Match Championship schedule, allied to the amount of limited-overs international cricket played, has dramatically increased the workloads of players, umpires, scorers, statisticians and the media. The computer has become an essential tool and Paula Dixon's decision to drag me into the technological age back in 1984 was indeed a key moment. Only those who have compiled large statistical tomes using a typewriter and carbon paper will realise how word processors have eased and accelerated the entire operation.

Tests are now umpired by members of an ICC élite panel, supplemented by those on an international panel, members from the countries involved in a particular Test being excluded. Sadly, this has meant that home umpires can no longer officiate in home Test matches. Not all the best umpires are members of that élite panel. Peter Willey and Neil Mallender, two of the most proficient umpires at the highest level, both withdrew from the international circuit for domestic reasons. Neither was prepared to desert his family for a large portion of the year. Match referees have had to be introduced to enforce the Code of Conduct and report chuckers, although the latter are now given an extraordinary amount of leeway (15 degrees of elbow flexing).

Perhaps the most important recent innovation has been the introduction of the third or replay umpire, who sits beside the referee to adjudicate on decisions, mainly stumpings, run-outs and boundaries, referred to him by the officials on the field. The system was introduced in South Africa for the four-match 1992–93 series against India and was also employed in New Zealand throughout the three-match series against Australia early in 1993. Only after trials involving three televised limited-overs matches later that year, did the TCCB authorise the use of TV replay judgements for the Second Test against Australia at Lord's in June 1993. The system's first Test-match victim in England was Robin Smith in England's first innings of that match when the verdict on his legside stumping took ninety-three seconds.

Photography of county and Test cricket was the protected preserves of two agencies until the mid-sixties. At The Oval two enormous cameras using large glass film plates were situated below the Surrey dressing room at the Pavilion End and on the roof of the low Vauxhall Stand. Their shots were restricted to action immediately around the batsman. Patrick Eagar was the first freelance photographer to break this mould and open the floodgates for a host of others. Colour and the rapid advancement of technology have increased the range and versatility of cameras and the speed by which photographs can reach sports and news desks.

Scoring has moved into the computer age and all major matches in England are now recorded on laptops and their results transmitted to agencies that relay them swiftly to universal outlets. Most counties also keep a manuscript record. I have never used a computer to score with and do not intend to do so. Having been on the arts side at school, I derive considerable satisfaction from creating neat scoresheets and would gain no pleasure whatsoever from achieving a similar record by tapping a keyboard or wrestling with a mouse.

Cricket reporting involved typewriters, shorthand notebooks and newspaper copytakers until the mid-1980s. When I began reporting matches soon after that, I was loaned a Tandy computer that could transmit copy via telephone lines. Modern systems can transmit written copy from laptop to sports room via a mobile phone. Like all technology, it is magnificent when it works.

Without doubt, the most far-reaching innovation in professional cricket during the last century has been the introduction of the limited-overs game. The desperate financial position of county cricket compelled urgent action. In 1956 an MCC committee under the chairmanship of H.S. Altham examined the rapid decline in attendances at county championship matches and in the general tempo of the game, and came up with the idea of a one-day knock-out tournament. After a pilot scheme involving four midlands counties in 1962, a knock-out competition, sponsored by Gillette, was introduced the following year with a final at Lord's. When this finished in the dark, the number of overs per side was reduced from 65 to 60. The success of televised Rothman's Cavaliers matches, in which a team of recently retired England and overseas cricketers played most of the counties in 40-over games on Sunday afternoons, led to the birth of the Sunday League in 1969. A League Cup competition sponsored by Benson & Hedges arrived in 1972.

The first limited-overs international was a hastily arranged affair, played to appease the disappointed public on the final scheduled day of a rain-aborted Test match between Australia and England at Melbourne on 5 January 1971. Significantly, it attracted 46,000 spectators and produced receipts of $33,000. Kerry Packer almost totally transformed this form of the game, introducing coloured clothing, white balls, black sightscreens and floodlit night cricket. Incidentally, I was assured by one of his close advisors that Packer never intended that the 'pyjamas' would descend to the crude and garish colour combinations of the present day. He wanted single-colour shirts and trousers in pastel shades that would show up against the grass and backcloth of the crowd and stands. His WSC sides played in yellow (Australia), pink (West Indies – who were not over-pleased with the colour) and blue (World XI). The matches were played in two halves with an hour's dinner break around 6 p.m. Floodlit cricket provided great theatre, particularly at the Sydney Cricket Ground with that fabulous view of the sun setting behind the Monty Noble Stand.

Since Packer, fielding restrictions and sundry other innovations have arrived. The attraction of limited-overs cricket, was its simplicity. Both sides batted and bowled within an eight-hour span. Provided the pitch was reasonably flat, batsmen would hold sway, producing plenty of boundaries and some tense finishes. Gradually, coaches and captains worked out a basic method of playing a game now standardised to 50 overs. Matches became increasingly formulaic and predictable, beginning with a flurry for 15 overs while the fielding restrictions were in force, followed by the graveyard shift where the ball was nudged and nurdled for singles, and ending with happy hour in the final ten overs.

In 2003 the ECB introduced 20-overs-per-innings matches and they immediately attracted vast crowds and television coverage. Since a game lasted barely three hours, it left plenty of the day in which to do something useful. The attraction of these games to county treasurers has led to them banishing championship matches from the fixture list for three prime weeks in the middle of the English season. So far, only four have been played at international level but they are seriously threatening the survival of the 50-overs version. To protect the latter, the ICC cricket committee, a panel of former international cricketers meeting periodically in Dubai, came up with two major trial innovations. Both have proved singularly unsuccessful and have been roundly condemned by players, press and public. The first involved the use of a twelfth player who had to be named prior to the toss and who could replace one of the chosen eleven at any time. This gave a great advantage to the side winning the toss and changed the entire ethos of an 11-a-side sport. Mercifully, it was discarded in April 2006. The other change increased the overs of field restrictions from 15 to 20, with the first half being compulsorily taken at the start of the innings and the second being available in two batches of five to be taken in the next 40 overs at the discretion of the fielding captain. Had this committee held its horses until after the superb tied NatWest Series final between England and Australia at Lord's on 2 July 2005 they would surely have resisted such ridiculous meddling. Perhaps they had to justify their expensive missions in some way.

County cricket has changed immeasurably since 1965. Although Warwickshire introduced the Champions Pennant in 1951, 61 years after the championship was officially constituted, not until 1973 did the winners receive a trophy. It has been sponsored only since 1977. The format of the competition has been fiddled with bewilderingly. When I began watching county cricket in 1951, each of the 17 counties played the others home and way each season, a total of 32 games each. This had been reduced to 28 matches apiece by 1966. The programme was cut to 24 games in 1969 and further reduced to 20 in 1972. From 1977 to 1982 inclusive, each county played 22 matches. The tally became 24 from 1983 until 1987 inclusive. The following season four-day championship cricket was introduced, each county playing six four-day and 16 three-day fixtures. Durham were admitted to the championship in 1992, the final season of this hybrid format. Since 1993 all matches have been played over four days.

The most significant change occurred in 2001 when the 18 counties were separated into two divisions of nine teams, with three counties being promoted or relegated at the end of the season. The initial split was decided by final positions in the 2000 table. Each county plays the other eight twice on a home and away basis. After five seasons the jury is still out regarding the success of this format. The chief executive of the ECB has publicly declared his support for restoring a single division. Apart from interest aroused by the end of season promotion and relegation jousting, the split format has little to recommend it. The current champions can claim only to have been the best of half the teams in the competition. Proof that there is little difference between the standard of the first and second tiers came in 2005 when newly promoted Nottinghamshire and Hampshire headed the First Division. From 2006, only two counties qualify for promotion/relegation. Warwickshire won the 2004 title with a pitiful tally of five wins from their 16 matches.

Another significant change in championship cricket during my career was the introduction of the full covering of pitches in 1981. It was swiftly abandoned when first introduced in 1959 but it now seems here to stay. Uncovered pitches produced some spectacular batting and bowling feats when exposed after rain to a drying sun. Jack Hobbs reputedly had the best technique of any batsman on a drying pitch. Len Hutton was not far behind him. This change removed a major trump card from England's armoury in home Test matches. Pitches left open to the wiles of the elements were as surfaces from another planet to overseas batsmen. Don Bradman was not in the same class in such alien conditions, although 'sticky dogs' involving Australian soil were more vicious than their English counterparts. Many feel that full covering is the main reason for the total absence of quality spin bowling in England. When Ashley Giles was compelled by injury to withdraw from the Tests in India in 2006, England's selectors, after considerable searching, mustered three slow bowlers with three Tests and the same number of wickets, averaging 92.33 apiece between them. All three caps and scalps were the sole property of Shaun Udal, who celebrated his 37th birthday during that series.

Many pundits attribute England's recent success in Test cricket to the introduction of central contracts. Those players who are awarded them are paid and controlled by the ECB and not by their counties. Certainly, the 'Team England' ethos played a central role in last year's Ashes campaign. With coach Duncan Fletcher eager to rest all his contracted players as much as possible, the England stars rarely appear for their counties. Had this system been in operation in 1951, I would not have witnessed that memorable duel between Denis Compton and Alec Bedser on a drying pitch at The Oval. With the 2006 England programme involving seven Tests, 10 limited-overs internationals, a ridiculously expanded Champions Trophy in India, and the Ashes series in Australia, any sighting of Andrew Flintoff in Lancashire colours will be as rare as that of a cloudless sky in Manchester.

To compensate for the almost total absence of front-line home players, the counties have been allowed to field two registered overseas players in all competitions. These can be replaced in the case of serious injury or calls by their home boards. The addition of players with British passports courtesy of distant kin and those qualified through European Union passports and even trade agreements (à la Maros Kolpak, the Slovakian handball player who successfully took legal action against the German authorities) has made a total nonsense of county cricket. The 2005 Cheltenham and Gloucester Trophy, a Lord's county limited-overs showpiece, was won by a Hampshire team that included just four players born in England. From 2006, counties will receive financial bonuses from the ECB for producing English players. Thus teams that include excessive numbers of 'foreigners' will be severely penalised.

During the past forty years no decision has aroused such strength of emotion, ranging from considerable wrath to abject despair, among cricket statisticians and historians as that taken by the ICC to award Test match status to the Johnnie Walker ICC 'super test' between the Australians and a World XI at Sydney in October 2005. This decision followed three other contentious ones involving limited-overs international status being accorded to a Tsunami Appeal match, three games between Africa and Asia and a three-match rubber between Australia and the World XI.

Matches involving multinational teams cannot qualify for Test match or limited-overs international status. The ICC's own regulations confirm that only their full members can participate in Test matches. Conglomerates such as World XI teams most certainly do not qualify and it is ridiculous that a player should be able to represent two Test teams concurrently. The ICC's main committee was far from unanimous in this controversial decision. Moreover, the Association of Cricket Statisticians and Historians was consulted and opposed official status being given to this junket. As far as the superfluous 'test' is concerned, some of the players taking part were embarrassed by the ICC's decision to call it a Test. Adam Gilchrist publicly declared his unease with it.

Limited-overs internationals have scant importance historically and, frankly, their status is of no great concern. The latest meddling with their playing conditions had rendered them even more contrived and farcical. Having watched the Tsunami Appeal match on TV, it would appear that numerous factors, most importantly statements from players and commentators, confirmed that the result of the game was purely incidental. It was not an authentic contest and should not have any special or official status – in the same way that the Princess Diana Memorial match at Lord's didn't.

Test match and limited-over international records should be restricted to matches between teams representing national boards. They should not include hotchpotch multinational games that have no significance beyond fund raising. The records of authentic Tests have already been devalued by the inclusion of matches between excessively weak Bangladesh and Zimbabwe teams. Including so-called 'super tests' prostitutes them even further. A far stronger case could be made for including the 1970 England v. Rest of the World five-match series, which I scored for *Test Match Special*. At that time, I was also compiler of the records section of *Wisden Cricketers' Almanack* and I was consulted by the Secretary of ICC concerning the series' status. In fact, those games were accorded the full panoply of official Test matches and the BBC would not have broadcast them ball by ball if that had not been the case. England's players were awarded official caps and Gary Sobers, captain of the Rest of the World XI, was assured that his team's performances would be included in the official Test records. He subsequently told me that he would not have taken them seriously if they had been unofficial Tests and would have treated them just as exhibition games. Ironically, in view of their recent decision, it was the ICC who subsequently ordained that the 1970 games were unofficial matches and must be excluded from official Test match records. They remained a grumbling appendix in *Wisden* from 1971 until 1980, when a change of publisher persuaded the editor, Norman Preston, to drop them from the records section.

TWENTY-FOUR

THE ASHES SURRENDERED

OR AN ENGLISH SCORER – and pensioner – to be elected Patron of the German Cricket Board (Deutscher Cricket Bund) must be akin to C. B. Fry famously receiving an invitation to become monarch of Albania.

My appointment was the curious and convoluted outcome of answering a question about linear scoring from the only qualified Association of Cricket Umpires and Scorers (ACU&S) incumbent in Germany. Although a book published in Hamburg in 1796 included a detailed description of cricket and the first club was formed in Berlin in 1858, the game never attracted more than a tiny minority of British servicemen and ex-pats. In 1900 an Edinburgh school played Preussen CC in Berlin in an epic billed as '*Deutschland gegen Schottland*', but not until 1930 did the four clubs then constituting the Berlin League organise a tour to England. After the Second World War, German cricket was dominated by the British occupying forces and I enjoyed several matches there during my NATO sojourn at Fontainebleau in the early sixties.

A vast influx of Asians during the past decade has seen the numbers of cricketers grow considerably, and in 1999 Germany gained Associate Membership of the ICC. There are now more than 2000 registered cricketers representing over 60 organised clubs spread around five League areas (Bavaria, Berlin, Hessen, North Germany and North-

Rhineland). Most clubs have youth teams, and a recruiting pro-gramme for women's cricket was begun in 2005 and won an ICC award. It was the fact that very few followers of the game outside its boundaries are aware of the huge numbers of players Germany now supports that prompted the DCB to issue their invitation. I have tried to repay this honour with frequent mentions on *Test Match Special* and several visits to present awards at their cricket festivals and to give lec-tures on linear scoring.

I had expected my future cricketing travels to be confined to Europe when Peter Baxter dashed my hopes of joining the *TMS* team for the 2006–07 Ashes campaign by revealing that there were likely to be sufficient funds only for a local state scorer. So it was a great surprise when this decision was reversed six months before the Brisbane Test. After enduring my first long-haul flight for five years, I collected my luggage while my body was still being flown over the Arabian Gulf. Two days later I watched in bemused and jetlagged horror as a stress-stricken Steve Harmison scored a direct hit on his startled captain at second slip with the opening ball of the campaign. Sadly it set the scene for 22 days of almost unmitigated disappointment for England's players, travelling supporters and the millions at home nocturnally listening to or viewing broadcasts.

I should have listened to my immigration interrogator at the air-port or to several taxi drivers who advised me to load as much money as possible on Australia to regain the Ashes. Betting assessors rely on imminent past form and there was no comparison between recent Test match results. Excluding their anomalous frolic with a World XI, Australia had won ten of their 11 Tests since losing the Ashes in September 2005, whereas England had won five and lost four of their 13. Moreover the Aussie team had been strengthened by the recruit-ment of batsman and ace fielder Michael Hussey and metronome seam bowler Stuart Clark. Crucially, the Australians were desperately hun-gry to regain the Ashes. They didn't fire their coach, captain or selec-tors. They sat down and worked out what had gone wrong and played throughout with an intensity that stunned England.

England really didn't turn up at The Gabba. Their preparation had been virtually non-existent with only a single first-class match, and that a three-day affair on a totally different surface. After the Sydney Test, Bob Merriman, a senior, long-serving and greatly respected Australian administrator, revealed that the ECB was offered, and declined, up to four four-day first-class matches prior to the First Test and they were advised that the ICC could be persuaded to bring their Champions Trophy forward to accommodate this.

Over-protected against burn-out, Harmison had bowled a paltry 183.3 first-class overs in 2006, a tally that any of Fred Trueman, Brian Statham or John Lever would have comfortably exceeded in a fortnight. Fellow members of his attack included three players, in Andrew Flintoff, Jimmy Anderson and Ashley Giles, who were returning from lengthy absences after serious injuries involving surgery. England's selectors lumbered Flintoff with the burden of captaincy instead of leaving it with Andrew Strauss, who had shown proactive flair during a successful series against Pakistan. The most ludicrous decision, widely denounced by former Test captains, players and the touring media, was to replace Monty Panesar and Chris Read with Giles and Geraint Jones. Taken by coach Duncan Fletcher and the captain to bolster the tailend batting, it sent out all the wrong signals. Having enjoyed a successful series against Pakistan, Panesar and Read were unceremoniously dumped. Not only was it a grave injustice, it was also a totally negative decision that showed the opposition we were desperately worried about our batting. England deserved to lose.

Brisbane itself had changed out of recognition from the sleepy backwater I first visited 30 years ago. It is now Australia's fastest growing and most progressive city. Luckily full-blown summer had not arrived yet with its formidable heat and humidity. My rented Vulture Street apartment overlooked the Brisbane River towards the rapidly expanding high-rise skyline of the city. Just ten minutes walk along that busy one-way street was the entrance to Brisbane Cricket Ground in Wooloongabba. Gone were the greyhound track, the hill, the flaming poinciana trees and the quaint Queensland Cricketers' Club. The

Gabba was now a soulless concrete bowl, a stark replica of the vast mausoleum that awaited us at Melbourne. Policed by moronic stewards it produced an eminently forgettable intro to the series.

After Ricky Ponting (196) had declared at 602, Glenn McGrath, returning from a ten-month absence to care for his cancer-stricken wife, took six for 50 as England were despatched for 157. Much to the relief of Queensland's treasurer and caterers, Ponting did not enforce the follow-on. Declaring at 200 for 1 (Jason Langer 100 not out), England were dismissed for 370, to lose by a monumental 277 runs. Their only consolation came from a stand of 153 between Paul Collingwood (96) and Kevin Pietersen (92).

Jeff Thomson, who joined our commentary team for this match, provided its only humorous moment. Watching 'Blowers' dribble most of the contents of a meat pie down his shirt, Aggers asked 'Thommo' about the essential ingredients of Australia's staple diet. 'Road kill!' came the growled reply.

It was a supreme joy to escape Brisbane and revisit the elegant Adelaide Oval. The recent additions of the Bradman and Chappell Stands have enhanced the attraction of one of the most memorable cricket grounds in the world. I had a wonderful view of it as I flew in from Brisbane but sadly had left my camera in the overhead locker. Its only blemish was our commentary box, one of the smallest in the world, so narrow that only two could sit at the front desk (commentator and scorer), with the summariser perched on the stairs behind them. When I sneaked into the ground on Tuesday afternoon, Harmison, distraught after returning figures of 1 for 177 and determined to recapture his form, was alone in the nets with bowling coach Kevin Shine. Surely this should have been the formula before the series began. Figures of 0 for 111 in the Second Test were to prove that it was too little too late.

The Adelaide Oval has usually been a batting paradise. In ten first-class innings in 1962–63 and 1965–66, Ken Barrington scored 748 runs, average 93.5, with a lowest score of 51. Curator Les Burdett has worked hard to produce surfaces that will provide a more even balance between bat and ball. Anticipating a continuation of the current heat-wave, he had left a mat of thick grass and flooded the square earlier in the week. When the first four days turned out to be cool he was left with a totally benign pitch. Only on the last day did the sun burn down and present a bowler-friendly strip. It produced the most remarkable turnabout in Test cricket since Ian Botham and Bob Willis snatched victory after following on at Headingley in 1981. This time England seized defeat from the jaws of a safe draw.

Thanks to a record fourth-wicket Ashes partnership of 310 between Collingwood (206) and Pietersen (158), Flintoff was able to declare at 551 for 6, leaving McGrath and Shane Warne with combined figures of 1 for 274 from 83 overs. Australia replied with 513 (Ponting 142, Michael Clarke 124, Matthew Hoggard 7 for 109 in 42 overs).

Having survived a tricky 19 overs on the fourth evening, England began the final day 97 runs ahead with just one wicket down and 90 overs left in the match. At a Travels Tour forum with Mike Atherton, Peter Walker and Mark Ilott after that session, I had startled the audience by saying that only Australia could win the match and that England would have to bat until tea to secure a draw. I reckoned that Warne, with his incredible accuracy, sharp spin and constant chirping at both batsmen and umpires, would pose a tremendous threat. If I had uttered such an accurate prediction in the Middle Ages I would have been burned as a witch.

England began confidently and had reached 69 when Andrew Strauss was given out to a bat-pad catch when the ball clearly missed the bat. He had played Warne with great assurance, as had Ian Bell. The latter's run out when he steered a ball to backward point and responded late to a call from Collingwood precipitated a dire procession. It took only one ball for Warne to win his ego battle with Pietersen by looping a vast leg-break round a reckless sweep. Curiously it was a stroke that KP had totally eliminated from his century in the first innings. The rest followed like lambs despite a 198-minute resistance from that admirable battler Collingwood. The loss of nine wickets for 60 runs gained a worthy entry in the book of England's Most Dramatic

Collapses. Needing 168 off 36 overs, Australia reached their target with 13 balls to spare. Poor Collingwood. Only the third England batsman to score a double century in Australia, he became the first since Dennis Amiss in 1976 to score 200 for England and finish on the losing side. England's total of 551 became the highest losing declared total in the opening innings of a Test.

England's players, having controlled the match for four days, were devastated by this defeat. They were aware that no England side had ever drawn a series Down Under after losing the first two Tests and, in the entire history of Test cricket, only Australia had won a series (in 1936–37) after being 2–0 down. Their only spark of good news came with Damian Martyn's mysterious retirement and disappearance. Perhaps others would follow.

The main route to Adelaide's airport involves a long thoroughfare that has recently been renamed Sir Donald Bradman Drive at considerable expense to all the home- and business-owners living along it. An enterprising owner of one of the less salubrious establishments swiftly erected a sign proclaiming 'Bradman's Massage Parlour'. He was soon ordered to remove it but apparently the publicity it briefly engendered increased the number of his patrons considerably.

Perth provided no relief for Flintoff's besieged troops. Barely 462 days after regaining the Ashes, England surrendered them to a rampant Australian team that had then won ten Tests in succession. They showed no mercy at Melbourne or Sydney, extending their run to twelve and emulating the previously unique Ashes feat of Warwick Armstrong's 1920–21 team by completing a 5–0 whitewash.

The gross folly of the selections of Giles and Jones was confirmed when Panesar celebrated his return by taking eight wickets at the WACA and Read became the first keeper in Test history to claim six dismissals twice in successive innings of the same series. His nimble footwork and exquisite glovework earned comparisons with Alan Knott, the best keeper I have seen, from Ian Healy.

Australia won the last three Tests by 206 runs, an innings and 99 runs in three days, and ten wickets in four days respectively. At Perth,

Adam Gilchrist, having narrowly avoided a king pair, scored a 57-ball hundred, the second fastest in Test history. Having announced his imminent retirement from Test cricket, Warne celebrated his last first-class match on his home Melbourne soil by becoming the first to take 700 Test wickets. He reached this target when he trapped Harmison in front in the second innings. Public celebrations when he bowled Strauss on the first day erroneously allowed for the six wickets he had taken against the World XI. In a grand retirement finale in Sydney, McGrath and Langer joined Warne's exodus from the Test match arena. All had played major roles in one of their country's outstand-ingly successful eras. It will be surprising if their replacements prove half as durable. Certainly Australia can expect to spend much longer in the field when they resume Test cricket after a ten-month hiatus.

There will be no easy remedy for England's emphatic failure. It seems obvious that the central contracts system must be overhauled so that the players involved play sufficient county cricket to keep them in peak form. They must not be rested so that they may be fit in six months' time. The ECB's annual handout of television's largesse, some £1.5 million per county, should go to the County Boards for distribu-tion upwards from grassroots level, and not be given to the County Clubs to fritter on the wages of Kolpak and other players unqualified for England.

At a Testimonial Dinner for veteran leg-spinner Peter Philpott, I was privileged to renew friendships with several Australian legends. Bob Simpson, Neil Harvey, Doug Walters, Bob Cowper and Brian Taber were all critical of England's preparation and approach. However, all were convinced, such was the unity and purpose of Ricky Ponting's team that it was inevitable that Australia would have won convincing-ly – but not 5–0.

The most unusual email to reach me on this tour came from Colchester where ten-year-old Sam Crame, cricket-mad and a fan of *TMS*, named his inland Bearded Dragon after me. This Frindall was a three-month-old Pogona Vitticeps, a native of the Australian desert that is becoming increasingly popular as a pet. Appropriately, the dragon's staple diet consists of crickets. Sam's dad, Nathan, wrote: 'He has consumed nearly 100 crickets since we took delivery of him three weeks ago. He keeps us all amused with his varying sleeping positions, his favourite at the moment being pressed up close to the glass with one claw gripping his log and the other splayed on the screen. He has also taken to displaying his beard, we're not sure what it means or why he does it.'

Some mysteries are best left unsolved.

On New Year's Eve, Sydney celebrated the 75th anniversary of its famous Harbour Bridge with an unbelievably spectacular fireworks display. Tewkesbury-based Gullivers Sports Travel hired the cruiser *Sydney 2000* to cheer their 750 disappointed touring cricket supporters with a five-course meal, copious quantities of expensive falling-over water and a grandstand view of the fireworks. My reward for participating in cricket evenings during each Test was a surprise inclusion on their guest list. The bridge is known as the 'Coathanger' because of its arch-based design. A vast scarlet image of one, 300-feet wide, formed the centrepiece of this New Year extravaganza. Our ship doused its lights as, for 20 minutes, we were surrounded by a battery of multi-coloured explosions all around the city supporting the main event on the bridge.

On his first visit to Australia, Fred Trueman had been taken to the bridge by his host. 'What do you think of our bridge, Mr Trueman?' 'Your bloody bridge!' thundered Fred. 'It was planned by an Englishman [Francis Greenway, a convict architect from Bristol], built by the Yorkshire firm of Dorman Long and you buggers haven't finished paying for it yet!' Nor did they until 1988.

Soon after this edition is published, *TMS* will celebrate its golden jubilee, the first continuous ball-by-ball Test match commentary having been that covering the West Indies Test played at Edgbaston from 30 May to 4 June in 1957. Immediately after the four-match series ends on 19 June, Peter Baxter will leave the staff of the BBC. During his 34 years as cricket producer he has developed the programme's relaxed atmosphere while upholding its essential traditions. His successor will have a very hard act to follow and we await his appointment with not a little trepidation.

INDEX